MOON CAKES IN GOLD MOUNTAIN

From China to the Canadian Plains

J. Brian Dawson

with Patricia M. Dawson

Detselig Enterprises Ltd
Calgary, Alberta

Canadian Cataloguing in Publication Data

Dawson, J. Brian (John Brian), 1948-
Moon cakes in Gold Mountain

Includes bibliographical references and index.
ISBN 1-55059-026-X

1. Chinese—Alberta—History. 2. Chinese—Alberta—Social conditions. 3. Chinese Canadians—Alberta—History. 4. Chinese Canadians—Alberta—Social conditions. I. Title.
FC3700.C5D39 1991 971.23'004951 C91-091595-4
F1080.C5D39 1991

Detselig Enterprises Ltd.
P.O. Box G 399
Calgary, Alberta, T3A 2G3

Detselig Enterprises Ltd. appreciates the financial assistance for its 1991 publishing program from Canada Council and Alberta Foundation for the Literary Arts.

Printed in Canada SAN115-0324 ISBN 1-55059-026-X

To the memory of my mother

Dorothy Elizabeth Dawson

Contents

Preface

A brief look at the contents reveals that a considerable amount of ground has been covered in this book. Subjects range from China's progressively serious decline under Manchu rule from about 1800 on, to the cosmopolitan nature of contemporary Chinese-Canadian communities.

This book meets several objectives. First, a general, but wide-ranging history of the Chinese in Alberta is presented, covering the period from 1885 to the present. Secondly, the Chinese experience in Alberta is placed in a meaningful Canadian context; what appears, then, concerning Alberta is appreciated more fully, and the Canada-wide situation itself becomes clearer. Thirdly, distinct emphasis has been placed on assessing and explaining the components and essence of the Chinese community in Alberta. This has been done by attempting, as much as possible, to employ a Chinese perspective and viewpoint on significant topics. The use of Chinese oral testimony has been very valuable in this regard.

In summer 1974 I set up and administered an oral history program concerning Chinese pioneers in southern Alberta; the resulting, mostly translated, material has been invaluable to this study.

In 1985 almost sixty people were interviewed over several months, again to much advantage. Nicholas Ting was my research assistant at the time and conducted many of the discussions. I extend warm appreciation to him for excellent work. Finally, I conducted many discussions over the telephone from 1985 to the present, gaining much information only available from individuals.

The other main category of primary source material was newspaper articles. Various articles used herein I located in clippings files in archives and libraries; a substantial majority, however, were discovered by searching through a great many newspaper editions preserved on microfilm.

Most of the microfilm searching was done by my wife, Patricia, who was my research assistant for the summer of 1985; she also contributed to the written material included in the text. I cannot thank her enough for her fine contributions.

I extend considerable gratitude to my father, Lorne Dawson, who instilled in me a deep and abiding appreciation of learning and fine writing, especially in the historical realm. His enthusiastic backing of my M.A. thesis and this study was invaluable.

I cannot begin to list the many dozens of people who have assisted me in so many ways during the research and writing of this book; such a compilation would amount to a study in itself. My deep gratitude is extended to everyone who helped out; you know who you are: Thank you!

How did this study come about? Briefly, during undergraduate studies, I completed a survey course in Chinese history. I was captivated by the fascinating panorama of Chinese history and culture. In later years, several courses in Modern Chinese History followed. For my master of arts thesis (1976) in Western Canadian History, I assessed Chinese settlement and community formation to 1925 in southern Alberta.

In 1985 I was awarded a one-year grant by the Alberta Cultural Heritage Foundation to pursue further the history of Alberta Chinese. The great amount of work outstanding when the year ended, and the many commitments which arose since then, have resulted in the present release of *Moon Cakes in Gold Mountain: From China to the Canadian Plains*. I hope that you will regard your time spent with this book as worthwhile.

J. Brian Dawson
October 1991

1

The Search for Gold Mountain: Adventurers and Other Early Arrivals

Did Ancient Chinese Mariners Reach North America?

For over two centuries scholars in the Western world have debated whether or not Chinese mariners reached North America many hundreds of years ago. Relatively recent archaeological finds in California have highlighted the very controversial and intriguing subject once again.

In 1761 a book by the French Sinologist Joseph de Guignes was published. De Guignes had become convinced that a group of Buddhist monks from China arrived in the Americas a full thousand years before the time of Columbus. The author based his conclusions on his examination of the fifty-six-volume *Liang Shu* (*History of the Liang Dynasty*) written by Yao Silian (557-637 A.D.).

Therein, the astounded de Guignes found a detailed account of an 11 200-kilometre (7 000-mile) voyage across the "Great Eastern Sea" to a land called "Fu-Sang." Careful perusal and study convinced the Frenchman that Fu-Sang was Mexico.

According to translations of the account, a Buddhist priest, Huishen, arrived at Jingzhou, in Hubei province, in 499 A.D. The very old man stated that he had just returned from the land of Fu-Sang, which was 20 000 *li* (10 666 kilometres, or 6 666 miles) east of China. At this time Buddhism was in disfavor in China, and civil wars had fragmented the nation. Little attention was paid to Huishen and his accounts of adventure, strange peoples and customs, and the flora and fauna of far-off lands.

Three years later, Huishen was ordered to relate his amazing story to the new emperor, Wu-Ti, a Buddhist. "He presented an obsidian mirror and a sample of cloth from the Fu-Sang tree [to the emperor]. He was examined and cross-examined by the learned princes of the court before his story was accepted and entered in the history of the new dynasty."[1]

It appears that Huishen "was a disciple of a celebrated Buddhist prelate whose monastic name was Huiji."[2] In 458 A.D. evidence indicates that Huishen and four fellow Buddhist monks left China on a missionary voyage.

Currently, several authorities—having carefully assessed the Fu-Sang documentation, and having researched corresponding geographical, anthropological, botanical, and other available evidence—have concluded that Huishen's account is based on fact and, moreover, that Fu-Sang was actually Mexico.

The following presentation summarizes their basic interpretation of Huishen's story of his experiences and observations.

It has been maintained, then, that sailing to the northeast, the monks followed the Kurile Islands to Kamchatka, and then apparently followed the Aleutian Islands to Alaska. Huishen called the Aleutians "The Country of Marked Bodies," after the people's custom of placing painted stripes on their bodies and foreheads. Captain James Cook would later remark on the same markings when he visited the Aleutians.

The monks apparently became somewhat acquainted with the natives of Alaska and British Columbia. This region's coastal hinterland the monks chose to call "The Great Han Country," one translation of which is "Great Land of Rushing Waters."[3] The monks did not tarry long in these lands of Northwest America. Huishen remarked on the "rudeness" of the customs of the people, so, the travellers may have "considered the natives to be unworthy of their Buddhist teachings...but, whatever the reason, they apparently spent little time there before turning south for Mexico, which they named Fu-Sang. Strangely, it is almost as if they knew exactly where they were going."[4]

Concerning Mexico, or Fu-Sang, the account preserved in the Liang dynasty's history states: "The Fu-sang tree grows abundantly there and its leaves are similar to those of the Paulownia. The buds are like bamboo shoots and the people eat them. The fruit is pear-shaped, but red in color.

From the bark, cloth and garments are made. Houses are built of this tree. There are no walls around the cities. Records are inscribed on material made from the bark of the Fu-sang tree."[5] Botanists are in general agreement that Huishen's description of the Fu-sang tree matches that of the maguey or American Aloe.

Huishen described at great length the people and society in Fu-Sang. Modern archaeological data confirm much of what he related. Moreover, "his descriptions of the country's flora and fauna prove that he could have been in no other country but Mexico."[6] At some point during his forty-year stay in Fu-Sang, Huishen became separated from his fellow monks; accordingly, he returned to China without them.

The question arises, Could the monks have sailed from China to North America in the fifth century? There is no doubt that they could have. Chinese ships sailed neighboring seas as early as the fourth century B.C. By the second century B.C., ships capable of carrying sixty tons of cargo were being built. By the third century A.D., "Chinese sailors were able to calculate sailing speeds and the length of voyages and make use of the northeast (spring) monsoons."[7]

By the fourth century A.D., Chinese trading ships had reached the east coast of Africa. Huishen and his fellow missionaries may have embarked aboard an ocean-going junk, but probably they used a sea-going sailing-raft built of giant bamboo.

A few years ago, two finds were made of stone anchors which are 3 000 years old and Asian in origin. One find was made in shallow water off the Palos Verdes Peninsula, California. It consisted of two cylindrical stones and another in the shape of an equilateral triangle. The other find occurred in 1 000 fathoms of water off Point Medecino, California: it consisted of a large circular stone with a hole bored through the centre. The structure of these stones matches exactly the descriptions of anchors as related in ancient Chinese texts.

Professor James R. Moriarty, an archaeologist at the University of San Diego, has carefully examined these anchors. He has stated his professional conclusion that these discoveries "are beginning to provide solid scientific evidence of Chinese trans-Pacific voyages in pre-Columbian times and add real support to the theory that the ancient cultures of the Americas [were] influenced by ideas of Chinese origin."[8]

The Decline of the Manchu Dynasty

In 1644 China was conquered by the Manchus, fierce tribesmen from the northeast. They called their dynasty the Qing (Ch'ing), meaning "pure." Like the Ming dynasty traders before them, traders under the Manchus found it profitable to trade with the Portuguese confined at their colony of Macao. Other Western traders, too, came to China to do business. In 1757 the imperial court decreed that henceforth all foreign trade within the confines of the huge empire would be conducted at just one location, the great port of Canton (Guangzhou).

A trading system came into effect whereby a dozen or so Chinese firms, or *hongs*, monopolized the Chinese side of trade. The *hong* merchants were responsible to the Chinese government for the conduct of foreign trade and traders. Regulations essentially confined the foreign traders to their warehouses and offices which were outside the city of Canton. For many years the trading system held fast and benefitted both sides. Owing in part to trade with the *yangguici* (foreign devils), Canton "became by far the busiest and greatest trading centre of the empire."[9]

Until about 1800 China exported more than she imported. This state of essential self-sufficiency frustrated British and other traders, who were forced to bring large quantities of silver to Canton to make up the difference. After 1800 the British increasingly brought opium to Canton, instead of silver. The opium originated in British-controlled regions of India, and *hong* merchants paid silver to buy it.

Port officials and the *hong* merchants deliberately flaunted Chinese law and regulations when they permitted the entry of opium into China. Traditionally, opium served medicinal purposes in the Middle Kingdom. In 1729 opium smoking was prohibited in China; then, in 1800 smoking, importing, and cultivating opium were banned. For a while after 1800, the opium trade shifted away from Canton to the open seas or oceanside villages, but before long Canton again became the centre of the illicit trade.

By 1800 the corruption of public officials was a very serious and debilitating problem of the Chinese Empire, and domestic rebellion further weakened the government. "Opium speeded up the decay, for Chinese officials and soldiers, underpaid, discontented and often idle, were among the first to take up opium smoking, weakening their government still further."[10]

Over 1 800 tons of opium a year were entering Canton by 1836. The opium continued to be paid for in silver, and the great draining away of the precious metal created a national scandal. Opium addiction spread its pernicious tentacles widely because of its increased availability, and roughly one of every eight citizens of the empire became a habitual smoker.[11]

In March 1839 Lin Tse-hsu, the new imperial commissioner, arrived at Canton. Also serving as the governor of the provinces of Hubei and Hunan, Lin had received imperial attention and favor because of his assiduous attempts to eliminate opium smoking and provide addicts with medicine.

Just one week after his arrival in Canton, Lin demanded the surrender of all opium and promises that it would not be imported in the future. The Westerners did not respond, so Lin blockaded the warehouses until they complied and turned over 20 000 chests of the drug. All of the opium was promptly flushed into the sea by the commissioner's men.

The British refused to agree to halt the traffic in opium and withdrew to Macao. Long looking for any excuse to initiate hostilities, Britain soon initiated aggressive actions which inexorably resulted in what has become known as the Opium War. Actually, opium was not at all the primary concern of Britain, which sought both treaty ports at which they could trade freely and full diplomatic recognition.

After Britain's victory, these objectives—as well as the tremendously important cession of the island of Hong Kong to the British—were granted. In 1842 the Treaty of Nanking formalized China's humiliating concessions to a small, remote country which had defeated her in warfare.

Treaty ports were established in Canton, which was the provincial capital of Guangdong (Kwangtung), as well as in the cities of Amoy, Foochow, Ningpo, and Shanghai in the lower Yangtze valley. Henceforth, most opium entered China from ports other than Canton. The Treaty of Nanking "represented China's point of no return: hereafter, the tide of foreign penetration could not be reversed. A fault appeared in China's defense system, and through it poured the heterodoxy of the West which ultimately tolled the death knell of traditional China."[12]

The Taiping Rebellion of 1850-1864 posed a direct threat to the very existence of the Qing dynasty and seriously undermined society throughout south-central China. The leader of the Taiping rebels was Hung Hsiu-ch'uan, who had failed the civil service examinations four times. Having read a Christian pamphlet, Hung declared—after being in a coma for forty days—that he was Jesus' younger brother. Moreover, he stated, God had instructed him to destroy the Manchu rulers and establish a harmonious social and political order based on just treatment of all peoples.

Hung initially organized a small secret sect, the God-Worshippers' Society, in Guangxi (Kwangsi) province, not far west of Canton. The believers' sincerity, dedication, and high moral code attracted many adherents from among the poor peasantry; the unemployed; the dislocated; the disaffected and oppressed; and the hardy Chinese Hakkas, a distinctive minority group originally from northern China (Hung, himself, was a Hakka).

In 1850 Hung Hsiu-ch'uan issued the call to mobilize and 20 000 confirmed followers responded. Before long, city after city fell into the rebels' hands. Having declined considerably in terms of military and administrative preparedness and effectiveness, the weak Qing regime could do little to seriously impede the rebels' steady advances—let alone begin a large-scale campaign to defeat the Taiping forces.

The great city of Nanking fell to the determined rebel forces in 1853. Hung Hsiu-ch'uan proclaimed himself "Prince of Heaven" and called his kingdom the "Heavenly Kingdom of Great Peace." Communistic and collectivistic reforms were introduced. Not just another peasant revolt, "the Taiping movement had ideology and organization, preaching the overthrow of the existing order, the transformation of society, equality of all men, sharing of all property."[13]

In the summer of 1864 imperial forces attacked Nanking and, after fifteen days of fierce fighting, the city fell. Millions of people perished during the rebellion, and much of the countryside of seven provinces was devastated.

From 1842 onwards, China was increasingly humiliated by the Western powers. The empire was also subjected to governmental corruption and inefficiency; rebellions; social disruption; a disorganized economy; poverty; famine and natural catastrophes; and overpopulation in some areas. The chaos of the times, when coupled with the anger of the people, would eventually lead to the toppling of the Manchus' Qing dynasty in 1911 and its replacement by a republic.

Long before (and after) the revolution occurred, however, a great number of dissatisfied and desperate people chose to emigrate to a wide variety of lands scattered throughout the world in search of viable livelihoods.

Immigrants to Gold Mountain: Origins

Historically, substantial migration from China is a relatively recent phenomenon. The primary reason for this is that the Chinese believed that their civilization and culture were vastly superior to those of any other nation. In Mandarin, Imperial China was Jung Guo (The Middle Kingdom)—the centre of the world—and contact with outside "barbarian" countries was discouraged.

During most of the Qing dynasty (1644-1911), imperial decrees forbade anyone without a special permit to emigrate from China—the penalty being death—but provincial governors usually ignored such severe strictures, permitting some emigration. Bribing officials who were in relevant positions of authority also facilitated people's smooth departures. Emigrants were often looked down upon, however, and suspicion was sometimes entertained as to their loyalty to the empire and its dynastic rulers.

From the 1840s to 1930—in a great diaspora—over eight million Chinese left China and found new homes. Most who left their homeland were from the southeastern coastal provinces. About six million people settled in the East Indies, Taiwan, and Thailand. There was a strong demand for labor in various British, Spanish, Portuguese, and Dutch possessions; accordingly, many Chinese went to lands in Africa and Latin America. Others went to continental Europe, Britain, and New Zealand. A relatively small number made their way to North America to live and work.

Emperor Ch'ien-lung ruled from 1736 to 1795. There is a consensus among authorities that, within a few years of his death, "Ch'ing power had passed its pinnacle and the weaknesses of the dynastic cycle began to show in both domestic and foreign affairs."[14] Whereas the empire's population numbered 275 million in 1779 and 313 million in 1800, it stood at 430 million in 1850; nonetheless, there were no matching increases in food production or new economic opportunities.

The dramatic population increase, combined with "a shortage of arable land, led to a rice shortage throughout China. This problem was particularly keen in hilly Kwangtung [Guangdong] and Fukien [Fujian] provinces."[15] Indeed, since the early 1700s, the dense population and insufficient resources of these adjacent coastal provinces had prompted many men to put their lives on the line and migrate illegally to various areas of Southeast Asia.

Strong "push" and "pull" forces played a decisive role in the case of emigration from South China. Guangdong itself comprises about 130 000 square kilometres, an area about the size of the state of Oregon. In 1787 the province's population numbered 16 million. By 1911 the year the Qing dynasty fell, the population had virtually doubled to about thirty-one million, and the average density in populated areas stood at about 600 persons per square kilometre.

Guangdong's agricultural situation was unenviable; less than ten per cent of the land was arable, for example. In the eighteenth and nineteenth centuries, much of the cultivated land was used to grow commercial crops, such as sugarcane and tobacco—and not rice, people's staple food. Ordinary folk suffered from the ever-higher cost of rice; moreover, the introduction of commercial crops of high market value caused land prices and rent charges to soar, and short-term contracts replaced secure tenure.

Other serious problems aggravated the province's rural situation. Land distribution was extremely unequal. Absentee landlords owned most of the land; instead of hiring landless peasants, they rented land to tenant farmers whose lives were marked by poverty. (In 1888 seventy per cent of all farm families in Guangdong were tenants). Also, since Chinese did not practise primogeniture, farmers' plots were divided up equally among heirs; with each generation, then, family plots became progressively smaller.

Pioneer Joe How from Toi-san county aptly described prevailing conditions: "there wasn't enough land to make a living. People didn't have much money or equipment and did things the hard way. [It was] just like in Central America today: the rich had all the big plots of land, and the poor had nothing."[16]

Fred Yee, another pioneer, was born in Zhongshan (Chung-san), a village fifty kilometres south of Canton. He mentioned that dozens of villages were in the general Canton area (the Pearl River Delta region) and added: "I tell you, the people living there really struggled for a living. When I was a little boy [1910s], my mother used to carry me on her back while she delivered fruit on a pole to the landowners; they were the bosses, you know."[17]

The forcible opening of China's market to products from the capitalist West "seriously upset the domestic textile industry. The influx of cheap, machine-made foreign cloth of good quality...all but ruined the cottage industry which had provided peasant families with a source of extra income."[18]

Although Guangdong had fully ninety-eight *xian* (counties), the overwhelming majority of immigrants to Canada before 1924 originated from

Canton, which served as the provincial capital, and seven *xian* clustered around, or in relative proximity to, the great city.

The majority of emigrants to Canada and the United States lived in the region called Sze Yap (Siyi, in *pinyin* transliteration), or the "Four Counties." Southwest of Canton in the Pearl River Delta region, it consisted of the counties of Sun-wui, Toi-san, Yin-ping, and Hoi-ping (respectively, in *pinyin*, Xinhui, Taishan, Enping, and Kaiping). Toi-sanese, the most distinctive sub-dialect of Cantonese, is spoken in these four adjacent counties.

Also significant in terms of emigration to North America is the region called Sam Yap (Sanyi, in *pinyin*), or the "Three Counties." The region surrounds Canton and consists of three adjacent counties: Sun-dak, Nam-hoi, and Poon-yue (respectively, in *pinyin*, Shunde, Nanhai, and Panyu). Standard Cantonese is used in these counties.

The Pearl River Delta, heartland of Cantonese Guangdong, is a distinct region. Language distinguishes it, as does sub-cultural complexity. The Cantonese are self-consciously distinct, and their "sub-culture is noted for a fine regional cuisine and a distinctive tradition in the arts, poetry, and letters."[19]

Survival itself was the primary problem in the overpopulous delta. In the 1800s weak, ineffective imperial administration was part and parcel of socio-economic woes and political instability: flood control measures were abandoned, for example, and public granaries (to help people survive during droughts) were emptied to pay off war debts. By the mid-nineteenth century, when Chinese began arriving in Canada, "banditry [was] endemic in the countryside and private armies of all kinds were becoming a way of life in rural China."[20] With emigration increasingly essential for individual and group survival, many Cantonese peasants sailed to North America as soon as an opportunity arose.

The social organization of communities in Canada was a direct product of the rules and values of social conduct in China's agrarian society. In peasant society, kinship played a central role, and "economic organization, political power, sources of prestige, and religion were oriented toward kinship groups."[21]

The most elaborately-developed kinship system existed in southeastern China, where it dominated the regulation of most local matters. Indeed, in Guangdong, most villages had people with only one, two, or three surnames; the term "clan" can be taken to correspond roughly with "surname." Loyalty to one's village was reinforced a good deal by kinship ties.

Indeed, kin solidarities became interposed between an individual and the state. Inasmuch as imperial political regulation of rural villages was characterized by decentralization, village loyalties were markedly enhanced in contrast with any loyalty to the state.

The "individual's status was determined in part with reference to his family and his kin group. [The] local social system of which he was part was clear in its allocation of status."[22] With migration, however, this inclusive system affecting one's conduct was non-existent, and the migrant had no familiar, uniform community to provide support. "Nonetheless, his attachment to traditional forms was intense [and he sought] to remain involved, as far as possible, with his native cultural system."[23]

Traditionally, voluntary associations in China were common among urban migrants. Most were either economic groups, much like guilds, or "provincial (district) clubs," which mostly provided mutual aid to those required to spend time in the cities, away from native villages and districts. Some voluntary associations appeared in rural villages, usually for raising short-term credit.

Armed with knowledge relating to organizing and conducting associations, Chinese immigrants in Canada formed a variety of organizations—both to assist adaptation to a new society and to establish their own communities. Chinese in Canada, as elsewhere, "identified themselves with their clan, village, and dialect grouping. The overseas clan, village, [or district] leaders were accepted as legitimate substitutes for the village council."[24]

Vancouver Island's Eighteenth-Century Colonists

In 1788 ex-Royal Navy Captain John Meares entered into a personal partnership with a Portuguese merchant at Macao. Meares intended to engage in the nascent Pacific Northwest fur trade. He may also have sought to found a shipbuilding establishment in the Northwest. At Macao Meares hired about seventy Chinese carpenters, metalworkers, shipbuilders, and sailors.

In May of 1788 Meares's ship anchored at Friendly Cove on Nootka Sound, on the west coast of Vancouver Island. Meares acquired a piece of land from the local Nootka Indian chief, Maquinna. A reasonably strong fort was built there by the Chinese. A residence and shipyard were also erected. On 20 September a momentous event occurred at Nootka Sound: the launching of the schooner *North West America*—the first ship built on the Pacific Northwest coast. By means of these activities, Britain established a solid claim to proprietorship of the west coast of Vancouver Island and, by extension, to the Pacific Northwest coast.

The *North West America* set sail for the Queen Charlotte Islands with a mixed Chinese and English crew. Some Chinese remained behind at the small settlement. Subsequently, an additional seventy-four Chinese arrived aboard two ships to augment the small colony.[25] In May 1789 several Spanish ships reached Nootka Sound. Spain maintained that the Pacific Northwest coast was Spanish territory, and it now sought to enforce its claim and build a Spanish fort at Nootka Sound. In coming weeks, Meares's ships and crews were seized as they arrived; many of the men were soon freed on the condition that they return to China.

Because of the seizures, by spring of 1790 Britain and Spain were on the brink of war. Britain sought the support of Prussia and Holland, mobilized her navy, and prepared colonial forts for warfare. Spain garrisoned her North American forts and readied a fleet. Tensions were relaxed in June, when agreement was reached on conditions for negotiation. The crisis finally ended in October. Spain reluctantly gave in to British demands, but did not relinquish all of her claims to the Pacific Northwest coast.

The fate of the Chinese colonists is not entirely clear. Apparently, some were taken away by ship to San Blas, and what happened to them is not known.[26] Some or all of the remaining Chinese at Nootka Sound "decided to settle there, and sought shelter among the natives on the island."[27] Over the next forty-five years, several reports "told of the Chinese workers mixing well in native society, making their homes as settlers, raising families with native women and growing old in the New World."[28]

A Vital Chinese Presence is Established in North America

In 1849 news of the California Gold Rush swept through Guangdong, precipitating nearly a century of mass migration to the Western hemisphere. By 1851 fully 25 000 Chinese were seeking their fortune in unruly California. Most were gold miners, but few made substantial finds. Many decided that there was a future all the same in North America, which they called *Gum Shan* (Gold Mountain), a term still used today. Most hoped to accumulate sufficient savings to retire in comfort as respected elders in their native villages. While overseas, the men sent money regularly to their families, which often relied absolutely upon such assistance to pay for the necessities of life, that is, for their very survival.

In 1862 the United States federal government authorized the construction of a transcontinental railway. Two companies, the Union Pacific and the Central Pacific, received commissions to build the railway. Faced with a shortage of willing workers, the Central Pacific hired thousands of Chinese.

The men proved to be highly reliable, industrious navvies who would stoically brave severe weather conditions and hazardous terrain. One day, as the result of a wager on the part of one of the partners, a Chinese crew laid over sixteen kilometres (ten miles) of track. "It was an achievement that has never been equaled nor approached even by modern methods in the United States."[29] Chinese labor was so accomplished that the Southern Pacific and Northwest Pacific railways also relied considerably on Chinese to build their lines.

At the outset of the Fraser River gold strike of 1858, a group of Chinese miners arrived at Fort Victoria on Vancouver Island from California. It seems that Chinese miners who subsequently came to British Columbia did so by means of chartered ships which left San Francisco and Hong Kong. In 1860 some 4 000 Chinese reached Victoria, and even more arrived the following year. A fledgling Chinatown soon made its appearance on Cormorant Street. In 1861 at Port Douglas, B.C., the first Chinese baby born in Canada arrived.

In the early 1860s there were about 7 000 Chinese in B.C. The great majority were to be found in the gold-fields, and many worked diggings abandoned by whites. As the prospectors worked their way into the Cariboo area in the interior and up tributaries of the Fraser River, "the most advanced parties tried to keep the Chinese out of their areas, even by violent means."[30]

By 1863, nonetheless, about 4 000 Chinese were in the Cariboo area. In the heyday of booming Barkerville, the presence of enterprising Chinese in the town was most apparent: more than thirty boarding-houses were occupied by Chinese; a Chinese temple was erected there; and the third largest store was operated by the notable Kwong Lee Company of Victoria. Over 3 000 Chinese lived in Barkerville at its height.

Although gold deposits in the British colony became depleted in the late 1860s, many Chinese stayed. They found jobs as laborers, houseboys, coal miners, and gardeners, or they opened their own businesses. According to the census of 1871, there were 1 548 Chinese in B.C., but this number may have been on the low side.

The second wave of Chinese immigration to Canada occurred in the 1880s, when Chinese laborers arrived to build the B.C. sections of the Canadian Pacific Railway (CPR). The contractor, Andrew Onderdonk, arranged for more than 18 000 Chinese to come to Canada: some came from the United States, but the majority arrived directly from China aboard chartered vessels.

During the year of peak railway construction (1883), there were 6 000 to 7 500 Chinese working on various sections of track at any one time. The men set up their own camps, brought in and cooked their own food, and were highly mobile and self-reliant. They fearlessly hazarded treacherous sections of the Fraser River Canyon—without their labors the railway would have taken considerably longer to build. An estimated 1 500 Chinese died in the course of work, thereby indebting Canada forever to her Chinese citizenry.

When the CPR was completed, a serious recession began in the Pacific province; it battered the economy and very adversely affected the available labor force throughout the province. In makeshift camps along the railway line, many unemployed Chinese endured extreme deprivation and malnutrition for months. Fleeing such conditions, those who had sufficient savings sailed home to China; many others crowded into B.C.'s few Chinatowns, seeking life's necessities from their fellow countrymen.

It was during these difficult times that a number of enterprising Chinese crossed through the easternmost mountains to seek a new life in the North-West Territories. "The trek eastward was caused in part by Andrew Onderdonk's refusal to honor his pledge to provide railhands with a one-way ticket back to China. Many laborers were left destitute and stranded in a foreign land."[31]

Anti-Chinese Actions and Legislation

Despite their invaluable contribution to opening the American West, Chinese in the United States suffered from discrimination and persecution. Early on, white miners protested about supposed unfair competition from Chinese miners and, accordingly, a foreign miners' tax was imposed; this was merely the thin edge of a grossly discriminatory racist wedge.

In the 1850s Chinese were driven from many mining areas, and later they were chased out of various towns. In the 1880s all of the Chinese residents of Tacoma and Seattle were expelled. Killings were not uncommon.

What has been called the Anti-Chinese Movement gained momentum and spread throughout the land. Politicians by the hundreds regularly castigated the Chinese, thereby fanning the flames of mindless prejudice and hatred. "Scorned by officials, patronized by missionaries, defamed by labor leaders, and battered by mobs, the Chinese suffered nearly the full panoply of injustice that a racist society could impose."[32]

For over thirty years, commencing in 1852, California legislators passed acts intended to restrict Chinese immigration. In 1882 Congress and the president approved an exclusion act whereby no skilled or unskilled Chinese miner or laborer could enter the United States for ten years. In 1892 the severe *Geary Act* was passed. It restricted Chinese immigration for an additional ten years; stipulated that no bail be permitted Chinese involved in *habeus corpus* proceedings; and required all Chinese laborers to carry certificates of residence.

In 1902 another U.S. exclusion act was passed, but many Chinese entered the country by assuming the roles of merchants, teachers, students, and travellers—categories of Chinese eligible to enter the country. Other Chinese were smuggled into the country. Through these means, then, the rigidly-enforced laws were widely ineffective.

In 1884 a Canadian federal Royal Commission was held inquiring into the alleged problem of Chinese immigration. This course of action was prompted by the agitation of various labor leaders and politicians in B.C. This, despite the fact that in 1881 the Chinese in all of Canada accounted for only 4 383 persons. Fifty-one witnesses testified before the commission—significantly and indicatively, only two Chinese were among them. "Almost all witnesses manifested prejudice against the Chinese."[33]

As a result of the Royal Commission, a fifty-dollar "head tax" was imposed upon each Chinese who entered Canada. The only people exempted from paying the levy were merchants and their families, tourists, diplomatic personnel, scientists, and students.

When modest Chinese immigration continued, the head tax was raised to $100 in 1902 and to $500 in 1903. As a further deterrent to Chinese immigration, in 1904 a federal act was passed which required Chinese laborers to have $200 in their possession before being admitted to Canada. Moreover, after "June, 1917, a Chinese was liable to arrest without warrant if a policeman so much as suspected him of having entered Canada illegally."[34] No other immigrant group was singled out for such severe discriminatory treatment.

In 1875 the B.C. legislature forbade Chinese to vote in provincial elections. That meant that they were prevented, *ipso facto*, from voting federally and were also barred from various professions, including law, pharmacy, and chartered accountancy. In 1908 Chinese in Saskatchewan were likewise denied the vote in provincial elections and, accordingly, in federal elections as well. "Alberta, too, discussed the possibility of disenfranchising its Chinese. There was little support for the idea, however, and it was not pursued."[35]

In Saskatchewan an act was passed in 1912 whereby Chinese restaurant owners could not hire white women as waitresses. In B.C. a host of various acts and regulations were passed against Chinese over many years.

In the turbulent times which followed the First World War, agitation in B.C. against the Chinese—frequent scapegoats during periods of recession—increased dramatically. Chinese communities were confronted by hostile business groups, unfriendly trade unionists, and militant unemployed veterans. Anti-Chinese elements fostered unreasoned fears of an Oriental Menace to Canada in the form of imagined massive and uncontrollable immigration.

The federal government responded to pressures from the Pacific province: on 2 March 1923 the acting Minister of Immigration, Charles Stewart—a former Alberta premier—introduced a bill which would virtually exclude Chinese immigrants from entering Canada. Almost unbelievably, no one in Parliament spoke on behalf of the Chinese. What has become known as the *Chinese Exclusion Act* (it was formally titled the *Chinese Immigration Act of 1923*) was passed, despite protests from enraged Chinese communities and other groups.

The effects of the *Chinese Exclusion Act* were drastic. Over the subsequent twenty-four years, only a few dozen Chinese were legally admitted into Canada, and the number of Chinese residents in the country dropped significantly. Whereas there were 46 519 Chinese in Canada in 1931, there were only 34 627 in 1941.

Feeling unwanted and uncertain about the future, Chinese relied heavily on their own social, fraternal, and benevolent organizations. Chinese communities looked inwardly and became increasingly isolated. Worst of all, men were precluded from bringing over their wives and children: they were cruelly denied the comforts and meaningfulness of family life.

At long last—in 1947—the *Chinese Exclusion Act* was repealed; but Canadian immigration policy regarding the Chinese continued to be discriminatory until 1967.

2

Chinese Settlement and Frontier Oppression

The years from 1885 to 1910 were distinctive ones in the historical evolution of Calgary, Edmonton, Medicine Hat, and Lethbridge; the period was also highly significant in terms of the establishment of local Chinese communities. In 1885 Calgary was a small railway town, with some likelihood of expanding into a major transportation centre. Edmonton was a hamlet which had not lived up to its promise. Medicine Hat and Lethbridge were fledgling towns with an uncertain future.

By 1910, however, Calgary had been an incorporated city for sixteen years, and approximately 40 000 people resided in the city as 1911 approached. By 1910 Edmonton was the capital of the province with good prospects for a bright future, and it had been a city for six years. Medicine Hat and Lethbridge were both incorporated in 1906 and were bustling little cities by 1910. Within a generation, these four towns had been transformed into significant urban centres.

The first Chinese pioneers in Alberta arrived in 1885, but during the 1880s and 1890s there were relatively few Chinese in the area. As increasing numbers of immigrants and Canadians arrived in the territory of Alberta (which became a province in 1905), more Chinese settled in Alberta, residing primarily in the larger centres. By 1910 there were Chinatowns in Calgary, Edmonton, Medicine Hat, and Lethbridge; this was indicative of the increased number of Chinese pioneers in these centres. From this year onward distinct, recognizable Chinese urban communities can be said to have existed in Alberta.

Chinese Settlement in Calgary, 1885-1888

There is no written account of the arrival of the first Chinese in the territory of Alberta. As early as 1885, there was at least one Chinese resident of Banff, several Chinese lived in or near the Crowsnest Pass in southwestern Alberta, and some Chinese were living in the Calgary area.

The *Calgary Herald* reported in late January 1886: "Mr. Amos Roscoe, as subcollector of customs for this outpost of Calgary, has been appointed comptroller of Chinese immigration in this district. Every Chinaman at present residing in the district has to pay a fee of five dollars and everyone coming in hereafter fifty dollars. The latter have also to obtain a medical certificate that they are free from leprosy and other contagious diseases and no Chinese prostitutes are to be admitted at all."[1]

It is probable that the Chinese residents referred to were local launderers, inasmuch as the Chinese hand laundry—a hallmark of Canadian prairie settlement—made a very early appearance in frontier Alberta.

By 1888 several Chinese laundries had been operating for some time in Calgary. In June of that year, one Hop Sing arrived from Vancouver to open another laundry "where family and single persons' washing of all kinds [would] be done in first-class style at very low prices."[2]

The established laundries were soon forced into a price war by the newcomer: "Calgary's Chinese colony is just now in the midst of a bitter trade war. A recently arrived immigrant from the flowery kingdom opened the ball by advertising...reduced rates. Joe George and Sam Lee, two oldtimers, immediately raised him, coming out with a tariff which threatens ruination to the manipulators of the wash board and flat iron, if kept up for long."[3]

The price war continued into the fall season, by which time Hop Sing was apparently forced out of business. In late September the four remaining laundries established fixed rates for laundering. Their new tariff was to come into effect 1 October 1888 and was advertised under the heading "Chinese Laundry Association Prices."[4]

The stability of the local laundry business was short-lived, however. The interloper again decided to upset the status quo: "Hop Sing informs us that the Chinese washing combination are not to have it all their own way, as he has made arrangements for a number of men to come in from Victoria when he will resume work at his old stand near H. Collins' Ivy Goods store at old prices."[5] The resulting events were not reported, but it is probable that the enterprising Hop Sing transferred the base of his operations to an area of pure competition.

This episode reveals that Chinese entrepreneurs had firmly established themselves in a particular service trade in Calgary in the 1880s. Also, the economic enterprise and competitiveness of the Chinese in the Canadian West is quite apparent. But, in an established frontier settlement there was little room for unnecessary competition in any service trade, because no one would benefit in the long run.

The Anti-Chinese Movement

Frontier oppression of Chinese in Alberta was but one example of what has aptly been termed the Anti-Chinese Movement: a rather amorphous, but determinedly purposeful and powerful, movement which found solid support in the United States and, later, in Canada.

Americans' highly unfavorable, stereotypical views of the Chinese as a people can be dated to the days of the China trade in the late 1700s. Pertinent documentation concerning the period 1785 to 1840 strongly demonstrates that a majority of American traders who visited China before the California Gold Rush concluded that the Chinese were "ridiculously clad, superstitious ridden, dishonest, crafty, cruel, and marginal members of the human race...."[6]

The meticulous scholarship of Stuart Miller has convincingly revealed that a very negative image of China and the Chinese people was consistently present in the United States from early China trade days on. Morally indignant and provincial-minded Protestant missionaries in China condemned Chinese on a host of grounds in the many books and articles they wrote about their experiences with the so-called pagan, hopelessly backward, corrupt, and servile Chinese people.

For their part, American editors emphasized the supposed xenophobia of the Chinese and China's allegedly uncivilized and barbarous society. This was particularly the case after the outbreak of the Taiping Rebellion (1850), which ultimately left much of south-central China devastated and a great number of innocent people dead, primarily through starvation and disease.

Overall, because of the traders', Protestant missionaries', and newspaper editors' essentially uniform and intensely negative portrayals of the Chinese people, their government, society, and culture, "an unfavorable image of China evolved and dominated American thinking during the nineteenth century...."[7]

Not surprisingly, when Chinese arrived in California, Sinophobia and anti-Chinese sentiment found fertile ground among many bigots and racists located along the Pacific coast. Serious hostility toward the Chinese was initially aroused by white miners opposed to Chinese engaging in gold mining: false accusations were made about great mineral wealth being siphoned off to China; disgruntled whites blamed Chinese for supposedly unfair competition.

Soon, Chinese labor in general was viciously and inaccurately attacked on various grounds, including the unfair competition complaint—even as white capitalists increasingly and shamefully exploited Chinese workers.

Later, in B.C., during and after the Fraser River and Cariboo gold rushes (1858 into the mid-1860s), the same pattern of unfair accusations, accompanying hostility, and Sinophobia manifested itself. British Columbians' reaction to the Chinese presence reflected the Americans' long-standing, intensely negative, portrayals and conceptions of the Chinese people.

Reaction to the arrival of Chinese in British North America and Canada was influenced, too, by indigenous factors. Canadians had been "conditioned by a tradition of racism implanted by the European empires as they sought to extend their dominion to the New World."[8] Social Darwinism was a major factor in this regard.

European powers had subjugated huge areas of Asia by the 1850s; so, clearly the Asians were inferior, concluded the English and other imperialists. The easy defeat of China by Britain during the Opium War (1840-1842) was interpreted as a convincing demonstration of Chinese racial inferiority. In light of the overwhelming predominance of English thought and institutions in Canada, "the pervasive attitude that Asians...were innately inferior was also part of the British legacy to Canada."[9]

Owing to the powerful and insidious influence of the Anti-Chinese Movement—whether expressed in its American or Canadian contexts—for decades, Chinese were singled out for substantial abuse on all fronts. In both countries Chinese immigrants were subjected to concerted attacks by labor lobbies; disgruntled working-class dissidents; crowd-pleasing politicians; and an odd assortment of ideologues espousing insular and ethnocentric arguments against Chinese immigration.

During the frontier era, the Anti-Chinese Movement directly and indirectly inflicted tremendous hardships upon Chinese communities. Legislative action at all levels created much misery, frustration, and consternation. American exclusion acts were passed, and Canada's extortionate federal head taxes were imposed on Chinese immigrants.

B.C. passed a host of laws directed against the Chinese; while some laws were declared unconstitutional, others were not. From laws barring Chinese from specific occupations to laws intended solely to harass Chinese businessmen, workers, and communities, anti-Chinese legislation in the Pacific province exacted a terrible toll in both personal and group terms.

By 1910 or so the Anti-Chinese Movement had become a less significant force, especially in terms of the intensity of its activities. In the case of Alberta, this was reflected in the absence of any acts of irrational, racist mob violence.

By about 1910, too, the garrison mentality of Alberta's urban centres was being transformed into an urban mentality with the beginning of a social consciousness appearing. In 1910 Chinese in Calgary successfully relocated Chinatown in an area of their own choosing, despite minor opposition. This clearly revealed that a more considered, moderate mentality was being formed in the minds of Albertans.

The 1892 Smallpox Riot

Before 1905 little notice was given to Chinese pioneers by southern Alberta's press, but in 1892 it became dramatically evident that the Chinese were not welcome residents of Calgary. In April 1892 the *Empress of Japan* docked at Royal Roads, British Columbia and a case of smallpox was detected.

Health measures were implemented, but within a few months the dread disease had taken seven lives in Vancouver and Victoria. Although the smallpox had been carried aboard a ship from China to B.C., a bastion of anti-Asian sentiment, "there was surprisingly little anti-Oriental feeling generated by [the episode]."[10]

On 28 June 1892 it was discovered that a Chinese resident of Calgary was recovering from smallpox in a local Chinese laundry. The man had returned from Vancouver several weeks previously, then fell ill and was attended to by fellow countrymen. The building housing the laundry and all its contents were burned the same day by civic authorities, and the occupants were quarantined outside the town in an empty shack. A detachment of North-West Mounted Police guarded the shack to enforce strict quarantine measures and a town doctor was placed in attendance.

The outbreak was taken very seriously, as were all similarly contagious diseases which, on occasion, resulted in epidemics in the Canadian West. Within a brief span of time, Calgary's Chinese laundries were inspected, disinfectants were employed in houses, most of the citizens were vaccinated, and "all of the lanes, yards and back premises in town" were inspected.[11]

In order to check the spread of the disease, various precautionary health measures were implemented throughout the prairies. In Manitoba medical examinations were instituted at the boundary with the North-West Territories "in the case of passengers going East."[12]

At Banff medical examinations were required before newcomers could enter the town, and at Medicine Hat civic officials absolutely prohibited east-bound passengers from "entering the town and Mounted Police [were] on hand to enforce the order."[13] At Sheppard, Alberta, "the Canadian Pacific pay car was not allowed to stop."[14] During the scare only two cases of smallpox occurred outside Calgary, and both patients recovered.

In Calgary nine persons eventually contracted the disease, and by mid-August three had died. The town's citizens placed blame for the disease directly on the local Chinese population, and it seemed that violence was imminent. The *Calgary Herald* issued a stern warning to civic officials: "The local feeling against the race is strong and it is as well for the authorities to recognize the fact. If the Chinese now at the quarantine be sent back into the town there will be trouble."[15]

Interestingly, two days later the *Herald* published a long editorial which did not blame Chinese as the transgressors. Rather, the Canadian Pacific Railway and the Canadian federal government were singled out for severe criticism. "There is a strong conviction throughout Canada [and] these Territories, that the Government authorities are greatly to blame for the introduction of smallpox into British Columbia....it is almost impossible to prevent the Canadian Pacific Railway carrying the disease along its entire system....Government officials dealt too easily with the officers and property of this powerful company....all Canada is alarmed at the consequences of this fatal neglect of duty."[16]

During the following two weeks, only one other indication of hostility toward the Chinese appeared in print, when a letter to the editor was published with the ominous title "The Chinamen Must Go." The writer contended that Chinese were "undesirable residents in any white community" and the only solution was to await the release of the quarantined Chinese and, then, "let them and all the others be told that they must go."[17]

On 2 August the four Chinese men in quarantine were released and went to a local Chinese laundry. Upon hearing the news, a mob of over 300 men—many of whom were drunk and had just attended a cricket match—led by seven or eight ringleaders, gathered in the streets to chase the Chinese population out of town. At about 10:30 p.m., they proceeded to the laundry where the released men were residing, but all of the occupants escaped.

The mob then surged on to two other Chinese laundries, where they smashed in the doors and windows. At the second laundry the men unsuccessfully "attempted to burn the place down" and subsequently: "[The mob] visited the Chinese store....One or two Chinamen were badly treated in the melee, though no bones were broken and no serious injury was sustained....The outrages might have been stopped at the outset by the prompt interference of the police, but they were not to be seen until too late. The Mounted Police were finally brought up, but by this time the excitement had spent its force."[18] The total lack of any response by the town's authorities was quite remarkable.

North-West Mounted Police Inspector R.A. Cuthbert's report on the riot is revealing. Inasmuch as he had heard rumors that the Chinese "were to be driven from town," Cuthbert sent an officer on 2 August to notify the mayor that the men were about to be released, "in case he should deem it necessary to take some steps to anticipate a possible disturbance."[19] During the riot several Chinese fled to the Mounted Police barracks for protection. Fearing further outrages, Inspector Cuthbert sent messengers to the mayor offering support; the mayor, however, had "left town shortly after seeing my messenger from quarantine."[20]

Although the North-West Mounted Police rarely acted as town constables, "a squad of men" was dispatched into the town. The inspector explained his action: "...the row seemed to continue and several persons asked me to take some steps to stop it....the matter seemed to be going too far; none of the municipal authorities were disposed to assume any responsibility in dispersing the mob which had gathered or in restoring order....On arrival of the squad in town and the effecting of a couple of arrests the last of the crowd dispersed."[21]

It is beyond question that for a number of hours a large and unruly anti-Chinese mob roamed the streets of the town at will. Fortunately, there were some cool-headed individuals present who checked the roving bands from inordinate acts of physical assault.[22] "More than any other single event in Calgary's history, the smallpox riots [sic] of 1892 illustrated how perilously close the peaceable Canadian frontier came to emulating its more lawless American counterpart."[23]

Calgary's Chinese residents were naturally very badly shaken up by the violence. For the next few nights a number of Chinese arrived at the Mounted Police barracks to join their fellow countrymen. Other Chinese spent the nights at homes of clergymen. The Mounties discovered one terrified fellow in a weakened state hiding in a railway culvert near Gleichen, about fifty kilometres east of the town.

Threats against the Chinese continued, reported Inspector Cuthbert, and "the situation was becoming absurd when the town authorities were urged to take decisive action."[24] The mayor finally requested that the Mounted Police patrol the town. After three weeks of both day and night patrols, the contingent was withdrawn as there appeared to be little likelihood of renewed violence.

The *Calgary Herald* deplored the rioters' actions as a "thoughtless demonstration," adding that "everything approaching the mob spirit is to be condemned."[25] But, the newspaper made it clear two days later that it sympathized with the motives of the rioting element when it advocated a boycott of Chinese businesses. "[By boycotting the Chinese], in a short time, without violence, without any interference with personal liberty, we can be rid of what the majority regard as an obnoxious element....If public opinion decides that he shall go the country will not be a loser by his absence."[26]

Such reporting, even encased in editorial parlance, could only foster hostility and antipathy toward local Chinese. The abusive editorial policy of the *Herald* lasted many years and was typical of almost all Alberta papers.

The *Calgary Tribune* expressed a more tolerant viewpoint than its rival during the smallpox episode. Although the newspaper felt that the alleged harboring of smallpox was wrong, there were no accusatory condemnations of the Chinese as a people. The *Tribune* heartily denounced the rioters, and from the outset, "called for the punishment of its ringleaders."[27] Also, a *Winnipeg Free Press* editorial of 5 August 1892 was reprinted which condemned the un-British behavior of the "cowardly pack" in Calgary and remarked on the "[Chinese] characteristics deserving of admiration."[28]

While positive aspects of the Chinese community were not singled out for praise by the *Tribune*, two letters to the editor were published defending the Chinese. The first letter, submitted by "JUSTICE," called upon all loyal Englishmen to honor Queen Victoria's commitment to China, whereby she expressly guaranteed the immigration of any number of Chinese into Canada and promised that full legal protection for them would exist, unlike the situation in the United States.

The second letter, submitted by "D.C.," advocated establishing "a local Health Society" for all Calgarians' advantage and then related Lord [Garnet] Wolseley's opinions of the Chinese; Wolseley "believed the Chinese to be the greatest race in the world; they possess all the elements of being a great people; they have courage, physical power and absolute contempt for death...."[29]

Nonetheless, at the time, the great majority of Calgarians held the Chinese in derision and disrespect. In mid-August about 600 citizens packed the Opera House to listen to an anti-Asian lecturer, one Locksley Lucas, whose topic was "the Chinese question."

Lucas spoke "at considerable length into the reasons why Chinamen are not desirable residents of any country,"[30] presumably excluding China. The audience "frequently and forcibly expressed their approval of the views promulgated by Mr. Lucas."[31] At the end of the meeting, a provisional committee was formed to establish a branch of the Anti-Chinese League: it consisted of Mayor Lucas (no relation to Locksley), and Councillors Orr and Freeze.

Locksley Lucas was secretary of the Vancouver Anti-Chinese League. While he was in Calgary, he sent his clothes to a Chinese laundry to be cleaned. Word of this leaked out and, not surprisingly, he was subjected to ridicule by some residents. On 17 August, the day after his address at the Opera House, he attempted suicide by taking an overdose of morphine. (In 1894 Lucas died in prison while serving time for seducing an underage girl, his sister-in-law).

Calgary's clergy gave the largest measure of support to the Chinese. At a special meeting with the town council, three representatives of the local clergy expressed concern that no prosecutions had been laid concerning the riot although the leaders were well-known local citizens. Mayor Lucas calmly expressed the opinion that, if prosecutions were laid, "it would be almost impossible to keep the people quiet."[32] The clergy did not press the point and no charges were laid.

The ministers present, however, felt that the town council should assure the Chinese that they could expect full and complete protection under the law. The clergymen's petition for the council to condemn the riot was discussed, but not acted upon.

Mayor Lucas's behavior was openly hostile toward local Chinese. At a council meeting he maintained that the Chinese "deserved to be punished."[33] Moreover, the mayor's calculated absence from town was hardly coincidental. Not only did a Mounted Policeman warn him on the day of the riot of the impending release of the men in quarantine, but Lucas blandly told the council that "some of them [Chinese] had come to his house several hours before the riot and asked for him, intimating that there was going to be trouble."[34] Chief of Police English was out of town for the week, and the mayor decided to absent himself as well and let events take their course, whatever happened.

Councillor Wesley F. Orr, a man of similar racist sentiments, offered a double lot of land free of cost to any white person who would thereupon construct and operate a laundry employing only white personnel. He hoped that this would "make the presence of Mongolians in our midst totally unnecessary."[35]

The 1892 Smallpox Riot was an isolated act of concerted violence directed against Calgary's very small Chinese population. It revealed that the majority Anglo-Canadian population regarded the Chinese as an undesirable group in "their" town. The incident and its shameful aftermath—when racial rage simmered and seriously threatened to boil over into concerted violence—clearly demonstrated the presence of a "garrison mentality"[36] in the town. In other words, the town's citizens held deep convictions as to what, and even who, was right and proper for the continuing community good.

Prairie isolation in Calgary and other frontier towns reinforced the strength of existing principles and the sense of community. The Chinese "outsiders," as a whole, were condemned by Anglo-Canadians in this instance as carriers of disease into "their" town: it was not the sick man and those who cared for him who were blamed, but all local Chinese.

The 1892 Smallpox Riot was the most dramatic example of widespread hostility to Chinese in early Alberta history. Pervasive prejudicial attitudes in Alberta regarding Asians transcended political orientations and class allegiances, although anti-Asian sentiment was stronger in southern Alberta.[37] Especially before 1910, the press and politicians of the province were vehemently anti-Asian on many occasions, and few citizens in the province expressed any public support for the Chinese.

Chinese Settlement in Lethbridge and Medicine Hat

Most Chinese who settled in the Canadian prairie provinces became owners or employees of small businesses. This phenomenon resulted primarily from Chinese experience in B.C., where operating stores had proved "quite profitable [and thus] when the Chinese penetrated to the prairie and eastern provinces, most of them opened business for themselves."[38]

Chinese businesses in Alberta—as throughout the Canadian West—consisted overwhelmingly of restaurants, laundries, and grocery stores. Chinese entrepreneurs took full advantage of any perceived opportunities and set up service-sector enterprises in hamlets, villages, towns, and cities dispersed throughout Alberta; through patient work, long hours, and good service, they maintained their enterprises on a highly competitive basis.

In Medicine Hat, as in Lethbridge, the number of Chinese residents was not large; however, occasional items concerning local Chinese appeared in newspapers, providing some insights into what was happening.

The first Chinese resident in Medicine Hat appears to have been Lee Turn who opened a laundry in late March 1887. Lee, referred to as "an intelligent Chinaman,"[39] shortly thereafter remarked that he had all the work he could handle and was "well pleased with the prospects in Medicine Hat."[40] In 1889 another Chinese laundry opened, as well as a Chinese restaurant. In the next two decades additional Chinese businesses were founded in the growing town, including laundries, restaurants, and several stores specializing in goods from China.

The Chinese presence in Medicine Hat did not lead to serious instances of violence against local Chinese. In an apparently rare act of violence, a broken wagon wheel and the shafts of a light wagon were thrust through the windows of a local Chinese laundry. The *Medicine Hat Times* castigated the men involved for committing "a dastardly [and] most cowardly act."[41]

The so-called "Chinese question" was apparently not a local issue, even during elections. It is noteworthy, too, that the *Medicine Hat Times* severely denounced the 1892 Smallpox Riot. The previous year the newspaper had published an editorial entitled the "Enterprising Chinese," which remarked on the construction of a rice mill and a salmon cannery by Chinese in B.C.[42]

Although local Chinese launderers were severely criticized on occasion for spreading ashes in lanes and depositing dirty water into the streets, condemnations of Chinese as a people did not appear on the pages of Medicine Hat newspapers.

The absence of a relatively large Chinese population was almost certainly a factor in the remarkably moderate Medicine Hat attitude toward Chinese residents. Also, more personalized and informal relations were possible in a small urban centre, but this alone does not at all account for the atypical Medicine Hat situation.

One very prominent Chinese merchant, the owner of several businesses, was referred to in the press in 1910 as the "genial and popular Quon Koy,"[43] an indication of the general acceptance of the Chinese presence in Medicine Hat. This Chinese pioneer undoubtedly did a great deal to establish in the minds of community leaders and the general public a very positive image of the Chinese people—of which he was clearly a very worthy representative.

A small Chinatown grew up in Medicine Hat on North Railway Street, where a number of Chinese businesses were located.

In Lethbridge Chinese settlement followed the same general pattern as in Calgary and Medicine Hat. By May 1890 there were three Chinese laundries operating in Lethbridge. In the next two decades, as the town expanded, additional Chinese businesses located in its centre. During this period, a Chinatown came into existence on Second Avenue South, between Second and Third Streets.

Shortly before the turn of the century, a substantial number of Chinese market gardens were established in the Lethbridge vicinity because of very favorable climatic conditions. The market gardens conducted by Chinese could be as large as twenty acres in size each. By 1902 about 300 Chinese in the Lethbridge area depended directly or indirectly on market gardening for their livelihood.

The Chinese presence in Lethbridge and district was not as acceptable to local Anglo-Canadians as was the case in Medicine Hat. One factor was the relatively larger number of Chinese in the area and the more readily apparent Chinese presence. Secondly, nativist sentiment in Lethbridge was quite pronounced during the period under consideration. In addition to the Chinese, the presence of many Mormons, Mennonites, and non-Anglo-

Saxons in the immediate Lethbridge area accentuated negative Anglo--Canadian responses toward minority groups.

Anti-Chinese sentiment in Lethbridge was not readily apparent until after 1900, although in 1892 the response of the *Lethbridge News* to the Calgary Smallpox Riot was to refer to Calgary's Chinese residents as "plague breeding celestials."[44] In 1899, too, Reverend Charles McKillop complained to the town council that, among other technically illegal matters, the police were ignoring Chinese who worked on Sundays.

From 1902 to 1909 a number of incidents and editorials demonstrated the prevalence of hostile attitudes toward Chinese residents. One indication of press attitudes was that Chinese market gardens and laundries were occasionally denigrated. In 1902 the *Lethbridge News* lamented the Chinese take-over of the market garden industry and thundered against supposedly unsanitary Chinese practices in that endeavor.

In 1905 when the first modern steam laundry opened in the town, the *Lethbridge Herald* urged its readers to give Chinese launderers "the go-by"[45] and patronize "a white institution."[46] Nonetheless, the steam laundry was an utter failure within a year.

Lethbridge newspapers strongly advocated the disfranchisement of Chinese in Alberta, when that question became an issue in B.C. The press even advocated segregation of the local Chinese community. Regarding the former, in 1907 the *Herald* stated: "The Alberta Government would be well advised if it passed legislation making it impossible for a Chinaman to have a vote in this province. Make these yellow men understand we are not going to allow them to secure any influence in our affairs. They have no right...to compete with white votes."[47]

Regarding segregation, in early October 1905 the *News* stated: "[A] matter which calls for prompt attention is the restriction of Chinese to certain quarters. This is done in other towns and should be done here."[48] Several days later the *News* was even more blunt: "The Chinese in Lethbridge should be assigned to certain quarters and made to stay there."[49] Clearly, from time to time before 1910, there was a perceived—if contrived—Chinese question in Lethbridge, as in Calgary.

On Christmas Day 1907 Lethbridge hostility toward the Chinese population resulted in a riotous attack on Chinese business premises. The episode originated when a disturbance broke out in the Columbia Restaurant. When the Chinese owner told an unruly, though popular, local customer to leave his premises, the man refused and created a disturbance;

the distraught owner felt compelled to hit the disorderly patron with a hammer. No appreciable damage was incurred, however, and the slightly stunned patron turned up shortly thereafter at a Christmas dinner party, apparently none the worse for wear!

All the same, a rumor originated and quickly spread that the man in question had died from the hammer-blow. A crowd of some 500 obstreperous men soon gathered in the streets.

A "spontaneous movement to clean out the supposed murderers...and all their fellow countrymen"[50] then ensued, buoyed by the liberal consumption of holiday spirits. At the Columbia Restaurant a gang of men demolished "everything in sight," and "the Chinamen were roughly handled but finally escaped."[51] Nearly every other Chinese restaurant in the city was then visited; the angry mob threw stones through any visible windows and caused further damage.

The tumult continued, and the extremely dangerous situation was approaching a virtually uncontrollable level of intensity. The mayor, "as soon as he saw the magnitude of the disturbance, 'phoned the Mounted Police, swore in a lot of special constables and made a speech to the mob."[52] Things quieted down upon arrival of the police squad, who guarded all Chinese businesses, and the arrival of the Mounted Police ended the wild affair. The riot was an isolated example in Lethbridge of frontier violence toward the local Chinese population.

A by-law was passed early in 1909 "to remove Chinese laundries, etc., from the centre sections of the city."[53] Two Chinese laundry proprietors were charged with violating the by-law, and they retained a lawyer to test the city's authority to pass it. It appears that they lost their case, because in September Mah Wah was tried by a magistrate for running a laundry in a downtown area, contrary to city by-laws. He was remanded for a week, having promised to move his business by then.

In March 1909 North Ward ratepayers presented a petition to the city council asking that Chinese restaurants and laundries be banned from their part of the city. The council unanimously favored the petition and decided not to grant a licence to a restaurant-owner already in the area, should he apply for one. Council announced that it would soon consider establishing "a restricted district."[54]

In September the city board of health met "to discuss the matter of Chinese laundries being within a certain area. They found that it was outside their power to do anything in the matter."[55] Nonetheless, until a new sewer was put in working order, the laundries were directed to dispose of waste water appropriately. A few days later the *Lethbridge Daily News* editorialized that it was regrettable that the city council did not have the power under the licence by-law to refuse licence applications and added: "A Chinese laundry...is decidedly objectionable in a residential district and should not be allowed."[56]

On 21 September—probably in response to the lengthy editorial of thirteen days earlier—three aldermen were appointed as "a committee to map out a district where Chinese laundries may be located...."[57] By-law No. 83 was passed in November 1910, and it took effect as of 1 January 1911. By its terms Chinese laundries were confined to the area from First Avenue to Second Avenue South, and from First Street to Fourth Street. This came to be called the Restricted Area. Chinese laundries were confined there for over five years, until the by-law was rescinded.

Stereotyping of Chinese was well-established in North America by the late nineteenth century. Among various supposed negative characteristics of Chinese behavior, were female slavery and smoking opium. These issues were of at least some concern in Lethbridge and typified cultural conflict.

Writing of 1908 or 1909, James Carpenter, a former Lethbridge police chief, has remarked: "Early unfounded fears of opium use and white slavery were reflected in the attitude of some citizens who felt it their duty to draw to Council's attention that some of the Chinese operating laundries, cafes and restaurants were hiring white girls. Chief Gillespie was instructed to report on the matter and then Council instructed the City Solicitor to see if a prohibition of this practice could become law." Carpenter has also noted that: "As late as 1930 there was disapproval if a white girl was employed by a Chinese."[58]

Chinese Settlement in Edmonton

Ten years before the first Chinese pioneers settled in the town, the *Edmonton Bulletin* remarked: "The Victoria Colonist demands the exclusion of the Chinese from British Columbia. While the paper is right in saying that we should have the right to choose the immigrants we want, it has not been shown that the Chinese are injurious in any way, and in fact they are helping to develop the natural resources by their cheap labor."[59] Such moderation and tolerance on the part of the *Bulletin* would, unfortunately, be reversed with the passage of the years .

Chinese did not settle as early in Edmonton as they did in the other major centres of Alberta; nor did as many settle there as in Calgary. The first Chinese settler was Chung Gee who arrived in July 1892. Formerly a resident of Calgary, he wanted to escape from the rampant anti-Chinese sentiments ominously simmering there during the smallpox affliction. He opened the first Chinese laundry in Edmonton.

The same summer witnessed the arrival of Wing Lee and several other Chinese, possibly "refugees" from the violence and racial tension in Calgary. Wing Lee opened the second Chinese laundry in Edmonton.

The winter of 1892-1893 was extremely cold. "Chung Yan, a laundryman, had trouble keeping warm, and then on top of that, bore the brunt of intolerant neighbors. During March he inadvertently caused a minor fire by throwing his ashes out on the back of the lot. For a while he was in grave danger of mob action."[60] Referring to the episode, the *Bulletin*'s editor said that Albertans could do without Jews, Mormons, and Chinese. The newspaper's tolerant editorial stance of a decade earlier regarding the Chinese had disappeared altogether.

The Chinese population increased slowly. By 1899 there were only thirteen Chinese in the town. Most or all of these men would have worked at the two Chinese hand laundries and one Chinese restaurant operating at that time. By 1911 there were 130 Chinese in Alberta's capital city.

Before the turn of the century, a Chinatown was in existence at Jasper Avenue (the major downtown road) and 97th Street. A goodly number of Chinese occupied small cottages on 97th Street, while others lived in the general vicinity.

In 1908 the *Edmonton Bulletin* published what it regarded as an exposé of the state of affairs of local "Celestials From the Kingdom of Teeming Millions." One purported reason for the article's appearance was "the acute nature of the threatened yellow peril on the Pacific coast." The reporter who wrote the article made a one-night tour of Chinese premises. He and his editors deemed these few hours of general observation quite sufficient as a basis to document the inside story about the Chinese way of life in the city.

The astute, overnight authority provided an overview of the Chinese community early in his report. "There are restaurant keepers, there are laundrymen, domestics, gamblers and there is one lonely cobbler who does work for the Celestials in the shoemaking line. They are divided into three main divisions, the leaders of which are Wong Fook, Mah Jim and Sam Sing."

In the course of his encounters, the wordsmith and self-proclaimed explorer mustered enough courage to visit stores featuring varied merchandise. "In the Chinese stores queer wares were on sale: the long, strange pipes of the Celestials, strange looking masses of Chinese foods, lacquer work, ivory carvings, silk clothing and other curious and unknown articles." In one store all of the basement was "connected from end to end with mysterious doors and passages." There, he found a number of bunks and an assortment of Chinese musical instruments.

The intrepid investigator dared not disappoint readers who were seeking sensationalistic tidbits of a lurid nature. "In one room a half dozen Chinamen lay in various stages of bliss induced by the smoking of opium, the acrid fumes of which hung heavy in the air. One...shrunken specimen of Chinese manhood lay like dead with his flat chest barely moving. He was in the supreme power of the powerful drug and was dreaming poppy dreams of Chinese joy. Another was just recovering and his languid and stupid actions bore testimony of the after results of his debauch."

Apparently, it was possible for whites to be admitted to the "opium joint," but: "To succeed in gaining admittance one must have the backing of the best of the Chinks in command and then he is watched pretty closely until he has demonstrated without doubt that he is really on a par with the yellow slaves of the poppy product."[61] Importing, manufacturing, and smoking opium were perfectly legal in Canada at the time this article was written, and many whites throughout the country regularly smoked opium. To bolster his sensationalistic, racist account, the *Bulletin*'s reporter conveniently neglected to mention these crucial facts.

In 1909 a play, *King of the Opium Ring*, was presented at the opera house. The producer engaged two local Chinese to appear in it. As reported at the time, "The Chinamen are in no way essential to the production of the play, but Manager Allen was anxious to have them for scenic purposes only." The scheduled appearance of the men in such a production caused a "commotion in Chinatown" and the *Edmonton Journal* reported that "real if not serious trouble is brewing."[62]

Such flagrant and demeaning exploitation was bound to upset the Chinese community. If the two men supposedly hired actually appeared in the presentation, they undoubtedly did so because of serious economic necessity, inasmuch as they certainly lacked the blessing of most fellow Chinese.

During these times the city's Chinese residents were occasionally subjected to police raids. In September 1910, for example, twenty-eight men were arrested following a Saturday-night raid. Mah Quong Gee was charged with running a gambling house. When the others were acquitted on the charge of frequenting a gambling house, it looked as if Mah would also go free; presumably, this is what happened.

As related above, the Chinese were held in disrespect by Edmonton newspapers. After the Calgary Smallpox Riot—and in contrast to some other Canadian newspapers—the editors of the *Edmonton Bulletin* made it amply clear that they sympathized with the riotous mob. They referred to "foreign heathens who may choose to engage in the distribution of opium, leprosy, small-pox and diabolism generally in their midst."

The editorial continued: "...we have a Chinese question [to face] in all its hideousness and harmfulness; and as if that were not enough a part of our own press must use Chinese dirt...to besmirch those who believe that the highest and best charity is that which begins at home. It is quite possible that what these people are pleased to call the Calgary outrage is not sanctioned by law, but let the action of the Chinese which led to the so-called outrage be considered...."[63]

The equating of "charity...at home" and the outrageous actions and intents of the Calgary mob was quite remarkable; besides, Calgary was also the "home" of the victimized Chinese; but this seemingly was either not accepted as being the case, or else the self-evident fact did not make a conscious impression on the mind of the bigoted editor.

In September 1907 the Edmonton Trades and Labour Council adopted a resolution protesting against the admittance of Japanese and Chinese laborers into B.C. Copies of the resolution were sent to Victoria and Ottawa. This prompted a long letter to the editor by Emilia F. Murphy. She praised the Chinese for helping to build the Canadian Pacific Railway and for their contributions to the coal industry and salmon canneries. Because of the rarity of whites publicly defending Chinese in this time period, her remarks are worthy of note:

> One might imagine from hearing these axe-to-grind unions talk of "the Chinese invasion" that Canada was about to be converted into a dependency of the Chinese Empire....at present, when our country is so sparsely populated, it is a grave error in statesmanship to exclude any law-abiding worker

> save for reasons moral, financial and sanitary....while they may carry their dollars out of Canada, it is manifest that they cannot take the result of their labors away. The road is built, the land cleared or the fish netted....There are some few of us in Canada who think that the anti-Chinese clamor arises from the fact that the conservative oriental, with his immobile taciturn face, is too smart for us....He pays his debts promptly, lives up to his contracts, and weighs goods at sixteen ounces to the pound. The Chinese are a strong race physically. They are a strong race intellectually. Most of them can read and write in their own language....To sum the whole matter up, it is the Chinaman's virtues we are afraid of, rather than his vices.[64]

Perhaps her remarks prompted at least a few racist-minded readers to re-evaluate their biases.

In October 1907 Senator George McHugh of Lindsay, Ontario, arrived in Edmonton on a tour of the West. He spoke with an *Edmonton Journal* reporter, who noted: "The great question of the Oriental invasion now agitating the coast, he said, was a matter to be considered seriously and at once. If the yellow race is to be kept out of Canada there is an easy solution to the problem: if labor were refused the Japs and Chinese and only whites employed in every case where work is to be done, they would have to get out or starve, that's all!"

The question directly concerned race and patriotism, maintained the senator. "Canada is a white man's country. If there are some who would hire the Chinese and employ cheap labor, they are not true citizens of Canada and patriotic."[65] B.C.'s racist, and presumably Sinophobic, politicians clearly had like-minded counterparts elsewhere in Canada.

Also in 1907 W.R. Trotter, "Dominion Organizer of the Trades and Labour Congress, addressed a very large and enthusiastic gathering in the Mechanics Hall." It was reported: "The Chinese problem in both Australia and Canada received his attention to a considerable extent. It was explained in a concise and a very conclusive manner how the Australians handled the very perplexing question. They simply made it so hot for the Chinaman that he had to get out and it was almost an impossibility for him to live in the country."

The speaker then added remarks designed to thoroughly unsettle his listeners. "Mr. Trotter told of the existing conditions in British Columbia, how the Chink and the Jap were superseding the whites at every turn. If it were not stopped they would soon control the labor and the business of the country."[66] Trotter's wildly exaggerated viewpoint was typical of labor leaders throughout much of the country at this time.

In March 1908 an "opium den" was found to be operating "right in the heart of Edmonton, within hailing distance of the police station." The reporter observed: "On the ground floor is an imitation business, a bluff. Upstairs are twelve or fifteen bunks.... Alongside each [is a] smoking outfit—a spirit lamp and small jar of opium....Not that all Chinamen smoke opium. Many do not do so. In fact, only a minority smoke, but those who do so must have their 'dope'....Their faces have [a] darkness that characterizes the opium fiend....Here is a man who smokes three times a day and attends to his business regularly." Contradicting the statement just quoted, the reporter concluded: "Opium is an imperious master and brooks no inattention, in fact the drug robs men of all interest in anything else."[67]

Apart from sensationalistic reporting regarding the Chinese community, Edmonton papers also freely printed racial slurs. For example, in 1910 the following appeared in the *Journal*: "A Toronto detective says that he secured evidence that the Chinamen were playing fantan by looking through cracks in the wall. In other words, he saw through the Chinks."[68] Among other disparaging epithets, Chinese were referred to as "Mongolians."

"The Chinese Question"

Before Chinese ever set foot in Alberta, the *Calgary Herald* unequivocally decided that they would not be welcome additions to the town. In September 1884 the paper chose to reprint an article from the *Hamilton Spectator*. In part, it stated: "We do not want Chinamen in Canada. It is desirable that this country shall not be peopled by any servile race....the million who will soon people the great Prairie of the West shall be children of the Indo-Germanic parents...not the degenerate children of the Mongols."[69]

Remarking upon the federal Royal Commission on Chinese Immigration, established in mid-1884, the *Herald* stated later the same year: "[the] experiment of introducing Chinese into America has proved a disastrous and terrible experiment...." A prognostication in the Alberta context was advanced: "We have a right to be indignant and a reason to sympathize with the British Columbians, for we are their neighbors, and what proves a curse to them will presently become a curse to us."[70]

Early the next year the *Herald* commented: "It is the fate of Chinese immigrants to occasion periodical fits of excitement among the residents of the Pacific coast. Let them take some Alberta advice. So long as Canada is a part of the Empire...she must bear a few of the Imperial burdens and among others, the Chinese infliction, for it is certain if Canadians are admitted into Chinese ports the Chinese must be admitted into Canadian harbors."

In the same editorial, however, the writer proposed a means whereby Chinese would have no choice but to leave Canada for good. "The Irish have, however, with the true genius which inspires that people, taught us the proper way of attaining desirable ends by constitutional means and the teaching may be taken to heart by the British Columbians. Let them boycott the pigtails. If they refused to employ Chinese help or labor, they would depart where the favorite people of Providence are better appreciated."[71] This was not the last time boycotting the Chinese was advocated by Alberta newspapers.

Three years later, clearly revealing strong elements of Sinophobia, the same paper reported: "The insidious almond eyed gentlemen from the walled empire continue to work themselves into Canada."[72]

In 1904 the Calgary city council passed a by-law "stipulating that no more Chinese laundries were to be allowed on Main Street, Stephen Avenue, and in any business streets in Calgary."[73] The by-law was not enforced, however. In 1905 "the Calgary Central Labour Union condemned the Chinese laundries as a menace to health, and the *Calgary Herald* demanded that the Chinese laundries be cleaned in order to avoid an epidemic."[74]

In September 1907 an anti-Asian rampage occurred in Vancouver. A mob of about 1 000 people who had just attended a rally of the Asiatic Exclusion League surged through Chinatown and the outskirts of the Japanese district to destroy property; many business premises were damaged, especially in Chinatown.

The *Calgary Herald* commented: "Every Western Canadian sympathizes with the protests of British Columbia against the Japanese invasion. Every Canadian...will deplore the unseemly and dangerous action of the Vancouver mob which attacked the Oriental portion of the city....A systematic scheme of immigration inimical to the best interests of Western Canada and pregnant with danger to the Dominion as a whole has been carried on with the full knowledge and even connivance of Ottawa."[75] The editor's real sympathies were obviously more with the rioting element, than with those who bore the brunt of the mindless attacks.

The stance of the *Calgary Albertan* was similar. "The *Albertan* has all sympathy for the Coast people who are making an effort to preserve Canada for the white race....The incident of last Saturday night was regrettable, because it was unwise and retards the efforts that are being made to...restrict the Asiatic labor in the country."[76] Three years later the paper's editors wrote in a similar vein: "The *Albertan* believes that Oriental labor, as far as possible, should be excluded from Canada."[77]

As has been seen above, the so-called Chinese question was of concern in Lethbridge. In 1907 the *Lethbridge Herald* stated: "the coming of thousands of Asiatic people to Canada, if not a menace at this moment will be in a few years. Surely we do not want to see a rich province like British Columbia in control of yellow men. This is what would happen if things were allowed to proceed as they have been."[78]

The same year, the *Herald* adamantly advocated disfranchising Asians. "We would like to see the Alberta government...pass a law preventing any of the Asiatic races having votes in this province. We do not want people without our ideals of government, without our aspirations as a province and nation to bear any part in the election of our representatives. We have enough poor stuff in the voting class now.... It is bad enough to have these races in the country but it would be incomparably worse to give them a voice in our affairs."[79]

In 1909 John Angus McDonald wrote a letter to the *Herald* announcing to electors of the Rocky Mountain electoral district that he would be running as an independent candidate in the 23 March election. "I stand for the disfranchising of people of the Asiatic race, such as Japs and Chinamen. These people take no interest in our institutions and they should not be given the franchise and I pledge myself if elected to deprive them of this right, also to prohibit their employment in or around the coal mines of the province."[80] There was much anti-Asian talk bandied about during this particular election.

In 1898 a Fort Macleod citizen wrote to the *Macleod Gazette*: "One of the most important subjects to deal with at the present time is the Chinese question....The washing is taken from the deserving half breed and the odd chores from the Indian worker, and the white cook is replaced by a celestial." In a rather contradictory vein, the writer continued: "There is no doubt of their being an enterprising, hard working people, and if they but spent their money like white people we would not care [but] as it is now, they affect us one and all....The only solution [is] to employ Chinese only when white labor cannot be obtained, and to deal and trade with them when you cannot do so well elsewhere. This vexed question is a social evil that demands a remedy."[81]

In response to the letter the editor remarked: "We are of the opinion, moreover, that our correspondent's suggestion to only employ Chinese labor when "white" labor is unattainable, is pretty generally acted upon. The almost total impossibility of getting good cooks and household servants is well known, and the Celestial cook and kitchen help is [sic] the only one left to fall back on."[82]

A few years later, in 1906, the Fort Macleod town council "placed a tax of one hundred dollars on Chinese laundries to discourage their operation."[83]

Hostility toward Chinese was not uncommon and was sometimes potentially very dangerous. One nearly deadly incident occurred in 1910. That summer an irrigation survey party was camped about fifty-five kilometres northeast of Strathmore, Alberta. As reported in a newspaper account, the Chinese cook "carelessly emptied some hot ashes on the dry prairie, and in a minute a brisk fire had started." The men of the party spent eighteen hours fighting the fire, which laid waste an area of sixteen-square kilometres and burned most of the men's belongings. When the men learned who had started the fire, they became "enraged" and "threatened to lynch him, and were only stopped by Engineer Rath, who was in charge of the party, and who stood in front of the Chinaman with a club and threatened to knock down the first man who touched him."[84]

The Chinatown Relocation Issue of 1910 in Calgary

Calgary's first Chinatown, established in the early 1890s, was located on the corner of Centre Street South and Ninth Avenue East, across from the Canadian Pacific Railway Station. By 1900 it consisted of two restaurants, a hand laundry, two groceries, and a twenty-bed rooming-house. The Kwong Man Yuen Restaurant at 815 Centre Street South in Chinatown had a "community room" behind its premises, where Chinese congregated after work to socialize and drink tea or perhaps Sam Suey, a Chinese whiskey.

After 1901 increasing numbers of Chinese arrived in southern Alberta, along with many thousands of European settlers. In Calgary the need arose around 1901 for a larger Chinatown: to meet the increased demand for goods and services, as well as for rooming facilities. The first Chinatown could not expand as, due to its restricted location, there was simply no adjacent unused land.

Accordingly, a second Chinatown came into existence in the immediate vicinity of the recently built Chinese Mission, and businesses opened along Tenth Avenue and First Street, South West. By 1910 this Chinatown consisted of twelve businesses, several community rooms, and rooming facilities. Chinese businesses in the first Chinatown, however, continued to operate for some years after 1901, and most Chinese residents continued to live in quarters behind their business premises, which were scattered throughout the city.

In 1910, however, Calgary's second Chinatown was forced to relocate. This resulted in a brief minor stir. In June 1910 the Canadian Northern Railway announced its proposed route into the city, and plans called for the construction of a mammoth hotel/depot on the corner of Tenth Avenue and First Street, South West. Property values in Chinatown immediately soared, and the non-Chinese owners of the real estate concerned sold their holdings.

The Chinese community was in full agreement that the best course would be to buy their own property and, thereby, have the say in the next Chinatown. Several wealthy Chinese merchants jointly purchased a site at the south-east corner of Centre Street and Second Avenue, South East; after submitting detailed construction plans, they received a building permit.

On 4 October 1910 a deputation of angry citizens, represented by Alderman James Short, K.C., approached the city commissioners and demanded that the proposed Chinatown be located on another site. The citizens, supposedly owners of property situated near the chosen site, advocated a segregated Chinatown. Alderman Short remarked: "It is for you to take up the question and set the Chinese in one section of the city as you would an isolation hospital."[85]

The city commissioners subsequently issued a temporary order to withhold any further building permits to Chinese until the situation was resolved. The Chinese took into consideration alternate locations and expressed considerable interest in property between Seventh and Eighth Avenues, South West, across from Mewata Park; at the same time they insisted that, if another site were chosen, they must be fully reimbursed for their investment to that date.

At a 10 October 1910 city council meeting, in "respect to the Chinese puzzle," a petition presented by three citizens was approved which recommended "that the commissioners, twelve citizens appointed by the mayor and twelve representatives of the Chinese should confer within the next few days and report back to the council."[86] The question at hand was: "What shall be done with the Chinese citizens of Calgary, will they be placed in a special quarter, or will they be permitted to go where they like?"[87]

On 13 October the representative parties met and discussed the Chinatown issue. Three white members of the Chinese Mission formed part of the Chinese delegation, "while prominent among the Chinese were Luey Kheong, president of the [Chinese Empire] Reform Association of Calgary, and Ho Lem, representing the laundry interests."[88]

Chinese delegation meets with city Commissioners.
October 13, 1910. Glenbow Archives, NA-2798-6.

The members of the conference passed "a resolution that no action be taken by the council in the matter of segregation but that they pass a by-law regulating sleeping and living space in houses."[89] Alderman Cameron stated after the meeting that: "Objection was taken to anything being said about segregation as we are all opposed to segregation."[90] A more careful reading of the episode reveals that whenever an alternate site for Chinatown was suggested, there were objections from the aldermen or residents of the area in question.

To all intents, the Chinatown relocation issue was resolved at the conference, and the initial phase of building a new Chinatown—one featuring a good deal of general Chinese say in significant matters—was able to proceed. In 1910, then, Calgary's third, and present-day, Chinatown had its origins.

Before long, the Chinese businessmen who had bought the site at the corner of Centre Street and Second Avenue, South East, had a fine two-storey brick block occupying the piece of land. A block and one-half to the south, Paul Dofoo's father, "Luey Dofoo, opened a grocery store on Centre Street in Chinatown in 1911. Slowly, more shop/houses were erected."[91] By 1912, as a Chinese pioneer noted, "there were...a few Chinese restaurants there."[92]

The Chinatown Relocation Issue of 1910 revealed that, although anti-Chinese sentiment was still prevalent in the city, there had been an overall improvement in the local standing of the Chinese population. For instance, when a petition opposing the proposed site of Chinatown was circulated in the general vicinity of Centre Street, only a small minority of people in the area signed it—just 38 of 450 eligible property owners.

Some prominent Calgary citizens also publicly supported the Chinese and maintained that they were deserving and desirable citizens. Alderman Stanley T. Jones remarked in part: "There is one reason the Chinese are unpopular and that is that they have got along well....Those discriminating are against them on the grounds of religion and race."[93]

The most revealing remarks uttered during the controversy were those of Mr. H. Haskins, a member of the "white delegation," who felt compelled to remark at the 13 October conference: "Many of them [Chinese] are among our best citizens. The only solution I see is that we leave them completely alone....They are a different class in Calgary to San Francisco and New York. We have some of the best of the boys....They are better citizens than lots of people...and I could point to some around me. If you want to do something good, let's turn to something else than getting after these hard-working honest citizens."[94]

At the same time letters to the editor by prominent members of the Chinese Mission, J.B. Henderson and R.H. Standerwick, lauded the provident nature of the Chinese people. The former wrote that he had personally drawn up the plans and specifications for the proposed brick block which were "better than...actually required." He added: "[Let us abide] by the strictest letter of the law, and show the same faith in the law and its administration that these people [the Chinese] have done."[95]

This liberal conviction was borne out during the relocation episode in a reply by Luey Kheong, a prominent Chinese merchant. In what was probably the first public rejoinder in a Calgary newspaper by a Chinese resident, the author demonstrated considerable political acumen and humor:

> Calgary, Oct. 6 — To the Editor of the *Herald* - I take your paper and see that some people in Calgary are saying some bad things about my countrymen here. This is not right. The Canadian government has given us the right to live here and pay our debts. We want to do honest business in Calgary, same as all men, and, Canada's law will protect us. You send missionaries to our homes in China, and we use them good; also English business men. If my people are no good to live here, what good trying to make them go to Heaven? Perhaps there will be only my people there. Thanking you for your trouble. I am, yours truly,
>
> *Luey Kheong*
> Chinese Merchant
> Member Chinese Empire Reform Association[96]

Such expressions of Chinese opinion rarely found their way into local newspapers.

More common to frontier-city journalism was the expression of segregationist opinion in favor of a relocated, distinctly homogeneous Chinatown. The *Calgary Albertan* feared that the city core would degenerate without segregation. "The Chinese are all right in their place, but their place is not in the heart of the business district of the city."[97] The *Calgary Herald*, on the other hand, regarded the recently acquired Birnie market site as the best Chinatown location and added: "The Chinese, wherever they locate, should not be allowed to establish their centre on a main thoroughfare as Centre Street."[98]

Such extremely harsh, haughty positions as these were almost certainly not characteristic of broader civic opinion. A poll of the city of Calgary's nine senior officials, for example, revealed that only one of them advocated segregation of the Chinese and, then, "only if it were carried out properly."[99]

3

Social and Cultural Affairs

Before examining the lives of Chinese pioneers more closely, some insights should be provided into the personal background of pioneers whose remarks and experiences are quoted or described throughout much of this study. For example, of interest and relevance are the ages of arriving immigrants interviewed—from a seven-year-old (Byng Lee), who sailed in 1910 from Hong Kong to Victoria, where his father awaited his arrival and that of his mother, to a twenty-five-year-old (Ook Wah Yee), who, having decided to emigrate, in 1912 promptly married and then travelled from Guangdong to Thailand, where his father had a business, to obtain from him the $500 required to enter Canada.

There was certainly a degree of diversity in age and background among Chinese entering Canada. This should be kept in mind since over-simplification in this respect is far too tempting. That this holds true is because most Chinese immigrants during the pre-Exclusion era tended to be quite similar in most important respects, even in terms of originating from a very few counties (or districts) in one particular south-eastern province, Guangdong, which was comprised of fully ninety-eight counties (*xian*).

Readers should keep in mind that ethnic histories—by definition and necessity—present most material in terms of the experiences and actions of peoples as a whole, distinguishing commonalties among their members, and generalities pertaining to group settlement and community formation and development.

Moreover, readers should never overlook the fact that everyone who was (or is) a member of the group in question had his or her own unique, very personal, flesh-and-blood life experiences, complete with all manner of hardships; achievements; frustrations; goals and expectations; toil; comradeship; loving; sorrow; longing; caring; and moments of happiness and contentment.

A More Personal View: The Pioneers

Of the nineteen male pioneers who were interviewed, five arrived in Canada when they were quite young: ages seven, nine, and eleven. Upon arrival, four, if not all five children lived with one or more members of their immediate family. One of these youths lived alternately between Canada and China from ages nine through twenty-one, travelling back and forth three or four times; all the while, however, he faithfully attended school in both countries.

Seven youths arrived when they were teenagers. Four of them attended school after coming to Canada; two were fourteen, and two fifteen years of age. One youth left school after just a few months because he was very unhappy there; another fellow attended for one-and-one-half years; another, for two years; because of economic necessity the fourth left after four years.

The three youths who did not attend school arrived at sixteen, seventeen, and eighteen years of age; the youngest initially lived and worked at his father's charcoal shop; the next eldest began work as a houseboy and, six months later, joined his father as a fellow cook at a hotel; the eldest youth worked initially at a restaurant, then did odd jobs, and for a while was a miner.

The seven remaining pioneers interviewed entered Canada as workers. As it turned out, fully five of these men were twenty years of age when they came to Canada; two were age twenty-five.

Also of interest are the years of arrival of the nineteen pioneers. Two pioneers arrived in Canada in 1910; one came in 1911; from 1912 to 1914, eleven arrived; the remaining five arrived in the early 1920s.

Individually, of course, every adult immigrant left south China because of particular circumstances. King Loo, for example, specifically recalled what had impelled him to sail overseas. "I left mainly because warlords and large bands of bandits and marauders were ravaging my country. I wanted to leave the chaos and danger behind."[1] Seto Gan, too, had a clearly defined motive for leaving China. "I migrated to Canada...from Hoi-ping, near Canton. There were too many people [there] and no work was available; so, I migrated here to try to get a job."[2]

Interestingly, a pattern of emigration based upon clan practice or convention soon emerged in terms of settlement in Alberta. Charlie Chew, for example, stated that his father first arrived in Canada about 1893. In 1913, at age seventeen, Charlie sailed to Canada and soon after his arrival teamed up with his father for life. Concerning his trip over, aboard *The Empress of Russia*, Charlie noted: "with me were some of my cousins who had previously lived and worked in Canada."[3]

In 1922 Frank Wong left China by steamer to join his father and grandfather in Olds, Alberta. Arthur Yee Mock's grandfather labored on the construction of the CPR. In 1914 Arthur's father was brought to Canada by an uncle of his, while in 1922 the father paid a $500 head tax so that Arthur could join him.

Joe How recounted in some detail the scope of his clan's emigration to Canada. "My grandfather and others were the first of our clan...to come to Canada. Then, they brought over their nephews and other relatives. My grandfather had four brothers and my father had three brothers. All of them came to Canada."[4] He added: "One of my grandfather's nephews...and some other relatives worked as cooks at ranches west of Calgary. For years they cooked for the big ranch crews."[5]

During their anticipated sojourn, Chinese in Alberta regarded the absorption of Anglo-Canadian culture and ways of behavior as essentially irrelevant; moreover, any serious attempts in this direction proved quite difficult. Learning the English language, for example, was a formidable task. There were neither significant similarities, in terms of grammar or usage, for instance, nor was there any common heritage between Chinese and English—such as that existing between two Romance languages, for instance—upon which one could build and, thereby, pursue a program of study and learning. English had an alphabet and Chinese had ideograms.

Besides, most Chinese worked very long hours for six and even seven days a week, and little or no time was available for language study. In this context, Charles Lee recalled: "At that time, [the inter-war period] most Chinese [adults] did not go to school and they learned English solely by contact with Canadians."[6] What English was learned in this manner, was almost invariably very rudimentary.

Lee Pin Kam, known as Lee Bang, servant to photographer R. Randolph Bruce in Calgary, 1893. Glenbow Archives, NA-2307-32.

Chinese immigration to North America occurred through a process of chain migration, whereby a relatively few counties in Guangdong province provided the vast majority of immigrants. This type of migration pattern had the effect of transferring native loyalties and societal characteristics quite easily to the new homeland.

One authority has concluded that, during the early decades of this century, the Chinese in south China "conceived of themselves primarily as members of local extended kin units, bound together by ties of blood and language and only secondarily, if at all, as 'citizens' of the Chinese Empire."[7] Moreover, he states: "Chinese emigration was an organized affair in which kinsmen or fellow villagers [with] wealth or status acted as agents and sponsors for their compatriots."[8] As a result, such "emigration acted to transfer the loyalties and institutions of the village to the overseas community."[9]

Like many immigrants of this period, they brought few possessions along. Toe You Mah, who sailed to Canada in 1912 at age sixteen, recalled: "My luggage contained only a couple of articles of clothing, a bedsheet, and towels."[10] Ook Wah Yee emigrated the same year. "I was twenty-five years of age and brought only a change of clothing and a blanket with me. I wore Chinese clothing when I left China but changed into Canadian clothing as soon as I arrived."[11]

Almost immediately after arriving in Canada, Chinese immigrants secured employment. Paying back loans incurred to pay the extortionate $500 head tax, was the crucial—and extremely burdensome—inducement in this regard. Charlie Chew encountered such a situation. "I had had no option but to borrow $500 in China to pay the head tax. The lenders charged me a high rate of interest, and I had to get right to work to start paying back the loan."[12] Such a state of imposed employment—necessarily of long duration, too, because of the formidable interest-bearing debt incurred—was very common among Chinese immigrants.

Scarcely any substantial information is available concerning the initial Chinese residents of Alberta and their activities. It is known that in the late 1880s and early 1890s Calgary's Chinese residents were engaged primarily in the hand laundry business; a few other Chinese commercial operations also appeared, though how long they operated is uncertain.

Joe How's father worked near Revelstoke, B.C., clearing away bush just before the CPR rails were laid. When his job ended he headed to Calgary and opened a store in 1885 or 1886 with his two brothers. They "sold general merchandise: groceries, silk imports from China, and the like."[13] The store did not operate for very long, however.

Ook Wah Yee settled in Calgary in 1912. He recalled: "Chinatown was small then. Most Chinese worked in laundries [where they also resided; these were scattered throughout the city]; a few worked in restaurants."[14]

Chinese bellboys, Lake Louise, 1905.
Glenbow Archives, NC-53-94.

Charlie Leroy, Banff pioneer, about 1910. Charlie Leroy came to Banff in 1885 and built the National Park Hotel in 1887, the forerunner of the Alberta Hotel, known later as the Cascade Hotel. Glenbow Archives, NA-2512-1.

The same year, June Jay Chang moved to Calgary. Upon arriving, he found that joblessness was a serious problem. "Many unemployed Chinese gathered in the basement of the Kim Sang store [still operating in Calgary's first Chinatown] to eat and sleep."[15]

When King Loo came to Calgary in 1913, he concluded that the 500 or so local Chinese had a "very poor" standard of living. Almost everyone "either worked in laundries or restaurants. They worked sixteen to eighteen hours a day for approximately ten dollars per month. They tried, too, to support their families in China from this low wage!"[16]

Urban Community Growth and Occupations: An Overview

In the generation preceding 1925, Chinese urban communities in Alberta experienced considerable growth, both in terms of the number of Chinese residents and of the number of Chinese businesses in Chinatowns and elsewhere. Overall immigration to Canada was not significant in the decade after 1892, but after 1902 the policies of the Minister of the Interior, Clifford Sifton, opened an era of immigration which resulted in the Canadian West being truly settled. During the rather chaotic "boom" years from 1902 to 1910, over 400 Chinese settled in Calgary, about 140 settled in Edmonton, and others found a livelihood in such centres as Lethbridge and Medicine Hat.

The Chinese in Alberta were overwhelmingly located in urban centres. Of all ethnic groups in Alberta in 1926—including English, Irish, and Scottish—the Chinese had the largest percentage of urban residents, namely, 85.45 per cent. This is explained by the nature of occupations Chinese were engaged in performing.

The interior of a Chinese restaurant in Lacombe, Alberta.
Glenbow Archives, ND-2-112.

The interior of the Wing Chong laundry, High River, Alberta.
Glenbow Archives, NA-2979-5, NA-2979-6.

An upright stove with "sad" irons heating.
Glenbow Archives, NA-2979-9.

The ironing area with a "mangle" iron.
Glenbow Archives, NA-2979-10.

Chinese who settled in Alberta had arrived hoping to take advantage of increased opportunities, and many new Chinese businesses were established after 1902. Because of cultural barriers and the continuing discrimination against them, most newly arrived Chinese had virtually no choice except to work at menial occupations. Chinese business enterprises in Alberta were predominantly restaurants, laundries, and grocery stores.

Chinese had to work very hard to make a living, and in business the need to remain competitive was ever-present. Restaurants and groceries had to open early in the morning and close late in the evening in order to make a profit. Laundry work was especially wearisome, because it meant the soaking, scrubbing, and ironing of clothing solely by hand; moreover, prompt and high quality service was necessary to keep customers satisfied. Workers in laundries and groceries received the going wage of twenty-five dollars per month, and despite long hours the work-week was seven days. For the majority of Chinese, then, the daily routine was almost solely working, eating, and sleeping.

There were a few other occupations available to Chinese, including hotel workers, laborers, and domestic servants. In the countryside, too, Chinese cooks were hired by ranchers on a seasonal basis, and they customarily returned to an urban centre during the off-season.

J.C. Brokovski, Calgary lawyer, and Wing Lee, Chinese cook and houseboy, 1915. Glenbow Archives, NA-3186-1.

After 1900 a greater number of Chinese in Calgary were employed as domestic servants, owing to the needs of wealthy Calgarians, whose spacious residences were increasing in number. "Maids, Chinese houseboys and coachmen were viewed as status symbols, and were also expected to lighten the domestic burdens of the family. [By the beginning of the century] more employers began to employ Chinese servants, who also were in short supply. Paid twenty-five dollars a month, a Chinese houseboy was quick to give courteous service, and generally worked hard. Employers of houseboys as a rule had little difficulty in training them in the ways of servanthood."[17]

Some Chinese houseboys also found employment outside the spheres of the social elite. In Lethbridge and Calgary, as elsewhere, they were frequently employed by madams to do all manner of household duties in local bordellos.

During the period 1902 to 1925, the number of Chinese grocery stores, restaurants, and laundries in Calgary all reached a peak in 1915 (See Appendix: Tables Four and Five). This was a direct, significant result of the tremendous influx of people into Calgary in the immediate pre-war years. Also of interest is the fact that, in the three business categories considered, the total number of Chinese businesses was one hundred in 1915, sixty-three in 1920, and seventy-two in 1925. Business prospects in Calgary in the immediate post-war years were clearly markedly inferior to those of five or six years previously, at least in the public service sector. During the next five years, business conditions did improve somewhat, however, for the Chinese.

Wing Lee Jr., c. 1920. Wing Lee brought him to the J.C. Brokovski home after a return visit to China. Glenbow Archives, NA-3186-2.

Chinese businesses in Edmonton, Medicine Hat, and Lethbridge are also of interest. (See Appendix: Tables Six, Seven, and Eight). Briefly, Chinese merchants and businessmen in urban centres played a relatively important role in the world of local business: particularly in Lethbridge, where Chinese owned most of the restaurants and laundries, as well as over one-quarter of the grocery stores (1924).

Market Gardening

In each of the centres mentioned, Chinese engaged in market gardening. Some Chinese-owned greenhouses were established in several cities. One of the relatively long-standing institutions of urban life in Alberta was the Chinese vegetable pedlar, who brought fresh produce to housewives at about the same time each week. At Christmas, the pedlars customarily gave packages of ginger and Chinese lily bulbs to their customers as gifts.

As mentioned in Chapter Two, many Chinese market gardens were established in Lethbridge in the 1890s. The number of men involved is hard to determine. Joe How referred to half of the city's Chinese being market gardeners in 1914, the year he arrived; this would indicate about fifty-five Chinese market gardeners operated at that time. Fred Yee said that in 1924 there were thirty-two Chinese market gardeners.

Market gardeners lived very difficult lives. Most lived in small cabins or shacks on plots of land rented to them by farmers or other land owners. The work was all done by hand. As Fred Yee related, "I tell you, you'd work all day year-round, and you'd be lucky to make $300 a year."[18] He recalled having no choice but to barter vegetables for clothing as a child in the 1920s. In 1929 he was forced to quit school to help his father on the farm.

Hing Wah Co., Chinese gardens in Calgary.
Glenbow Archives, NC-26-26.

Members of the Hing Wah family, market gardeners.
Glenbow Archives, NC-26-27.

The Rural Chinese

Many Chinese worked as cooks at ranches in the southern Alberta foothills, but: "cooking was a small part of the job. They did the laundry for cowboys, looked after barn chores, raised chickens, planted gardens and looked after them."[19] In at least one instance, notable creativity found expression in the course of routine ranch work by Chinese. "On the Hull Ranch along the Bow river, the ingenious Chinese cooks were credited with devising a unique system for serving a large crew of ranch hands at one sitting. A big round dining table was built, with another large, Lazy Susan style circle in the centre. Platters of food, salt, pepper, sugar etc. were placed on the Lazy Susan and the diners helped themselves as the food came around."[20]

A one-time resident of the Nanton area, in the foothills south of Calgary, recalled: "I remember the Chinese cooks we had each year. Nearly every ranch had one. Hired in the spring before haying began and kept until after the fall roundup, the cook took complete charge of the kitchen. He always had a list of groceries ready for any cowboy who might be going to town. If the cowboy forgot to bring flour, the shortage of pies and cakes was immediate and acute."

The narrator added that children tended to be deferential to these men; apart from other things, adults respected certain non-cooking skills of Chinese ranch hands. "Most of these men still wore hair in pigtails and some wore oriental clothing. Some were good horsemen and added to their prestige by their ability to 'skin' a four-horse team and a chuckwagon from camp to camp at roundup time. We children soon learned the penalties that could be levied for disrespect and the goodies that could be had for co-operating with this kitchen autocrat."[21]

During Alberta's frontier era and somewhat later—when scores of hamlets were springing up all over—one of the first arrivals was frequently the aspiring Chinese restaurant-owner or laundry-owner. In this respect, a writer noted in 1930: "When a new town is being built the Chinaman comes in with the gang building the station or the elevators. In northern Alberta once I passed through a little place all white and shining in its new, unpainted lumber. About four miles out of town I met a young Chinaman trudging along the road with a straw suit-case in his hand. The train came only as far as the next station eight miles away." The absence of a railway station at the fledgling hamlet would have dissuaded many businessmen from locating there. But, as the writer continued, "Two days later, on passing through the town again, I found the Chinaman serving ham and eggs to a couple of travelling salesmen and a farmer, while the carpenters were still at work tacking a roof over his head."[22]

"Mow," Chinese cook on "CC" Ranch, Mosquito Creek, Alberta. Glenbow Archives, NA-4571-30.

This individual's industriousness was typical of the many Chinese who went to small towns and hamlets throughout the prairie provinces in search of a reasonably secure future. If obtained, such a future was usually bleak in most respects. "In small prairie towns, the Chinese lived difficult, lonely lives. Occasionally they were accepted into the community. More often their ways of speaking and dressing were made fun of."[23]

Two exceptions to the shameful situation described above were expressed in the life experiences of pioneer Louie Hong and family of Cluny and in that of the pioneering Wong family of Olds.

Louie Hong arrived in Canada from China in 1909 at age twenty-five; a widower, he had to leave his three children behind with relatives. After a year working as a CPR cook, he joined the southern Alberta ranching outfit of the notable millionaire, Pat Burns, and cooked on the range for two years. Then, in 1913, he opened a small store/restaurant at Cluny, east of Calgary, at the time, Cluny had just a few residents, a grain elevator, and an optimistic Asian entrepreneur—Louie Hong. In 1914 he opened a laundry there, too, but soon hired two men to run it.

In 1916 Louie opened a general store; three years later, he built a larger structure himself and soon thereafter sold the laundry. Louie always kept prices low (for a large turnover) and did so well that he added on to the store a number of times. In 1926 he married and the couple had nine children.

Community-minded, generous, a reliable friend who had a fine sense of humor, he garnered a legion of friends over a very large area of southern Alberta. He passed away, in 1969, at age eighty-four: a very popular, fine man had gone, and many mourned.

A native of Toi-san county, Wong Yet arrived in Canada in 1895 to work for the CPR. He settled in Olds, Alberta, in 1897 and, using savings and a loan, established a hand laundry and a restaurant. In 1903 his son, Wong Pond, arrived to assist him; he managed the restaurant. After a 1912 fire destroyed both businesses, they built a restaurant called the Public Lunch on the town's main street.

In 1922 Frank Wong, son of Wong Pond, left China for Olds; he was twenty-two years of age. From then until 1972—fifty years—he served as proprietor of the Public Lunch. Over this half-century, the Wong family built a theatre, pool hall, and barber shop near the restaurant. Frank Wong married Irene Won in 1927; the couple had five children and prospered. During the Great Depression, they provided food and a hayloft for shelter to homeless men who arrived at their house seeking help in exchange for doing chores.

The family has long engaged in church activities, backed local sports, and been involved in worthy local projects. The Wongs have been well-regarded business people and residents for generations. Back in 1927 a very dubious Irene Won of Victoria was struck by the lack of racial animosity and discrimination in the town. Like the Louie Hong family, the Wong family has given much to their community; likewise, they have fortunately received equal measure in terms of friendship, respect, and general goodwill.

Many Chinese worked for mining concerns in British Columbia. This situation was not paralleled in Alberta, but some Chinese, such as those at Canmore (not far east of Banff), engaged in work at mines. "The Chinese never assimilated or integrated into Canmore society. They were employed by the Canmore Mines during the very early days possibly drifting in after the construction of the C.P.R. They worked in small groups at the surface of the mine....For many years they provided cheap labor."

Wong Yet's restaurant and laundry, Olds, Alberta, 1904.
Glenbow Archives, NA-1978-1.

Wong Pond in front of the Public Lunch, Olds, Alberta.
Glenbow Archives, NA-1926-1.

The personal component of their lives there was expressed solely within their own isolated little community. "They lived segregated from the town in large grimy boarding houses within two hundred yards of the mine tipple and power house of No. 2 Mine. They grew their own vegetables in large carefully cared for gardens behind high deerproof fences, and had a well stocked fowl yard. Apart from their work they kept to themselves."[24]

At the turn of the century, Lee Poon, a cook, worked at the Oskaloosa Hotel in Canmore.[25] It came about that a ten-dollar bet was made between Poon and another party; the wager related to the high jagged mountain dominating part of the town. To win, Poon had to ascend the mountain alone within a six-hour period; he would wave a white table-cloth to signify his success.

On a Sunday over 100 miners and some women and children arrived at the Oskaloosa Hotel to watch the climb. Some bets were made on the side: the odds undoubtedly went against Poon, who had no mountaineering experience to his credit.

Not far into his climb, Poon encountered serious difficulties: detours had to be found around huge boulders; a layer of extremely loose shale, stretching across seventeen metres, had to be crossed with great care. Then, he took a route behind the mountain and was not seen for about an hour. Steep inclines near the summit slowed his ascent. But, in a little under six hours, a white table-cloth was seen blowing in the wind at the summit. The crowd dispersed.

As twilight was setting in, Poon began his descent. Detours again had to be made; these were much more difficult propositions when one was going down the mountainside. Then, the wind picked up and water on the rocks began freezing. Finding shelter beneath an overhang, he decided to stay put until dawn. The night air was cold, and he did not sleep. After nightfall, some miners noticed that Poon had not yet returned. They agreed to form a rescue party and set out at daybreak.

At first daylight, Poon slowly extricated himself from a treacherous slope just below the spot where he had spent the night. At the timberline, he met the rescue party. That night, after a good sleep, he boarded a train bound for Vancouver. Because Lee Poon was the first person to climb it, the mountain was named Chinaman's Peak.[26]

Community Developments

Chinese in Edmonton evinced a desire, from time to time, to take part in civic affairs. In 1911, for example, they sought to participate in the celebration of the coronation of King George V. Concerning a meeting where these plans were discussed, it was reported in the local press that: "the Celestial kingdom was represented. With Jim Mah as their leader, the Chinese friends showed they could be as loyal to the King, in whose land they are living, as any who were present. When Jim was asked concerning the celebration, he almost shouted an enquiry as to whether he and his friends could take a large part on the 'big' day and build a triumphal arch."[27]

Chinese involved in this matter later decided against an arch and suggested to the committee in charge of celebrations that a grand parade be held; that houses and businesses be decorated; and that a home for convalescents be built to mark the occasion.

In December 1912 a fire occurred at a Chinese laundry on Jasper Avenue. Kwong Lang was awakened by the smoke, and he roused three occupants, who escaped. He then saved the lives of the remaining three occupants by lowering them to the ground in bedclothing which he had fastened together. He then tried to locate $600: both his and his partner's savings. This was his undoing and he perished in the fire. He was justifiably referred to as a hero in local news accounts.

One of the more interesting Chinese pioneers in Alberta was Sam Sing Mah, commonly referred to as Sam Sing, who became known in Edmonton as the King of Chinatown. He was born in China about 1864 and was extremely strong. A builder by trade, he stood nearly six feet tall. At twenty-five years of age, he emigrated to Canada and settled in Victoria. He lived there for ten years and then moved to Saskatoon. He stayed there briefly and at the turn of the century moved to Edmonton.

Sing established a hand laundry, which was later converted into Edmonton's first steam laundry. In 1907 he opened an import store, the Kong Lee Yuen ("Store of Big Profit"), in a two-storey frame building, located between 97th and 98th Streets on the south side of 101A Avenue. At the Kong Lee Yuen one could purchase Chinese groceries and herbs; moreover, the store served as a gathering place for Chinese during times of leisure or unemployment. "With two benches outside for lounging in the sun, a dozen Chinese might...be found at any time in the store—lounging, smoking or playing [games]."

Despite his physical prowess, "it was Sam Sing's strength of character...which established him as elder among Edmonton's more than 500 Chinese. He was the first person they turned to for help and advice. Once he made up the shortfall in a collection taken among the Chinese for beautiful parade floats."[28] A personal friend of many policemen, detectives, and judges, he was also the head of many gambling joints! Such was the nature of the Canadian West's generally captivating, sometimes seemingly contradictory, frontier society.

It was during these times that Ho Lem, the father of George Ho Lem Sr., led the way in Calgary in adopting Western ways. He "donned bowler, black jacket and pinstripe trousers in the proper British tradition and shocked his fellow Chinese by cutting off his queue."[29]

Ho Lem arrived in Calgary in 1901 by way of Canton and Vancouver. It seems that he chose to live in Calgary because he had heard that there were free English lessons at Knox Presbyterian Church. He attended classes and, thereafter, spoke English with a Chinese-Scottish accent. In Canada he worked variously as a dishwasher, cook, restaurant owner, and life insurance agent. He became the owner of a wool and knitting mill on Second Avenue South, east of Centre Street.

An assiduous worker for the Chinese Mission, he was one of its first converts. His labors continued when it became the Chinese United Church. He also belonged to the Knox United Church and served on the board of elders: he was the first Chinese in Canada to hold a position at this level. He lived to a ripe old age.

Chinese "Bachelor" Society

During the period being considered, the majority of Chinese in Alberta and throughout North America were males. Most of these men were so-called "married bachelors:" they had wives living in China, but their way of life was that of bachelors. Indeed, for decades the type of society constituted by Chinese urban residents can accurately be designated a "Bachelor" Society.

Despite general agreement about the pattern of early Chinese settlement in North America, some doubt has been raised about the extent to which Chinese immigrants were sojourners, or even if they were sojourners at all.

The term sojourner was first used by Paul Siu to describe the migration pattern of the Chinese to North America and the motivations behind it. Siu defined the sojourner as one who "spends many years of his lifetime in a foreign country without being assimilated by it."[30] The term could, then, apply equally to an old-time Canadian missionary in China or a Chinese worker in North America.

The sojourner usually left his village in China while in his teens or twenties. In Canada he worked at virtually any job he could readily find upon arrival. His goal was not primarily to establish a career of some sort for himself, but to earn sufficient money to support his immediate and/or extended family back home and—with luck—return to his village with enough money to retire in relative comfort.

As two authorities have commented: "Overseas emigration was an economic enterprise in which the male members of the *jia* participated to improve its material condition and prestige. A highly malleable institution, the *jia* could comprise only the conjugal unit of a single household or could include the extended family living in more than one household or dispersed across the ocean."[31]

Strong familial ties bound the sojourner emotionally and psychologically to the homeland village and its environs. "Even during his absence, the emigrant retained his sense of belonging to the family, his share of the corporate family property, and the opportunity to return to the care of the family upon retirement or in difficult times."[32]

Certain areas of China produced many migrants because of high population density, political disruption, and pronounced scarcity of arable land. Some families sent two, three, or four generations of males to work in North America. Almost invariably, men did not bring over their wives to join them, but sent for grown sons or nephews, who could be economically productive.

Most often, a man arrived in North America as a teenager; returned to China a few times to marry and beget children; but essentially spent his whole working life overseas. Siu postulated that, although the sojourner originally intended to stay as short a time as possible to achieve his goals, he would make some adjustments to his new environment and change his original goals somewhat over time.

Because sojourners generally had little interest in conforming more than was absolutely necessary to the surrounding society, they tended to group together in a cultural colony (Chinatown), where Chinese dialects could be freely spoken and where a more or less traditional diet could be followed. Home ties were maintained through periodic visits and participation in the social and political affairs of the mother country. Overall, "[the] special and unique character of their immigration required them to *adapt* [North] America and its ways to their own purposes rather than *adopt* it to the exclusion and surrender of their own values."[33]

Sojourners returning to China sometimes discovered that they had become changed individuals through acquiring various new skills and habits—no longer undeniably Chinese in all respects, but not too attuned to Canadian ways either. The Canadian-born children of Chinese immigrants did not truly belong to either society: racial prejudice and discrimination prevented them from becoming full participants of Canadian society, while Anglo-Canadian socialization naturally led them to think and act like most Canadians in various important respects.

In addition to the majority of Chinese immigrants who were sojourners, there were a "relatively small number"[34] who intended from the outset to make North America their permanent home and were as adaptable as any other immigrants. Among these were wealthy merchants who invested heavily in Canada; had the finances to establish their families in their adopted country; and had a distinct incentive to do so: their various involvements in Canada were much more complex than those of most other Chinese immigrants.

It has been argued, however, that the concept of the Chinese sojourner is a Western perception of historical reality with little basis in fact. Anthony B. Chan argues that the Chinese term which translates as "Overseas Chinese" indicates migration and not temporary existence.[35] He points out that in 1885 the Chinese consul general, based in San Francisco, claimed that many Chinese in the United States would live there permanently with their families if they were permitted to be naturalized.

If the concept of the sojourner did not originate with the Chinese themselves, where did it come from? Chan argues that it was a concept espoused early by both federal and provincial governments to justify systematic discrimination and policies which would force the Chinese to return to China, as soon as the demand for their labor slackened. As early as 1882, Prime Minister John A. Macdonald stressed that the Chinese would leave as soon as construction was finished on the CPR because they had not brought their women with them and were therefore unlikely to become permanent settlers.

Chan argues that the lack of women proves nothing about the long-term goals of the Chinese laborers, since women were not economically necessary for the frontier economy, and poor laborers could not afford passage for their families; also, Chinese were not the only immigrants to send part of their wages back home.

One could contend that many circumstances which made the Chinese appear unassimilable were less a product of their own desires and ethnocentrism than a response to institutional racism. In several provinces legislation and regulations which disallowed Chinese from engaging in various occupations resulted in the concentration of Chinese workers in just a few service businesses, especially laundries, groceries, and restaurants. Early participation in mining and forestry was diminished over the years, and laws denying Chinese the right to vote also meant that, in some provinces, they were thereby automatically excluded from the professions, including law and teaching.

It is possible to look at the formation of Chinatowns as a defensive—even potentially strategic (in the physical sense)—response to racism, rather than as an attempt to maintain cultural identity and adapt as little as possible to new surroundings. The formation of various organizations for mutual support and welfare would have been a natural response to the overall hostile attitude toward Chinese by the white community. Retreat from society at large, then, might well have been a natural response to being treated as members of some "inferior species."[36]

Chan maintains that one compelling reason for believing that Canadian Chinese were not sojourners was that they contributed very substantial sums of money to China's Kuomintang (KMT) republican party. An interest in Chinese political reform was natural, he claims, when Chinese were unable to participate in Canadian politics.

The Chinese in Canada, as he accurately relates, contributed a great deal more to the KMT than did their counterparts in the United States: mortgaging society buildings, as well as collecting many individual contributions. He maintains: "One could argue that if the Chinese were indeed sojourners, their major objective, as politicians, scholars and community observers have stated, would have been their return to China with enough wealth to purchase land and live in ease with respect and esteem; the Chinese, if they were sojourners, would be more interested in their own selfish ends of financial aggrandizement."[37]

At this remove, one cannot look into the minds of those men who came to Canada after 1858 and assess exactly what their motivations and long-term goals were in respect to emigrating. Nevertheless, if racism were the primary reason for the overwhelmingly scant number of Chinese families in Canada for many years, then it is extremely difficult to explain crucial relevant facts relating to the period 1904-1923.

During these years the onerous head tax was at its zenith ($500 per Chinese immigrant); frontier oppression was very evident; discrimination against Chinese did not abate (it likely increased); and anti-Asian feelings ran rampant, especially in B.C., and fostered passage of the *Chinese Exclusion Act* in 1923. Despite anti-Chinese racism raising its ugly head to such an extent during these years, this period witnessed the largest influx of Chinese families into Canada.

The establishment and growth of many Chinese organizations cannot be explained as a mere response to racism: far too much went on in many respects for this to have been the case. It should also be appreciated that Overseas Chinese might very well have regarded political contributions to the KMT as a wise investment toward their future residence in China. Moreover, Siu's definition of the sojourner and his way of life fully takes into account a flexibility regarding individual goals in response to the new situation and new environment overseas.

Whatever the particular motivations of various individuals, the overall circumstances of the mass migration of Chinese to North America and the establishment of a Bachelor Society in both Canada and the United States leads one to utilize the most accurate, pragmatic, and convincing term available: sojourner.

Characteristics of Chinese cultural exclusiveness were represented in almost all aspects of daily living. Most striking to the observer was the appearance of the Chinese, who retained their queues and traditional clothing until the overthrow of the Manchu dynasty signalled a departure from well-established cultural norms. (The queue was imposed upon the Chinese by their Manchu conquerors in 1644 to distinguish the Chinese from their rulers, who were similar in appearance).

Occupationally, the vast majority of Chinese in Alberta worked alongside their fellow countrymen, primarily in small business enterprises. Socially, partly by predilection, but also because of social ostracism by Anglo-Canadians, Chinese interacted almost solely with one another. The several mutually intelligible dialects of Cantonese spoken during this period facilitated an easy and comprehensible social dialogue. Chinese cuisine went unchallenged, and foodstuffs imported from China were readily purchased at grocery stores located in Chinatowns.

The focal point of urban community life was the local Chinatown which was, in essence, a Chinese sociocultural enclave. There were a number of reasons why Chinatowns were established in North America. Firstly, as an American authority has remarked, "Chinatowns grew out of vital and cogent needs of the immigrant Chinese."[38] The Chinese "[were bound] together because of a common language and common customs [and they found] themselves more comfortable in surroundings more similar to those found in the mother country."[39] The wide cultural gap between the Chinese and the majority population served only to accentuate Chinese cultural expression as exemplified in Chinatown.

Secondly, as the same writer notes, "the Chinese sought refuge within the boundaries of Chinatown for their own protection from the persecution wreaked against them during the late nineteenth and early twentieth centuries."[40] Thirdly, Chinatown met certain psychological needs of those Chinese who regarded themselves as solely sojourning members of Canadian society; hence, during their anticipated sojourn, Chinatown was a culturally active, functional centre which concretely represented some basic features of Chinese culture and society.

In Chinatown many wants and needs of urban Chinese residents could be effectively met. In addition to business premises in Chinatown, various social institutions and political associations were invariably situated in the heart of Chinatown. This was the case in Chinatowns in Alberta's larger centres. A Chinese person might easily live, work, socialize, and function solely within a Chinatown.

Chinatowns are far from being only a North American phenomenon: "That North America's Chinatowns are not merely creatures of the American environment is indicated by the relatively similar institutionalization of Chinese communities in other parts of the world. The diaspora of Chinese in the last two centuries has populated Southeast Asia, the Americas, Europe, and Africa with Oriental colonies [which have established] 'Chinatowns' not unlike their North American counterparts."[41]

Chinatowns throughout the world have been established by Chinese seeking to maintain traditional life-styles and to perpetuate their cultural heritage. In addition to the factor of frequent discrimination and oppression, the sojourning nature of Chinese migration also prompted the formation of spatially distinct, compact Chinatown areas. The sojourn was made more endurable when the illusion of being present in the social surroundings of southern China could easily be experienced by spending some time in Chinatown.

For those who never managed to acquire sufficient savings to retire in China, their lives increasingly came to centre around Chinatown and its activities. Chinatown played an ever more crucial role to sojourners as the long years dragged on and their stay appeared permanent.

Born and raised in Chinatown, Paul Dofoo also spent most of his working life in the district. He remarked that during the early decades of the century, in particular, Chinese settlers "supported each other financially and socially. Often, they got together in Chinatown where they could find friendship, companionship, social familiarity, relaxation and some consolation."[42] Moreover, "for them Chinatown acted as a partial buffer against prejudice and hatred from hostile people. They also regarded Chinatown as a place to preserve their cultural identity."[43]

Gambling and Drug Use

Because of the social distance between Chinese Canadians and the Anglo-Canadian population, the majority of Chinese in Alberta engaged in traditional recreational and leisure-time activities rooted in the rural landscape of Guangdong province. Two types of such activity among North American Chinese have received a prodigious amount of attention by writers and newspaper reporters, namely, gambling and drug use. Sensationalistic newspaper and magazine articles about these pursuits served to establish and perpetuate very negative images of the Chinese, and they led many North Americans to mistakenly conclude that Chinatowns were centres of vice and crime.

The presence of widespread gambling among North American Chinese during the nineteenth and early twentieth centuries was largely a direct outcome of the existence of a Bachelor Society. Denied the comforts of family life and subjected to frontier oppression and social ostracism, Chinese sojourners had few options available for leisure-time pursuits. Gambling was one option and many Chinese indulged in that pastime. The favorite game among North American Chinese was *fantan* (in free translation, the game of repeatedly spreading out); next popular was *pak kop piu* (freely translated as the game of white pigeon ticket), commonly referred to in the Canadian West as the Chinese lottery; of lesser importance overall, but frequently played, were a number of games employing dice or dominoes.

In Guangdong gambling was a socially acceptable leisure-time activity, and many Chinese immigrants were quite familiar with the indigenous games. A Chinese scholar has remarked: "[In Guangdong during] winter there is not much to do on the farm, and it is then that many of the villagers indulge in gambling."[44] Also, it should be appreciated that: "the Chinese laborer entered the 'dens of iniquity' as an individual, and perhaps only in these places was it possible for him to obtain a sense of his personal worth. [One function of gambling] was to provide an opportunity by which the undividuated [sic] Chinese could *acquire* a status."[45]

The possibility of winning a large amount of money was naturally most appealing. The proprietors of gaming establishments frequently made a good livelihood from their operations.

Chinese residents of Alberta were not immune to the tantalizing temptations of games of chance. Because Calgary had the largest Chinese population in Alberta, information on Chinese gambling activities was occasionally reported in local newspapers, especially in the decade 1910-1920. While Chinese gaming establishments in Calgary functioned at least as early as the late 1890s, there was little public or police interest in their activities until much later.

Unlike *fantan*, the Chinese lottery was solely a matter of chance. It proved to be a popular enterprise among Alberta's Chinese population and also had many regular occidental patrons. It is uncertain when the Chinese lottery first appeared in Alberta, but reference was made in Calgary as early as 1913 to Chinese "lottery fiends,"[46] whatever this appellation was meant to imply.

Little, if any, further notice of the operation of Chinese lotteries appeared in Calgary until 1917, when ten local Chinese residents were arraigned on lottery-related charges. In the subsequent court testimony, Inspector D. Richardson and Police Chief Alfred Cuddy remarked that it was common knowledge to the Calgary police force that Chinese lotteries were openly operating in downtown Calgary.

During the relatively few trials in Alberta which concerned Chinese lotteries, their operations were explained. The lottery functioned essentially as follows. A lottery operation was managed by one or two men who employed up to four or so "runners," or lottery vendors. The lottery's activities were managed at specially outfitted premises, which were usually rented rooms above Chinatown businesses. Runners were paid on a daily commission basis when they turned in the day's proceeds and picked up the lottery "cards" for the next day. Lottery cards consisted of eighty printed Chinese characters, and the buyer chose ten characters on the card as his choice for the draw.

Draws were held in the morning and the evening every weekday; so, there were two lotteries each day per lottery company. The lottery cards used in Alberta were specially printed by Chinese printing firms in Vancouver. In order to win, a buyer had to choose at least five characters of the twenty characters randomly picked from a container at the draw: the more characters a buyer successfully chose, the greater his winnings. Cards could be purchased for as little as ten cents each, or as much as five dollars or more. The Chinese lottery lasted into the 1930s.

A long-time resident of Medicine Hat recalled years ago that: "the lottery-man, who was always two years older than God, wore a long brown overcoat. He wore it all year, and summers in Medicine Hat are hot. His route never varied, from the Chinese store on North Railway, up to the cafes by the depot, across the tracks to just about every business place in town....It spread all over town if someone happened to hit a nine spot, about equivalent in those times to winning the Irish [Sweepstake]." In light of the lottery's apparently widespread appeal, the following closing remarks of the resident make a good deal of sense. "I guess it was illegal, but I never heard of the police stopping it. In a town the size of the 'Hat, I'm sure they knew."[47]

In Lethbridge gambling companies were formed, and each partner put in about $500. The companies would rent rooms in Chinatown and operate there. "[Each] company would rent a room for each game [held]. Every night practically every building open had a game going."[48] The most popular games were *fantan*, *do far*, *mah-jong*, and *pi-gow*. From about the 1940s until fairly recent years, the "older Chinese played *mah-jong* pretty well all day long and always played for money."[49]

Among other places in Lethbridge, games were operated at the Kwong On Lung building, the Bow On Tong building, and on the main floor of the Freemasons' building. Joe How recalled of gambling over the years: "Games would open say from one o'clock until three o'clock, or from seven until nine, whatever it was; they had regular hours....Professional Chinese gamblers would go from place to place. They'd break the banks. I saw it happen: $500 at a crack and they'd break the bank and pull out."[50]

These outside gamblers "weren't really welcome. A call would come and police would close a game down until the outsiders left town. The Chinese couldn't offend these men, who were associated with criminal-type groups."[51]

Ex-Police Chief James Carpenter also related that occasionally complaints from Chinese would lead the police to close down games, "but there were very, very few complaints [and these] usually related to fights among the gamblers."[52]

Comparable in scope to the image of the Chinese as inveterate gamblers was the similarly negative image of Chinese as drug fiends and opium addicts. The stereotyped imagery invoked by the use of such terms was prejudicial, distorted, and extremely unfair to Chinese communities in North America. Many Chinese occasionally indulged in smoking opium, and a few took to other narcotic drugs; but drug addicts formed a very small minority of the Chinese populations of Canada and the United States.

As discussed previously, opium was introduced to China in large quantities by the British East India Company, and it became "the substitute for alcohol in the Orient."[53] Thus, the opium-smoking of Chinese immigrants was something in the order of cultural baggage from China; however, it is more realistically viewed as a direct by-product of British imperialism.

In Alberta the majority of Chinese residents from 1885 to 1925 and later were sojourners. A significant number of these men were unsuccessful sojourners, that is, they were not in a position to return to China with the fortune they had hoped to amass and had virtually no hope of so doing. The majority of Chinese drug users in North America fell into this category. Although arrests were occasionally made and convictions secured in Alberta's major centres, virtually no information on the lives of individual drug users has been retained, and there is an absence of reliable statistics.

The non-medical use of drugs during the period was widespread. Solid evidence demonstrates that there were a great many more Anglo-Canadian opium addicts than Chinese addicts. Research demonstrates that: "...many Canadians, representative of all segments of society, were acquainted with the euphoric and addictive effects of opium obtained through an extra swig of opiate-based cough medicines or of various pain killers, long before the Chinese arrived with their habit of smoking opium for pleasure. Opium use was as common to the Canadian of the late nineteenth and early twentieth century as is aspirin today."[54]

Until 1908 it was legal in Canada to import, manufacture, and use opium. By the late 1890s, though, Anglo-Canadians were concerned about its growing popularity.

In 1903 Lethbridge's town council approved a resolution requesting that the town's solicitor both investigate the council's power to suppress the use of opium and instruct the town's lone policeman "as to the course he shall pursue to obtain a conviction of the keeper of any house where opium is consumed."[55] This concern would have been at least partly directed toward the Chinese. Joe How related that before 1908: "My uncle and some others were smoking an ounce of opium a day. My other uncle was a [part-time] gambler. In those days, things were wide open!"[56]

Some opium was still brought into Lethbridge after 1908, but its use by Chinese residents seems to have decreased considerably. Mr. How noted: "When the opium law came into effect, prohibiting it, then it was all gambling [for Chinese]."[57] George Fong grew up in Lethbridge and recalled: "I never saw any opium abuse among Chinese, or any trouble connected with it. But, plain-clothes squads of Royal Canadian Mounted Police would conduct raids with warrants on supposed opium users. I don't remember any Chinese being caught, though."[58]

Charlie Chew remarked of past years: "In Lethbridge's Chinatown, quite a few men smoked long water pipes."[59] James Carpenter has written of this: "The smoking of opium by the Chinese was not nearly as bad as the rumors would have had [the 1903] Council believe. Most of the water pipes of the Chinese were used only for tobacco but to the uninitiated it would [have been] quite easy to believe the Chinese were [smoking opium] when they saw and heard the gurgle of the water pipe in action."[60]

Festivals

In Alberta the most popular festivals celebrated over the years have been the Moon (Cake) Festival, the Dragon Boat Festival, the Spring Festival, and Chinese New Year. Festivals provided an opportunity for Chinese to take some time off work and enjoy themselves, as they had done in their homeland villages. The celebrants usually congregated in association halls, where splendid banquets and festivities were held.

The Spring Festival, *Ch'ing Ming* (Pure Brightness Festival), is a springtime event when homage is proffered to deceased ancestors of families and clans. The occasion often has religious overtones. A ceremony is held at the gravesite of a particular ancestor. Food—such as pork, shrimp, fish, tofu, chicken, Chinese pastry, and fruit—is offered. Tea and whiskey may also be offered to the ancestor. Candles and incense are occasionally burned, and a prayer said. False paper money is burned, in order that the ancestor will have enough money to spend in heaven. Sometimes, "food and incense are placed at a neighboring plot, to symbolize generosity and friendship."[61] After the ceremony the food is taken home.

The Dragon Boat Festival is celebrated on the fifth day of the fifth lunar month. The festival "fulfills two purposes: to serve as a day for people to protect themselves from disease and danger, and to commemorate the suicide of the great poet Chu Yuan (340-278 B.C.)."

The poet, a devoted patriot, lived in the state of Ch'u during the so-called Period of the Warring States. Ambitious leaders of the state of Ch'in decided on one occasion to detain the king of Ch'u and then invade his state. Chu Yuan proposed that the invasion be resisted, "but the king, under the influence of courtiers who favored appeasement, banished him from Ch'u. Unhappy and concerned about the destruction of his state, Chu Yuan weighted himself with a rock and drowned himself in the Mi Lo River in protest. In admiration of his loyalty, his countrymen dragged the river with boats for three days in an attempt to find his body, and later threw bamboo tubes containing rice in the river to mourn him."[62]

In China and other locations throughout the world, Chu Yuan is remembered by dragon boat races. In Alberta, as in China, the day is remembered by eating *tsung tze*, glutinous rice wrapped in bamboo leaves and steamed.

The Moon Festival is held on the fifteenth day of the eighth month according to the Chinese lunar calendar. This festival celebrates several ancient stories.

One story concerns a Chinese monk, Chu Hung Wu, who lived in China during the oppressive Mongolian imperial rule. It is said that he "kept up the morale of the peasants [around 1367 A.D.] by hiding secret messages in mooncakes (a Chinese pastry) which he passed around. The monk organized the people to stage a vigil protesting the empire, which was held on the legendary night that the moon is at its fullest. For centuries people in China have carried lanterns, made mooncakes and celebrated in the streets on this night...to mark the legendary event."[63]

Another story is that "the wife of an alchemist, Chang-Ngo, stole the drug of longevity and flew into the clouds and landed on the moon."[64] Immortal, she became the moon goddess. The festival also heralds the taking in of the harvested crops.

In China the Moon Festival is second in importance to Chinese New Year. There, children wearing new clothes "are given lanterns of various shapes to illuminate the night. Everyone...sits outdoors in back yards and parks to admire the moon until the next morning. Lovers especially look forward to this night and many romantic songs and paintings are produced for the occasion. During the Sung Dynasty, [the] Chichang River was [lit] by thousands of small floating lanterns...made of dried lotus leaves or goatskins, creating the impression of a milky way."[65]

As in China, Alberta's Chinese celebrate the occasion by eating moon cakes made of yellow or black bean paste. Before eating them, some Chinese place moon cakes on the window sill as an offering to the moon.

Chinese New Year was, and is, by far the most important annual event among North American Chinese. Alberta has not been the exception to the rule. The novelty and excitement of celebrations frequently attracted curious citizens, and the festivities were often reported in local newspapers. For residents of the larger centres, at any rate, New Year's celebrations would usually last one or two days and—though not the extravaganza that was held in China—it was a joyous occasion.

Chinese preparing for a parade in Calgary, 1905.
Glenbow Archives, NA-2622-31.

Long-standing debts to fellow countrymen were absolved, and enmities between individuals were supposed to be mended. Lavish family and clan association banquets were indulged in; lion and dragon dances appeared on Chinatown sidewalks; and occidental patrons of Chinese businesses were customarily the recipients of Chinese candies, nuts, and other treats.

For the Chinese traditionalist, there are many customs associated with the New Year's season. One popular tradition, for example, holds that there is a Kitchen God in every household who departs for heaven five days before the New Year arrives. To symbolize this event, ghost money is burned by the family to provide their Kitchen God with an all-expense-paid return trip. While the deity is making his annual report on the family's affairs, family members customarily clean the house from top to bottom to create a favorable impression on him when he returns New Year's Day.

New Year's Day is devoted to the family. Children receive "lucky money" wrapped in red envelopes from their parents, and they reciprocate by giving gifts also wrapped in red, traditionally a lucky color. A fine, sometimes lavish, family dinner highlights the day's events. Subsequent days will find one visiting friends and attending any concerts or other get-togethers sponsored by Chinese organizations.

In Medicine Hat during the period under consideration, New Year celebrations were quiet. At least one businessman, a restaurant owner, however, made certain that the occasion was not overlooked. In February 1910 the *Medicine Hat News* observed: "The Chinese New Year festivities are now being observed and last evening the genial and popular Quan Koy entertained a number of well-known citizens to a royal feast of Chinese delicacies brought all the way from the Celestial Empire. Needless to say that everybody enjoyed himself to the limit."[66]

The following year Koy held a similarly generous event, which was also noted by the *News*. "Last night Quan Koy, the general proprietor of the E.R.A. Restaurant on North Railway Street...entertained a dozen or more of his friends among the business men at a swell supper in the restaurant. The menu was without doubt the most elaborate seen in this city. Those present did full justice to the good things provided, and united in wishing Quan Koy many returns of this unique New Year, which has so many associations which are close to his heart."[67]

Chinese New Year was a celebration which, at times, served to improve relations between Chinese and Anglo-Canadians.

In Lethbridge Chinese New Year received more attention by the Chinese community. In 1904, for example, a local newspaper noted that: "Crackers and other fireworks were discharged to chase away evil spirits and hospitality was liberally bestowed upon callers."[68]

In 1909 a more complete news report described the rejoicing of Lethbridge's Chinese community. "A general holiday is being kept for two days during which all the luxuries dear to the Chinaman's heart, denied all the other days and feasts of the year, will be very much in evidence. Last night some thousands of firecrackers were lit off according to ancient custom not only to keep the festive season but incidentally to scare away any evil spirits who might be loafing around."

During this particular celebration, time and expense were devoted to observing customary formalities. The same news account made note of this. "[In one Chinese store, a big table is centrally located] which is draped with a richly embroidered cloth [and there are] many sticks of burning incense emitting a pungent, perfumed odor. On the table is a profusion of dainties [and] on the corner is a space reserved for the card, or long red paper, of the visiting Chinaman, which if accepted by the host is returned with a similar message of good-will."[69]

In Calgary Chinese New Year was often a noisy and colorful affair which attracted public attention. A veteran reporter of long standing remarked that, in years past, "the Chinese New Year...turned Chinatown into a festive explosion. There were Lion dances, Chinese plays in a building on 2nd Avenue, east of Centre St., and family dinners."[70] With the arrival of Chinese New Year's Day in Calgary, "so many firecrackers used to be exploded that pedestrians the next morning waded knee deep through the red-paper remains of countless squibs and giant crackers."[71]

The event was royally celebrated early in Calgary's history. In 1911, for example, a local newspaper reported that on Chinese New Year's Day, wherever a few people gathered, there was "great rejoicing" and the community "celebrated the event with much merrymaking. Fireworks were induced to splutter and crack in ecstatic delight."[72]

Firecrackers were also a big part of celebrations in Edmonton, as were family and association banquets.

Religious Activities

Although Chinese urban communities in Canada remained essentially culturally exclusive enclaves during the period being considered, some Anglo-Canadians sought to instruct the Chinese in basic aspects of Western culture. The leading force which did constructive work was the Protestant segment of Canadian society. The Presbyterians, Methodists, and Anglicans, in particular, did their utmost to teach Canada's Chinese population the fundamentals of Christianity and the English language, the latter being a prerequisite to understanding the doctrines of the former. In Calgary and Edmonton some Protestants seriously undertook to educate Chinese in these fields.

It appears that Calgary's Methodists were the first denomination to take an active interest in the education of the local Chinese along Western lines. For over thirty years the Methodists conducted a special class for interested Chinese. "The class actually began during the 1890s, in the Calgary Methodist Church which stood on 2nd St. West, between 5th and 6th Avenues. The Chinese class appears to have originated from a desire to Christianize the young men recently arrived from China, but the project immediately took on a second function because of the fact that they spoke little or no English."

This great barrier to any meaningful instruction and conversion itself had to be overcome. The Chinese students therefore "received as much instruction in English as they did in Methodism....Primarily because of the language difficulty, the ratio of students to teachers was high [sic], and the two women who founded the class taught five men each."[73]

The class reached a peak size of twenty-five to thirty men before its demise in 1930. Interestingly, the room where classes were held (in today's Central United Church in the downtown) continues to be called the Chinese room.

Despite the existence of the Methodist classes, there was a strong need for further instruction of those who evinced a sincere interest in learning the basics of the English language. Around 1900 some young men began to attend Sunday School classes at Knox Presbyterian Church with the intention of learning English. Their efforts did not result in a warm welcome, however, as at this time "any attempt made by interested persons to teach the Chinese people English and a smattering of the Scriptures was thoroughly thwarted by many Calgarians."[74]

The minister of the church, Reverend J.C. Herdman, concluded that separate premises were essential for any Chinese classes. This news reached Thomas Underwood, a devoted Baptist who was the mayor of Calgary from 1902 to 1903. Underwood, a prominent contractor, provided a room at nominal rent for classes; shortly thereafter, in November 1901, he built a three and three-quarter metre by four and one-quarter metre wooden building, consisting of two rooms, on property he owned.

Within a year the building became overcrowded and on the same lot at 215 Tenth Avenue, South West, Underwood built a new Chinese Mission at his own expense. The building cost $5 000 and was a wooden two-storey structure. There was "classroom space downstairs for thirty-five pupils, and five bedrooms and a little kitchen upstairs where some of the men might board."[75] Years later it was recalled that: "Mr. Underwood founded the Mission with the object of bettering the relations between the white people and the Chinese, and at a time when feeling was very bitter against the Chinese here."[76]

In 1911 a new mission building, which cost over $12 000, was built at 120 Second Avenue, South West, near the centre of the new Chinatown, just then beginning to take form. About half the cost was raised by the

Chinese themselves. A minister of the Chinese United Church, the late Reverend David Wen, recalled that: "Mr. Underwood donated the land for the Mission and then raised the money to build the building. He was really good to the Chinese, who at the time really respected him...like a father you know."[77]

The new mission had rooming facilities, a meeting hall, and an area for physical education purposes. "From the beginning the Mission was deliberately non-denominational, and workers from all churches came to help out in the work."[78]

Teaching the members of the mission was a top priority. Every evening of the week, volunteers from the various churches arrived at the mission to conduct English lessons; however, "on Sundays the Bible took preference." If one could afford it, tuition cost one dollar per month; if not, there was no charge expected. "Between the years 1901 to 1910 ten to fifty Chinese would attend these evening classes at a given time. To attend Sunday School, however, the Chinese had to go either to the Knox Church or the Baptist Church where separate classes were conducted for them."[79]

Executive and teachers of the Chinese Mission, 1921.
Glenbow Archives, NA-3971-1.

After 1911 when the third mission was built, "evening instruction in English continued...with an average daily attendance of about sixty."[80] In 1922, due to continuing broadly based interest in language instruction, it became necessary to conduct an afternoon class "to provide an opportunity for those who could not attend the night classes."[81] In 1917 the first ladies' class began and those attending "were taught English and simple hymns."[82] "In 1922 open air meetings and services were conducted at St. George's Island and at Centre Street, the object 'being to take the Gospel to those who did not attend the regular services at the Mission'."[83]

Religious matters were naturally an integral feature of the mission's activities. In 1911 Reverend Chong Fee Tong was appointed to the mission; the first Chinese minister, he conducted Sunday services in Chinese. For all mission members, "a regular Gospel service [was] held every Thursday evening from 9 to 10 p.m."[84] presided over by visiting clergymen from all denominations.

In the early 1920s the mission supported a Chinese man from Calgary who was studying for the ministry in China, and it also paid the expenses of a Chinese missionary who worked full-time among Chinese throughout southern Alberta. Chinese girls had their own religious and social club at the mission by the 1920s, and they presented popular concerts to the public,

Pupils and teachers of the Chinese Mission, 1902.
Glenbow Archives, NA-2575-4.

on occasion. By 1921 a mission member could deliver an address which "dwelt upon the success of the Mission and called particular attention to the fact that it was self-supporting."[85]

Although the Chinese Mission was not an insignificant factor in Chinese community life, the number of converts to Christianity was not large. The failure of Protestant and Catholic churches to attract large numbers of Chinese into their congregations was prevalent throughout North America, and many devoted church workers were discouraged by the meagre fruits of their labor. One authority has observed that: "Protestant missionaries had chosen an extremely difficult task and, in consequence, they enjoyed less success than they must originally have anticipated. The greatest of all obstacles was the indifference, if not opposition, of most Orientals to the message of the Gospel. Clinging to the customs of their former homes and lands, Asians usually proved reluctant to embrace Christian ideals."[86]

Betty Lee Sung, an American author, has explained that the traditional Chinese attitude toward religion is a "practical" one. After pointing out that writers on China refer to Confucianism, Taoism, and Buddhism as the three major religions of China, she states that a "Chinese may be a Confucianist, a Taoist, and Buddhist at one and the same time." This is the case because "to the average Chinese all religions are good as long as they teach man to be good and ethical. To believe in one religion is not to exclude the other, and insistence upon such exclusion only tends to antagonize rather than convert him. That is why the Chinese will accept Christianity for its teachings, but not for its dogma."[87]

Calgary's Chinese residents did not appreciate being the recipients of evangelism when it was thrust upon them, as became apparent in 1913. In September of that year some local citizens proposed "to employ a missionary who [would] devote his time exclusively to the promotion of religion among the Chinese of Calgary."[88] However, "[the announcement was] received with hostility by a large number of the local Chinese."[89]

The *Albertan* interviewed "one of the most prominent Chinamen in the city" who explained the Chinese response. "We know where the churches, Sunday Schools and meeting halls are....When we want to go to church we will go. When we do not want to go we will stay at home, or do whatever else we please....While the Chinamen are friendly to the Christian religion and Christian people they have no desire to have a missionary appointed to do nothing but work among the Chinese here."

The prominent spokesman found it racially and/or communally insulting that such a proposition had been advanced at all. "We do not see why the Chinese should be chosen as the special objects of a missionary any more than the Greeks, French, Jews, or even Americans, or any other people who come here."[90] The proposal of the well-meaning, but rather uninformed, laymen was dropped.

Various Chinese who were converted to Christianity became very devoted and active supporters of the mission. Among the earliest converts were Wong Wah, Ho Lem, Mrs. Lem (or Lim) Kwong, and Luey Dofoo, all of whom contributed a great deal over the years to the successful operation of the Mission.

Wong Wah "was one of the first Chinese to be converted in Calgary [and he was] a member of the Board in the early days."[91] Ho Lem was one of the first members of the Mission, when he joined the body in 1902, and his contributions were many. Mrs. Lem Kwong was "one of the original members and officers of the Mothers' Club, being President of this group for many years. Under her leadership the group flourished."[92] Luey Dofoo, one of the earliest converts, was a leading figure in the establishment of the Mission, and he served the body faithfully for many years in various capacities. Together with other dedicated Chinese and Anglo-Canadians, these people made the mission a focal point of community life for many local Chinese residents.

In Edmonton missionary work among the Chinese seems to have begun around the turn of the century. Various activities were held at the Westminster Church, where Methodists and Presbyterians sponsored English classes and religious instruction for local Chinese.

In 1908 an article in the *Edmonton Bulletin* reported that students and instructors at Alberta College had voluntarily been assisting local Chinese for a few years and that "excellent work" had resulted therefrom. A minimum of ten Chinese attended classes regularly to learn to read and write English. Christian scriptural teachings were also part of the curriculum, and, as reported, the students were seemingly very interested in Bible study sessions.

The reporter added: "The idea of the mission is to educate, civilize and ultimately Christianize the Chinaman....The class who attend the school are mostly the domestics and restaurant men....one Chinaman who received his preliminary education in the school is now studying to be a missionary in his own country." The endeavor apparently faced considerable challenges, however; the reporter stated that the "great majority of Chinamen in the city do not pay much attention to the mission."[93]

In Lethbridge and Medicine Hat no such mission work seems to have been undertaken. In a related context, however, in 1915 a joint committee was established in Lethbridge to conduct rites for the deceased and to supervise the Chinese cemetery. Three Chinese grocers shared these responsibilities. "The owners of the three groceries would rotate the responsibility among themselves organizing visits and rites at the graveyard three times a year."[94]

Recreation and Education

Despite considerable gambling and some drug use, other ways of spending leisure time developed. In March 1912 a meeting was held at Calgary's Chinese Mission, and about seventy-five Chinese attended; the men decided in favor of establishing a Chinese Young Men's Christian Association (Y.M.C.A. or the "Y"). As reported by the *Albertan*: "The Calgary branch will be the first Chinese Y.M.C.A. to be organized in Canada. In China the organization is active and many of the branches have Chinese officials and workers. While the plans of the local branch have not

Boys at Chinese Y.M.C.A., Calgary, c. 1913-19.
Glenbow Archives, NA-2193-8.

been mapped out in detail one of the objects to be kept in view will be that of cooperation with the organization working in China."[95]

The Chinese "Y" membership reached forty by 1914, and on New Year's Day of that year its members made their first public appearance, demonstrating gymnastics and other skills.

The Chinese "Y" was an active organization. As early as January 1913, "the officers and members of the Chinese Y.M.C.A. [presented a program] in honor of their teachers and friends."[96] There is at least one reference to "the noted Chinese baseball team,"[97] which was comprised of "Y" members. Public performances were feature events. In 1921, for example, the Chinese "Y" presented a "Christmas tree and entertainment in their rooms on Second avenue"[98] to a packed house. Some of the program included "a class of boys who gave a very creditable showing on pyramid building...to the delight of those present [and] a physical drill by a class of Chinese girls."[99]

The Chinese Y.M.C.A. ice hockey team, Calgary, 1917.
Glenbow Archives, NA-2799-2.

By March 1921 the "Y" and its success was the topic of a speech by a prominent community figure. "The value of the Chinese Y.M.C.A. to the young China boys of the city was emphasized by Mr. Ho Lem [at a National League meeting]. Mr. Ho Lem spoke of the great good that has been accomplished by the 'Y' since its inception, and said that the daily attendance there is ample proof of its popularity."[100] Clearly, the Chinese "Y"—like the Chinese Mission—provided an opportunity for Chinese residents to spend their few leisure hours in pleasurable and educational enterprises.

In Edmonton a "Chinese Y.M.C.A. was set up in 1921 by Henry Mah, a Chinese church worker from Medicine Hat, with help from the Methodist and Presbyterian missions."[101] In 1922 Mr. Mah returned to China. "A Chinese minister, Rev. Mah Seung from Winnipeg, came to work for the Chinese 'Y' during 1924 to 1927. Rev. C.P. Leung took over the youth organization in 1927 till 1930, when it was closed due to destruction caused by some unruly members."[102]

The Chinese Public School in Calgary was founded in 1920 by Chinese parents who believed that their children should have some knowledge of their cultural heritage. "In 1906 the first child of Chinese parents was born in Calgary and in 1920 the number of Chinese children had reached about thirty. In order to transmit the language, traditions, and customs to their

A Chinese Y.M.C.A. group in front of the Chinese Mission, Calgary, 1914. Glenbow Archives, NA-2121-1.

offspring, the Chinese raised sufficient funds to buy a building on 126-2nd Avenue South West for the purpose of establishing a school."[103] Students attended classes in the evenings.

The first group to receive instruction comprised only six children, but the number increased as time passed. "Both teachers and pupils often lacked the enthusiasm to study Chinese after a regular school day [but Chinese parents believed that it was] worthwhile to give their children an additional education in their own ethnic background."[104] The establishment and operation of the school was a clear indication of the desire of parents to perpetuate Chinese culture.

In Edmonton the Chinese Public School "was established in 1915-17 with financial contributions from the Chinese community. The record indicates that a total sum of $2 300 was collected during the formative years of the school."[105] The donation of such a large sum of money clearly indicates that parents and other community members in the capital city were determined to see that Chinese children were given a thorough grounding in their cultural heritage.

4

Social Institutions, Political Organizations, and Factions

The subjects in this chapter relate directly and crucially to ethnic community formation and development. Although the general period covered is roughly 1910 to 1930, activities of groups discussed herein continued well beyond 1930; in fact, at present, some groups mentioned are more active than ever. As for the phenomenon of factionalism, it has always appeared in sizeable Overseas Chinese communities and continues to do so. This is to be expected within a racial/ethnic group which features many local community activities and which has established a wide range of organizations.

Social Institutions

By 1910 the Chinese presence in Alberta's urban centres was securely established. Until the outbreak of war in 1914, Chinese immigrants continued to join their fellow countrymen in prairie towns and cities. From about 1910 to 1930, the formal organizational infrastructure of the two largest communities—those in Edmonton and Calgary—was established. As a result the nature of personal relationships was modified, and community life in the two cities was conducted largely along institutionalized lines.

In terms of structuring their communities, the Chinese adapted traditional institutions to suit the North American situation. Four traditional Chinese institutions were transplanted to Canada and the United States: the *fong* (headquarters); the clan association (also referred to as the surname or family association); the *hui kuan* (mutual aid society); and the secret society.

The *fong* was the elemental unit of organization among North American Chinese. It was established whenever a sufficient number of Chinese resided in a town or city. In its full literal context, a *fong* was "a room or headquarters for people from the same locality, village or district."[1] It served as a meeting-place for socializing; sleeping and cooking facilities were available at a very reasonable cost for the temporarily unemployed, newcomers seeking employment, and men visiting from out of town. A *fong* served as the usual mailing address for its members, who would read letters from their home villages there and exchange news among themselves.

The majority of Chinese immigrants to North America came from the county of Toi-san in Guangdong province. In the United States, for several generations, about sixty per cent of all Chinese immigrants came from Toi-san, and the remaining forty per cent came primarily from five adjacent counties.

In Canada no adequate statistics are available in terms of a breakdown over time of immigrants' districts of origin. Nonetheless, indications are that the situation was very similar to that in the U.S. One authority on the history of Chinese-Canadians has implied that the proportion of people of Toi-sanese origin in Canada may be higher than that in the U.S.: "Canada's Chinese are culturally similar. Indeed, the only countries where there are more homogeneous Chinese populations are Great Britain [and] Jamaica."[2]

In Alberta a majority of Chinese pioneers were Toi-sanese. When Chinese pioneers of today (as was the case many years ago) speak together in Chinese, the dialect most frequently used is Toi-sanese, a rural dialect of Cantonese; the two are not mutually intelligible, however. Because Toi-sanese people hailed from the same locality and spoke the same dialect, the organization of *fongs* in both the larger and smaller centres of frontier Alberta was easily facilitated and a practical, essential, move.

At least one *fong* existed in Alberta about 100 years ago. The community room behind the Kwong Man Yuen restaurant and the nearby rooming facilities in Calgary's first Chinatown indicate that a *fong* was in operation in the 1890s. Similarly, there were community rooms and rooming facilities in Calgary's second and third Chinatowns. *Fongs* appeared, too, in Edmonton, Lethbridge, Medicine Hat, and elsewhere.

Clan associations in North America were an extremely important component of Chinese communities. The crucial role and pervasive influence of clan associations can be directly attributed to Chinese customs, tradition, and social organization in southern China. In China the family was the primary unit of social organization and control, however, the family relationship was "a link in a much larger chain of kinship."[3] The Chinese kinship system, a complex and intricate system of relationships, found its organizational expression in the operation of clan associations.

The members of a given association included all adult males of the village in question who possessed the same surname, and thereby claimed a real or imagined common ancestor. Clan associations assumed virtually all legal and social responsibilities and obligations of their members, as well as their economic and personal well-being. In Guangdong it was common for whole villages to be comprised solely of one, two, or three clans: an indication of the enormous importance of kinship in local affairs.

By instituting "appropriate structural changes and innovative functions,"[4] clan associations transplanted to North America met many of the needs of urban pioneers. In Alberta, as elsewhere, the associations provided rooming facilities, reading-rooms, and recreational areas for their members; the organizations assumed generally broader responsibilities than *fongs*.

In Alberta, almost without exception, the associations owned houses in Chinatown, where homeless members, the indigent, and the aged could live comfortably at nominal rent. Additional services were also provided. "[Clan associations set out] to protect the members of each family, to help them in sickness or poverty, to assist them to become familiar with the laws and customs of their adopted country, and yet not to forget their fatherland, language and family codes: in general, to supervise and lift them as if they were at home."[5]

Fellow clan members participated in various social gatherings and celebrated the more important traditional Chinese festivals. Clan associations "which stressed the values of mutual help, protection, benevolence, and stability were used in the overseas settings to express collective solidarity and fraternity."[6] Associations did their utmost to obtain jobs for unemployed members, and sometimes loans were made available.

In Calgary clan associations were established in the period 1910-1929. There were two associations for the Wongs: the Wong Kung Har Tong and the Wong Wu Sun Society. The Wong clan in Calgary, as in Vancouver, had "two overall associations [because of] earlier rivalry between factions that has since disappeared."[7] The two Calgary associations merged in 1968 to form the new Wong's Affinity Association, or the Wong Wun Shan.

Seven other clan associations still existing today were created prior to 1929. These were: the Gee How Oatkin Association; the Lim Shai Hor Association; the Lung Kong Association; the Mah Association; the Sue Yuen Tong Society; the Leong Chow How Tong Association; and the Yee Fong Toy Tong. All of these associations have remained voluntary "local autonomous organizations with headquarters in Vancouver."[8] The associations in Calgary performed services for fellow clansmen resident throughout southern Alberta.

In Lethbridge the larger clans operated on an informal basis. These included the Mahs, Wongs, Lees, and probably the Yees. These clans "had groups [and] would pay dues to the clan associations' headquarters in Vancouver."[9] Though not formally structured, some clans still used association names. Fellow clansmen in the towns around would contribute money if a need arose.

Joe How, who arrived in Lethbridge early in the century, summarized the nature of things: "In the old days it didn't really matter if they had organizations as such. If there were ten [clansmen] together somewhere, they'd form a fraternity. 'Whether you like it or not, you have to assist me' was the way it was. If anyone was in trouble his clansmen would back him right up: financially as well as morally."[10] If a good job was available, one would inform his clansmen first.

Jimmy Lee, son of a pioneer, related: "We Lees didn't have a formal meeting-place or executive. Some meetings were held here when I was young, I vaguely recall. Almost certainly these would have been held at the Cosmopolitan Restaurant and Hotel, a hangout for Lees."[11]

Way Leong relocated to Lethbridge from Vancouver, British Columbia, because of the many Leungs ("Leung" is the usual spelling of this surname) in the city and area. One of his sons, James, recalled that from Calgary to Lethbridge to Medicine Hat there were Leungs in nearly every small town. Periodically or regularly, they all came to Way Leong's Bow On Tong store to buy Chinese groceries and herbs.

Way Leong arrived in Lethbridge in 1929 and formed a Leung clan association, the Leong Chong How Tong. He served as lifelong treasurer and provided premises for the association on the second floor of the Bow On Tong building. Leungs south of the town of High River could belong; those to the north joined the Calgary Leung association. In 1967 Way Leong died and the association died with him.

A member of the group might be given help to set up a business; or, if someone was getting older and wanted to return to China but did not have the money, he would be assisted. Needs such as these were met. Charlie Chew, actually a Leung, remarked: "I used to attend some of the meetings of the Leung clan association. Usually meetings were called when there was some sort of trouble or other. There weren't that many meetings. A few times the association helped me out."[12]

During the traditional Spring Festival, all members were invited to come and celebrate in Lethbridge. On this occasion if you wanted to donate some money to the association, you would do so during the banquet. Not that much business was conducted during the celebration, however. During the period when there were many Leungs in southern Alberta, the Spring Festival gathering was an annual event.

In Edmonton the Wong clan association, now called the Wongs' Benevolent Society, was formed in 1917-1918. At first, premises were rented, but a few years later a building was purchased. The Gee Clan Association was formed in 1920, and it obtained its own premises. The Mah clan association, now called the Mah Society of Edmonton, was founded in 1913. Until 1923 nearly two-thirds of the local Chinese population were Mahs.

The *hui kuan* were "mutual aid societies which appeared in nearly every Chinese city and in all substantial overseas Chinese communities."[13] Members of the societies were men from the same district (or "county") or sub-district, or men speaking a common dialect. The services and responsibilities undertaken by North American *hui kuan* were in most instances broader and more inclusive than those assumed by clan associations. These additional services included credit and loan agencies for members; the arbitration of disputes among members and between members of different *hui kuan*; and employment agencies.

In North America "the relationship between clans and '*hui kuan*' was complex, sometimes overlapping but in other instances cross-cutting in enrollment."[14] Both institutions, however, were established to provide social, benevolent, and fraternal services to pioneering immigrants, who were striving to survive in an almost invariably hostile environment, where society in virtually all respects was markedly dissimilar from that which they had known in the homeland.

In the U.S. the *hui kuan* have historically maintained immensely stronger control over Chinatown affairs than has been the case in Canada. A few *hui kuan* have functioned in Calgary over the years. The first to appear was the Shon Yee Benevolent Association, which was established in 1922. Members originated from the county of Chung-san, directly adjacent to Macao; the county was known as Heung-san earlier this century; in *pinyin* romanization, it is referred to as Zhongshan. (The Chung Shan Association, another organization representing the same county, was established in Calgary in 1954).

In light of the predominance of Toi-sanese people in Alberta, it was to be expected that residents from other districts would band together for mutual assistance; it is surprising, however, to discover that over the years in Alberta—as across Canada, excepting Victoria and Vancouver—few district associations were in fact established.

It seems that no *hui kuan* have operated in Medicine Hat and, until a few years ago, Edmonton.

One *hui kuan* operated in Lethbridge. It was located at the Kwang Sang store in a Chinatown building presently called Man Sang. The store was owned by Kwang Sing, and it served as headquarters for all Chinese who originated from Hoi-ping county in Guangdong. Like all district associations, it was "concerned with the welfare and development of that county and the well-being of county residents overseas."[15]

Many people belonged to the association. They did all their banking there, and Kwang Sing would send remittances to family members in Hoi-ping. A brother-in-law of his in China was a senior clerk; he handled business affairs at that end. Detailed records were kept of all transactions. When Kwang Sing died, his brother and nephew managed the association; but it fell apart in the 1920s, when the brother-in-law in China died.

Over the years a number of Chinese lending clubs operated in Alberta's larger centres. The term for this type of lending system is *do wei*; *do* means participate and *wei* means association. Everyone who belonged would put in a certain amount of money per month, usually ten or twenty dollars. If twenty people belonged, then $200 would be available each month. A long-term Chinese resident of Lethbridge related that: "Whoever wanted to borrow would gather, and they'd write down on a slip what rate of interest they would pay; the highest bidder would get the pool. If someone needed money, he'd start up the pool and would bid heavily."[16]

Payments for loans were made over time. If someone wrote bad cheques or left town without paying, the club would stop running. So, these were intermittent enterprises.

The final institution indigenous to China and transplanted to North America was the secret society. Traditionally, throughout south-eastern China, there was a proliferation of various secret societies and brotherhoods which, on occasion, rose up in revolt against the imperial order. This was particularly the case in turbulent Guangdong and Fujian (Fukien) provinces, which were traditional hotbeds of revolt, rebellion, and social unrest in China.

Of all the many separately organized and variously named secret societies in China, the famous Triad Society (sometimes called the Heaven-and-Earth League or the Hung League) was the largest and most powerful. Before their arrival many Chinese immigrants to Canada and the U.S. were already members of the Triad Society; so, it was natural that "nearly every overseas Chinese community formed secret societies which were either chapters or models of that order."[17] The primary objective of the Triads was the overthrow of the reigning Manchu dynasty (1644-1912) and its replacement by descendants of the Ming dynasty (1368-1644).

In North America it appears that there has been only one secret society which could rightfully claim to represent the Triad Society and its political and ideological objectives. This secret society was the Cheekungtong (Zhigongtang), often simply called the CKT. It was apparently first established in Canada at Quesnel Mouth, B.C., in 1876. It is possible, however, that several chapters of the CKT existed in rural B.C. as early as 1858: organized by Chinese miners who arrived from California to join in the Fraser River Gold Rush.

Until the mid-1880s, the CKT was the only Chinese association or organization among the Chinese in Canada; by its nature and from necessity, the society bound together the solidarities of clan, language, and district of origin.

The Cheekungtong spread from San Francisco, where the head chapter was located, throughout the length and breadth of North America. Branches of the society served as fraternal associations, and boarding-houses and meeting-halls were usually maintained for members' use. The primary objective of the secret society, however, was most definitely political: its members constituted an underground, overseas revolutionary party, which followed political events in China with intense interest.

With few exceptions the inner workings and activities of the CKT in Canada and the U.S. have remained cloaked in secrecy; nonetheless, the society would have had branches in Alberta and the other prairie provinces by the turn of the century, if not earlier. The Chinese in Alberta became most actively involved in CKT activities in the decade preceding the 1911 revolution; this was the case throughout North America.

In 1908 several hundred members of the secret society met clandestinely somewhere in Calgary, presumably to discuss policy matters. At this conference Morris Abraham Cohen, an influential and ardent confidant and defender of Alberta's Chinese population, was admitted into the ranks of the CKT. Cohen regarded his investiture, even many years later, as a very personal matter and felt keenly the obligations and duties of membership in the secret order.

He did, however, note the following in his memoirs concerning his admission in Calgary: "[We went up a stairway into a large room] where there must have been a couple of hundred Chinese there sitting silent and solemn....there was some sort of a vote, and I was formally asked if I'd join the lodge. Having agreed, I was initiated. It may sound silly, but even now I am unable to tell you how it was done....I took an oath not to reveal any of their secrets and that oath still binds me."[18]

It is quite likely that Cohen was the only non-Chinese member of the secret society in Canada and that he was admitted only because of his deep friendships with Chinese and his defence of them, sometimes in violent circumstances.

The CKT claimed wide allegiance throughout North America and "during the height of its power...a branch existed wherever sojourners and their kinsmen resided."[19] During the early part of the twentieth century, most branches of the CKT and its affiliated secret societies in North America began to refer to their societies as branches of the Chinese Masonic Order; thus, the appellations Chinese Masons and Chinese Freemasons soon gained currency.

The reason for this was that, by this time, the true Masonic Order had largely accepted the idea that Freemasonry was an old and established movement in China. This "mythical history," states an authority, "inadvertently provided an avenue of legitimation for Chinese secret societies in the Occident [which began] to demand the rights and privileges accorded to the Occidental order."[20]

In Alberta CKT chapters began calling their members Chinese Freemasons shortly after the successful 1911 revolution in China. In Calgary the Chinese "Freemasons" were founded in 1911, when they opened their organization's headquarters at 107 Second Avenue, South East, and were formally called the Chinese Masonic League of Calgary. Within the Calgary organization was an inner lodge, the Dart Coon Society (or Dart Coon Club), which was common to many Chinese Masonic lodges. Members of this inner lodge were "the most trusted Freemasons [who, in the early years of its existence] were often entrusted with whatever fighting the Freemasons were engaged in."[21]

In Medicine Hat the local branch was called the Chinese Masonic Lodge. It held meetings as early as February 1911 and owned its own headquarters.

In Lethbridge the Chinese Freemasons were established in 1922, although CKT members had undoubtedly been active for many years. Initially, there were forty-eight members. Construction of a hall began in 1923 under the trusteeship of Joe Fong, Jung Shung Yen, and Mah Shue. The building was completed in 1924, donations having been received from Chinese Freemasons throughout Canada. The same year—to honor the occasion—Chinese Freemasons held their national convention in Lethbridge. The convention apparently lasted two weeks, and delegates arrived from fully sixty lodges.

Like its Calgary counterpart, the Lethbridge lodge had a Dart Coon Society. Members of it "gathered in secret meetings apart from the other membership in the basement of the Chinese Free Masons building."[22]

In Edmonton the Chinese Freemasons were not formally established until 1954. This occurred because of the comparatively superior numerical strength of the Mahs until after the 1940s: various Mah clan association executives belonged to the Chinese National League, a rival of the Freemasons for many years.

As secret society members, Triads and their overseas counterparts devised many secret coded words and mannerisms, both to identify themselves to one another and to detect spies. In China the Triads were outlawed, and the penalty for membership was death.

According to a longtime Freemason, James Leong: "There are many ways of identifying yourself to others as a Mason. If you walk into a great big room, because of the way you do a certain thing, any Mason there would know you are one. An infiltrator, who knew just a few Masonic ways, would easily be discovered. In many everyday things you had to be consistent."[23] Mr. Leong added: "If you are a Mason you are allowed—it is a male organization—to tell your wife things about the organization. Secrets. Everything. But, not your son: he might join a different party."[24]

A number of days were regularly honored by Freemasons. September 1st—the day the Triad Society was founded—was one of these; another was October 10th, the Double Ten, the date when the Triads and other revolutionaries toppled the Manchu dynasty. Other days of remembrance were Chung Yung; the birthday of a heroic Chinese general who fought the Manchus; and a day honoring martyred Triad monks.

During the decade prior to 1911, when it backed Dr. Sun Yat-sen's revolutionary movement, the CKT exercised its greatest influence in China's affairs. In Canada, the United States, Europe, and Asia, the Triad Society in its various guises collected huge sums of money from Overseas Chinese to help finance the successful revolution. Although non-Triad people overseas also donated significantly to the cause—as did merchants and others within China—the financial contribution of the Triads was very considerable.

Chinese Freemasons' national convention, Lethbridge, 1924.
Glenbow Archives, NA-1891-1.

After 1911 the Triad Society and the Overseas Chinese in general maintained a constant interest in China's affairs, "but this interest never again achieved the unified political action that characterized the period of Sun's triumph."[25]

Political Organizations

The four indigenous Chinese institutions transplanted from China were not the sole organizations among North American Chinese. In addition to the notorious fighting *tongs*—which did not operate in Canada—there were several important Chinese fraternal associations which were, in essence, political organizations. The most important of such associations in Canada were the Empire Reform Association and the Chinese National League, or Kuomintang (often called the KMT).

The Empire Reform Association was a voluntary fraternal association: there were no membership restrictions based on surname, speech, locality, or other considerations (this also held true for secret societies and the KMT). The Empire Reform Association was established in Vancouver at the turn of the century, following a visit to the city by the famous Chinese reformer, Kang Yu-wei. The association grew rapidly in Vancouver and advocated the introduction of Western technology and constitutional monarchy into China.

Members were recruited primarily from the prosperous, progressive merchant elite, who were quickly becoming Westernized in dress, manners, and attitudes. The association did much to foster a favorable image of Canada's Chinese population, and in B.C. it "was accepted with considerable interest and sympathy"[26] by Anglo-Canadians.

The Empire Reform Association had several branches in Alberta. There were about 200 members of the Calgary association in 1910. The president of the Calgary branch was Louie Kheong (also spelled Luey or Louis in the newspapers), a prosperous merchant who was highly respected by Chinese and non-Chinese alike. It was he who founded the first enduring Chinese store in Calgary, the Kwong Man Yuen, in the early 1890s; later, he served the Chinese Freemasons as president of the Dart Coon Club. At the time of his death, the *Calgary Herald* remarked that: "Many and varied were his contributions to the welfare of his fellow-countrymen and to the community which he organized."[27]

Some information is available concerning the president of a small Medicine Hat branch of the association. Quan Koy arrived in Medicine Hat in the 1880s or 1890s, after having "made a reputation for himself as a chef on the C.P.R. boat *Moyie*, on the Kootenay lakes."[28] A highly enterprising man, Koy and his wife soon established and operated a number of businesses in Medicine Hat, including a store specializing in goods from China, a laundry, and several restaurants.

The industrious entrepreneur was regarded by *Medicine Hat News* editors as a good Canadian citizen who promoted China's advancement in the world. "Quan Koy is one of the advanced members of the Chinese nation, and takes a great interest in the work of the Empire Reform Association. [His E.R.A. Restaurant has been] named after this movement for a more enlightened Orient. In his many years residence in this city Quan Koy has proved himself to be wide awake, public spirited, and progressive in his citizenship."[29] Progressive-minded and popular Chinese community leaders such as Quan Koy and Louie Kheong provided and enhanced a very favorable image of Chinese to Anglo-Canadians.

In 1912, with the overthrow of the Manchu dynasty, the monarchic, reform-minded association changed its name to the Constitutionalist Party, but it steadily declined in influence thereafter.

The Chinese National League proved to be a far more significant organization than the Empire Reform Association. The league was founded in 1911 after Dr. Sun Yat-sen's lecturing and fund-raising tour of most large Canadian cities, including Calgary and Edmonton. The organization was established as a political organization supporting Dr. Sun Yat-sen's republican cause in China and was not at all involved in Canadian politics. To all intents the Chinese National League was the overseas extension of Dr. Sun's Kuomintang party, and the league itself is commonly referred to as the Kuomintang.

The Calgary branch of the Chinese National League was set up in 1913 and had an original membership of thirty-eight men. The league soon established itself as a major organization in the Chinese community. For the first few years, a hall was rented. Membership soared, and in 1919 nearly $8 000 was spent to purchase premises at 109 Second Avenue, South East. A local newspaper remarked at the time on "the rapid growth of the league membership,"[30] then under the presidency of Ho Lem. The grand opening of the new headquarters was held in April 1920: a gourmet dinner was held, accompanied by the music of a six-piece Chinese orchestra.

The following year, the Calgary branch was chosen to host the Dominion convention of the Chinese National League, which lasted a full week.

The *Calgary Albertan* outlined the objectives of the delegates to the conference: "the objects of the league are [primarily] political, insofar as the affairs of the Chinese republic are concerned. The league strongly upholds the republican form of government established in China some years ago..."

In relation to disturbing early manifestations of the upcoming warlord era in China and other onerous problems which seriously undermined Dr. Sun Yat-sen's political efforts, the article added that the league "is engaged in efforts both in Canada and in all other countries where people of Chinese race reside, to strengthen the hands of the republicans against the dark forces of reaction which are seeking to undo the progressive work accomplished by the reform party in China."[31]

The Chinese National League in Calgary could boast of 450 members by 1923. In the early 1920s the organization conducted evening classes in public speaking in Chinese; hence, "each member when called upon had to speak, and the result was a general broadening of views, as well as increased proficiency in speaking."[33]

The headquarters consisted, in part, of a large assembly hall and a library which contained "the latest books of an educational nature [and subscriptions to] all the leading Chinese papers in Cuba, San Francisco, Canton, Shanghai, Sunning, Vancouver, Victoria and New York."[34] The Chinese Nationalists followed the course of Chinese affairs with avid interest, particularly in regard to turbulent China.

Canadian newspapers followed the course of events in China with some interest, and various articles outlined the progress of the Kuomintang in its political and military endeavors. Not surprisingly perhaps, the Chinese National League in Alberta almost always received "a good press." This was in vivid juxtaposition to most reporting of local Chinese news.

Informative reporting appeared from time to time concerning the league, as in the following from a 1923 article: "The membership is chosen by the ballot procedure and to become a member, a Chinaman must be held in esteem by his fellows, and show signs of industry. He must be law abiding, a Republican, and willing to assist in any cause when the majority of the league decides that action will be taken. The league is not a secret society. It has no ritual and its meetings are always open to the general public."[35] In 1921 it was estimated that eighty per cent of Calgary's Chinese population belonged to the Chinese National League, making it by far the largest local Chinese organization.

The Chinese National League had branches which owned their own buildings in Lethbridge and Medicine Hat. Information concerning the Medicine Hat branch is scarce, but as early as 1917 it sent delegates to a Nationalist convention in Lethbridge. Medicine Hat's Nationalists regularly sent delegates to subsequent conventions of the republican league, demonstrating their interest in its activities. In Lethbridge the local newspapers provided more coverage of the local organization's activities than was the case in Medicine Hat.

In 1915 republicans organized a Lethbridge association and located their party headquarters on Second Avenue South, where "the new flag of the Chinese Republic [floated] beneath the Union Jack."[36] Over 100 local Chinese, other Lethbridge citizens, and "several eminent Chinamen from Calgary [and] Medicine Hat"[37] celebrated the formation of what was first called the Chinese Revolutionary Party.

The general secretary of the association, Fing Wee, "a well known local Chinaman [who spoke] excellent English"[38] was interviewed by a local newspaper and explained some of the association's background. The following formed part of the resulting report. "[The association] aims to instruct the young Chinamen of the city in the politics of their native land and has for its express purpose the downfall of the Royalist faction in China....the movement is practically a Y.M.C.A. [and] reading rooms, games and physical classes [are] part of the plan. The best Chinese current literature is at the disposal of the boys."[39] Wee himself mentioned that: "telegrams of congratulations were received from similar organizations throughout Canada and the U.S."[40]

The Chinese republicans in Lethbridge hosted annual conventions of the Chinese National League, which commemorated the founding of the association by Dr. Sun Yat-sen. Chinese wisely took advantage of these occasions to foster goodwill with Anglo-Canadians.

In June 1917 a two-day celebration was held in the city, and Chinese delegates from many Alberta centres attended. The occasion began with a fireworks display "at which many local people were present,"[41] and the following day a meeting was held. "Many local Chinese and also many businessmen and other friends of the league gathered at the league headquarters, Second Avenue, and participated in the celebration, which was one of the most unique [sic] of its kind ever held here,"[42] commented the *Lethbridge Herald*.

At the meeting's end, "the Chinese national anthem was sung and refreshments were served. The city orchestra was in attendance and photographs were taken of the gathering."[43]

Before the celebration was held, the *Herald* outlined the objectives of the Chinese National League. "[The league aspires to further the] progress of China under republican government, to maintain the unity of politics, to expand local self-government, to enforce the assimilation of the race, to adopt the best policies of socialism and to maintain national peace."[44] It was largely due to the progressive, modernizing program of the Nationalists that they were able to foster interest and support among Alberta's Anglo-Canadians.

In June 1919 a similar convention and celebration in Lethbridge again demonstrated Nationalist strength in the city and Alberta in general; it also provided an opportunity for members to hear the views of Anglo-Canadians about Chinese concerns. The main speaker, Ernest Y. Dong, addressed the gathering "in excellent and fluent English."[45] After explaining some recent troubles of the league in Canada, Dong "stated that the Chinese National Leagues, of which there [were] 57 in the Dominion, were for the purpose of educating the Chinese along democratic lines of government. He welcomed the English-speaking visitors in that the leagues looked to them for support in carrying on their progressive policies for the enlightenment of the local Chinese."[46]

Seven prominent local Anglo-Canadians then delivered short speeches, which were not reported by the press. "Following the oratorical part of the program, a photo of the Chinese along with their guests was taken and a sumptuous tea with refreshments was served to the accompaniment of a Chinese orchestra."[47]

Over the years, the organization maintained its primary political role; members did not receive financial assistance from the league, for example. Social needs of members were met in various respects, however. "Members would congregate at the headquarters to socialize. There was a large reading-room there with periodicals; this still exists."[48] Upstairs, rooms were maintained for renting members. During the 1920s the rental rate for a room was about ten dollars a month. Tenants had use of the hall, including the reading-room with its library, a kitchen for cooking, and fridges at the back. At times members would engage in a game of *mah-jong* on tables at the back of the hall.

In 1925, after Dr. Sun Yat-sen's death, the local league honored his services to China. "There was a mock funeral service, and a parade was held in Lethbridge's streets and in Chinatown. Chinese in the parade wore top hats and tails. Dr. Sun's portrait was carried and a large number of people turned out. A big book, over one inch-thick, was compiled which contained the eulogies to Dr. Sun."[49]

The National League always had more members in Lethbridge than did the Freemasons. Elections were held every year. Quite often, Lee Duck served as president. Regular general meetings and regular and special executive meetings were held. These were conducted in the modern parliamentary fashion, with the president acting as chairman. "The secretary would read the minutes of the last meeting. Once a month the treasurer would show his figures."[50]

In Edmonton the Chinese National League was founded in 1913. Unfortunately, its activities were largely overlooked by the local press.

In 1919 the Chinese National League was accused of being responsible for the assassination of a Chinese government cabinet minister, who was visiting Victoria's Chinese community when he was murdered. The league's activities were banned for a brief period of time by the federal government, but after an investigation proved that the league was not involved, the ban was lifted.

"No sooner was the news received than the Edmonton branch of the league prepared for a meeting which...was especially well attended."[51] Two months later a bigger celebration was held by the branch to honor the league's reopening. A banquet was held after two hours of speeches; then, a parade of a dozen cars took place, followed by yet another banquet.

Chinese voluntary fraternal associations formed for political reasons were a very important component of Chinese urban communities in Alberta. They reflected widely shared concerns of Chinese about the future of their native land and an increasing interest in political affairs in general. Chinese utilized these associations to acquaint Anglo-Canadians with their political and social aspirations: thereby, enhancing understanding of their concerns to some extent and providing a meeting ground for the useful exchange of ideas.

The Chinese Freemasons also constituted a voluntary fraternal association formed for political reasons. But, despite the fact that after 1911 the CKT in Canada was registered as a political party, it continued to operate as a secret society.

There was some Chinese Freemason-initiated interaction with white Masonic lodges for a few years in Western Canadian cities. Basically, though, this simply involved inviting white Freemasons to various Chinese ceremonies, including that of initiation. No official ties were made between the Chinese Freemasons and the white Masonic Order in Canada.

Factions

Although scattered newspaper accounts in Alberta's press provided some insights into Chinese community life, tensions and conflicts within the community usually went unnoticed unless an act of violence, or a court case of some interest, appeared: marring the image of seemingly serene interpersonal Chinese relations. Disputes between parties were—whenever at all possible—settled by arbitration within the community. Only when traditional approaches had failed completely were the police and courts utilized; such situations were relatively uncommon.

Soon after their establishment in Alberta, it has been remarked that: "the tongs [clan associations] soon grew in size and power, and intense rivalries developed between them."[52] Although clan rivalries may have persisted for a long time, there is an absence of documentation on the subject. There are, however, informative accounts available which document conflicts between Chinese political associations.

During the First World War, a serious state of conflict manifested itself between the Chinese National League and the CKT—by 1920 referred to as the Chinese Freemasons or Chinese Masons. The Chinese Freemasons' explanation for the rivalry between the Freemasons (along with their counterparts throughout the world) and Dr. Sun's Kuomintang party and its overseas adherents is essentially as follows: "According to them [the CKT or Chinese Freemasons], Sun Yat-sen betrayed the Freemasons after the revolution of 1911 by closing them out of the newly-formed Kuomintang, although they had provided much of the support among overseas Chinese without which Sun would certainly have failed. For instance, the principal Masonic buildings in North America were heavily mortgaged to provide Sun with funds."[53]

Information relating to Nationalist-Freemason rivalry in Alberta reveals that political and cultural differences were also factors of some significance in the prevailing state of conflict between the two groups.

Nationalist-Freemason hostilities reached their apex in the province from late 1917 to 1922. During that period, a number of violent incidents and bitterly-fought criminal trials laid bare the serious cleavages in urban communities. The most serious episodes occurred in Calgary. In December 1918, for example, one or more Chinese Freemasons armed with heavy iron bars "beat two of the Nationalists into insensibility and nearly caused the death of one of them."[54] One man was subsequently charged with assault, but no conviction was obtained.

The Freemasons then launched a perjury trial against Nationalist witnesses; with dismissal of that case, the Nationalists concerned launched a similarly unsuccessful, and very bitter, perjury trial against their former accusers.

James Short, K.C., was the prosecutor in the assault case and many other cases involving local Chinese residents. His remarks to the attorney-general of Alberta concerning the case indicated his interpretation of the hostilities. "There is the old faction of Chinese Masons and the new faction of the Nationalist party. The Masons represent those who cling to the old [order] and the old customs generally....The Nationalist party is republican and is for reform and progress [and] as I see the matter it is a war between the two factions who desire to make the Courts of Justice the scene of their conflicts."[55]

From Short's remarks, one concludes that hostilities were the result of conflicting points of view regarding both China's political future and Chinese cultural matters. The Freemasons were members of—or successors of—the Cheekungtong, which had sought to restore a traditional ethnic Chinese monarchy. On the other hand, Chinese National League members' political positions were in accord with those of Dr. Sun Yat-sen and his republican Kuomintang party (National People's party).

Nonetheless, it must be stressed that soon after the toppling of the Manchu dynasty and the nominal establishment of republican government, the CKT generally accepted the Chinese republic and did not seek to restore the Ming dynasty. In both China and Canada, the CKT soon registered itself as a political party, calling itself the Zhigongdang (or Zhigong political party).

International CKT conferences were held to create structures to co-ordinate concerted activities among the various CKT national organizations and also to facilitate building political support in important Chinese cities. Thereby, the CKT potentially became an active contender with the KMT for political power; hence, not long after 1911, the Chinese National

League and the CKT (Chinese Freemasons) competed avidly for influence and support in Canada's Chinese communities.

Probably the most explosive confrontation between the two factions in Calgary occurred six months before the above-mentioned assault. During a domino game being played in a Chinatown location, a Nationalist player claimed he had been cheated by a Masonic player: he flew into a rage; demolished the gambling table with an axe; and hurriedly departed.

That evening he and another Nationalist were walking in an alley in Chinatown; suddenly, they were attacked by four members of the Dart Coon Club armed "with heavy sword knives and iron bars."[56] The two men were badly wounded, but both survived the ordeal. Two young men were subsequently charged with attempted murder and another with discharging a firearm. After an arduous three-day trial, the former men were convicted and sentenced to twenty-three months in jail.

Factional hostilities also appeared in Medicine Hat and Lethbridge during this period. During a trial in Calgary in 1919, for example, a Chinese Nationalist witness admitted that he had previously been convicted "for fighting with the other society who supported Wong Lee [i.e., the Chinese Freemasons]. They had fought on the streets at Medicine Hat and he was fined."[57]

Hostilities within Chinese communities in Alberta were, however, not solely Nationalist-Freemason affairs. In 1917 a very serious instance of internal community disruption occurred in Medicine Hat after a Chinese resident was charged with robbing and assaulting a local Chinese storekeeper. Mr. W.A. Begg, crown prosecutor in the case, subsequently reported that: "When the case was called on January the 31st, the informant and the Crown's [two Chinese] witnesses had all disappeared, apparently at the instigation of the friends of the accused....Efforts were made to locate these Chinamen in Alberta and Saskatchewan, but without results."[58]

The incident made a definite impact on the usually peaceful Chinese community; as reported by Begg: "This case has, in my opinion, had a serious effect on the Chinese element here, and to my knowledge it is the first time they have attempted anything of this sort."[59]

Instances of factionalism also appeared in Lethbridge, where the Chinese Nationalists (as in Calgary) were a strong political body. In December 1917 a local Chinese resident claimed that, after a domino game, two Chinese Nationalist players robbed and assaulted him. The alleged culprits were consequently tried on two different occasions, but in neither case did the jury agree on a decision.

The alleged robbers subsequently charged several of the Crown's Chinese witnesses with perjury, but an acquittal resulted. In addition, a friend of the two alleged robbers was indicted on a charge of fabricating evidence. These charges, the preliminary hearings, and trials caused a great deal of consternation among the Chinese population during the nine-month duration of legal proceedings.

The situation was not directly an outcome of Nationalist-Freemason antipathy; rather, a bitter confrontation developed between local Nationalists and an apparently non-aligned Chinese faction. Remarks of C.F.P. Conybeare, K.C., the crown prosecutor in these and other Chinese cases, explained developments in the matter.

"[The man who originally claimed that he was robbed] was not a member of the Chinese National League. The trouble occurred in a gambling place of members of that league. The men who were charged with robbing him were members of that league, but unluckily Quong Sam, an old Chinaman, who before the days of the young Chinese movement, was practically the head of Chinamen here, seems to have interested himself in assisting the prosecutor. Whether he did this out of antipathy to the National League, which put his nose out of joint, I do not know, but it gave room for the cry that it was a fight between the Monarchists and the National League....The complainant was a Republican although not a member of the National League but nonetheless the headquarters of the National League in Vancouver seems to have taken the matter up as a fight between the factions, ordered an assessment of one dollar per head of every member of the League throughout Canada for the defence of the persons accused, and they also retained Mr. Robertson [an eminent Edmonton criminal lawyer]. All the witnesses for the defence were members of that League while the witnesses for the prosecution belonged to no party."[60]

The fact that one of the accused was the secretary of the local branch of the league certainly must have inflamed the animosity of the Nationalists in Lethbridge and Vancouver against their legal antagonists.

The tension caused by the confrontation apparently reached a climax in June 1918, when D.H. Elton, counsel for the two non-aligned men charged with perjury, sent a telegram requesting an immediate trial, stating: "Witnesses for accused may leave country and some are comtemplating doing so."[61] By late August Quong Sam—who had largely induced the rising tension—had died; his death meant that the key witness in the final case, that of fabricating evidence, was gone. The action was therefore discontinued.

By late August Conybeare remarked upon the clear relaxation of tensions. "As far as I can judge the trouble has now simmered down."[62] The following years were more peaceful ones for the Chinese community in Lethbridge.

Rivalry between the two organizations continued until the outbreak of the Sino-Japanese War in 1937, when the Chinese war effort essentially united Canada's Chinese residents in a popular common cause. A few attempts were made before then to improve Nationalist-Freemason relations.

Early in 1921, for instance, when the Dominion Convention of the Chinese National League met in Calgary, friendly overtures were made to the Freemasons. A local newspaper reported: "In an attempt to resume friendly relations with the Masonic league, for the good of all Chinamen in general, Ah Koon, a member of the Chinese Masonic league of Edmonton was invited to attend and he also addressed the meeting...."[63] The convention ended on a conciliatory note. "[The] members of the two factions, the Masons and the National league, agreed to bury the hatchet and sign an everlasting peace."[64]

But, the delegates' efforts proved futile and short-lived. Exactly one week after the accord was agreed upon, two Chinese Masons were badly beaten by several Nationalists during a free-for-all in Calgary's Chinatown. By the end of 1921, however, the most physically abusive period of the serious factional struggle was over.

In Lethbridge one poignant episode revealed how deep divisions could be. As related by Joe How, the family of a very successful local Chinese merchant, Kwang Sing, was seriously divided by contrary convictions. "The family split up because there were political differences between the father and his children. Kwang Sing was a monarchist and a member of the Chinese Empire Reform Association."[65] While Kwang Sing continued to operate his business, all other members of the family relocated to Moose Jaw.

Mr. How explained the context of political thought during this period which could result in a fractured family. "At that time [about 1917] almost everyone—especially the younger generation—was strongly republican. The young people, in particular, wanted to see things reformed in China."[66]

Feelings ran deep in the city. "Politics came right out into the open. If you didn't side with me and if I knew about any good [employment or investment] opportunities, I wouldn't tell you about them."[67]

Factionalism directly determined fundamental aspects of the nature of Chinese community life in Canada and the U.S. One authority contends that Chinese political factionalism in Canada was a central factor—as important as Anglo-Canadian discrimination—accounting for "[the containment of] the Chinese community within its own boundaries...Leaders tried to rally the Chinese to one party or the other and thus succeeded...in ensuring the cohesion of the Chinese community as a whole."[68]

5

Prejudice, Discrimination, and Racism

As described in Chapter Two, soon after the initial settlement of Chinese in Alberta, prejudice and discrimination against the Asian arrivals became apparent. Long-term "institutional racism" (discussed in Chapter Eight) would only have worsened anti-Chinese sentiment. Simultaneous with these trends, a stringent state of cultural conflict arose between Alberta's Chinese and Anglo-Canadians: further complicating the complex matrix responsible for prolonged widespread antagonism toward the Chinese.

The Nature of Cultural Conflict, 1910-1925

Before, during, and well beyond the period under consideration, anti-Chinese sentiment exceeded hostility toward other minority immigrant groups. An authority on Alberta's ethnic groups has concluded that, "Aside from the Indians, the Chinese were rated as the most undesirable ethnic group in Alberta—the group least likely to be assimilated and the most conspicuously remote in culture and 'race'."[1]

He has also maintained that the belief that the Chinese could not be assimilated was a major factor predetermining Anglo-Canadian responses. "Hostility towards [Asians] exceeded anti-European sentiment because [they] were more remote culturally and 'racially', and more Chinese behavior patterns [like gambling] violated middle-class values."[2] Anti-

Chinese sentiment essentially transcended political affiliations and class allegiances, but it was more pronounced in southern Alberta.

Rationalization of anti-Chinese sentiment in North America found conceptual expression in both the extremely negative stereotyping of Chinese residents and in the belief of an Asian menace to Western civilization. These two currents of thought had wide currency throughout Alberta.

Stereotyping of the Chinese in North America was very pronounced and well-established by the late 1800s. It has been noted in this respect that, in Alberta, by 1896, "a whole set of negative stereotypes [regarding Chinese] had developed and were later used in the opposition to the Chinese immigrants who came into the province in larger numbers after the turn of the century."[3] The terms Chink, Mongolian, and Celestial commonly appeared in Alberta's newspapers before 1925 and were indicative of the prevailing hostility against the Chinese presence. Essentially, the Chinese were regarded as a clannish, rather mysterious community of heathen people, who clung tenaciously to their traditional way of life.

Supposed negative characteristics of Chinese behavior were frequently harped on by elements of society hostile to the Chinese. Supposed unsanitary living conditions, gambling, opium-smoking, and female slavery were perpetual themes of self-styled moralists, who railed against their purported existence in Chinese communities. In this respect, some members of the Protestant clergy thundered against alleged social deviance. Chinese Canadians' ostensible peculiarities were consistently remarked upon and included the spoken and written Chinese language; Chinese dress; music; superstitions; foods; traditional Chinese funerals; medicines; and so on.

Other elements also contributed to the prevailing negative stereotype of North American Chinese. Pejorative terms such as *tong* wars, hatchetmen, highbinders, and coolie labor had a wide circulation and evoked images of a mysterious and sinister way of life in Chinese communities.

The supposed Asian menace to Western civilization included both the Chinese and Japanese populations. In Canada—particularly in British Columbia—the Asian menace scare was regarded seriously. In that province, fears for the continued existence of a white-dominated society appear to have been rampant, especially after the end of the Great War. Economic competition was certainly a major factor determining the hostile B.C. response to Asian immigration, but other factors were present. As one authority on this topic has noted: "Throughout the 1920s politicians and publicists exploited and exaggerated [the menace] making the Oriental threat to [B.C.'s] future as a white province seem much greater than it actually was. The idea of a 'menace' flourished on fear."[4]

In Alberta the Asian menace scare reached the attention of the public primarily through newspaper reports. As early as 1910 the *Calgary Herald* remarked on increasing Chinese immigration to Canada in an article entitled "Chinks Come In Thousands," which expressed concern about the situation. Clergymen sometimes spoke about the imaginary Asian menace at meetings. In 1908, for instance, a Methodist minister from Toronto delivered a speech at Calgary's Central Methodist Church and contended that it was virtually impossible for Canada to prohibit the entrance of Asian immigrants. He remarked, in part, "[Japan, China and India] were knocking peacefully at our western door [but] the day might come when they would knock with their cannon."[5]

Periodic scares of massive Chinese immigration to Canada—on a legal basis or otherwise—were reported in the press. In 1922, for example, the *Calgary Albertan* reported: "'No Chinamen are coming to Canada with the exception of a small handful of bonafide children of Chinamen who have been here for about 20 years. There is nothing to the big scare that the country is being flooded with Chinamen. It is ridiculous', said Arnold F. George, chief immigration officer for the Alberta district, yesterday."[6] In 1913 a visiting Baptist minister gave a public lecture in Calgary devoted to the dangers resulting from the immigration of Chinese "hordes," who were freely entering Canada.[7]

Articles concerning B.C.'s hostility toward Chinese residents and restrictive measures against them also appeared frequently in Alberta's newspapers, acquainting readers with anti-Asian sentiment in the Pacific province.

For many years, there was strong opposition against Chinese engaging in intermarriage with whites and miscegenation. One prominent issue was the supposed need for protection of white girls from Chinese employers or aspiring lovers. After Saskatchewan passed an act in 1912 which prohibited Asians from employing white girls, efforts of a similar nature were promoted in Alberta; however, they were unsuccessful.

Intermarriage between Chinese and whites was nearly unheard of in the Canadian West. An authority on Chinese-Canadian society, Dr. Peter S. Li, has concluded: "Although it is theoretically possible for some

Chinese to have married members of other ethnic groups, inter-ethnic marriages were rare [before 1947] because of social discrimination...."[8]

During the latter months of 1913 and the early months of 1914, Reverend A.D. McDonald, Superintendent of the Children's Aid Society of Alberta, spearheaded an attempt to prohibit Chinese businessmen from employing white girls. Rev. McDonald felt that immediate legislation was required to remedy "this important and vexed question."[9]

When an unnamed but "prominent local Chinaman" took issue with the clergyman's proposals, the minister stood firm in his position, remarking in part: "The very fact that such a law was passed in Saskatchewan bears out the truth of my statement to the *Albertan* that the Chinese are very often a moral menace to a community....While there are some respectable, moral Chinese in Calgary, the majority of them are not....Take the Chinatowns of New York, Chicago and other large American cities. They are cancers on the towns. Conditions are undesirable in our own small but growing Chinatown."[10]

In March 1914, after his society endorsed his proposals, Rev. McDonald advocated that black employers also be included in legislation prohibiting the employment of white girls. No substantive results came from his campaign, however, and no such legislation was ever passed in Alberta.

Shortly after the disgraceful Saskatchewan act took effect, the popular Calgary newspaper editor and publisher Bob Edwards remarked that: "This is a wise law and should be in force in Alberta....[The Chinese] have an unholy penchant for white girls, especially young ones, and seem to be able to obtain a strange, uncanny, unaccountable influence over them."[11] Edwards's remarks typify Anglo-Canadian ethnocentrism in Alberta in regard to the Chinese population.

Occasional incidents of violence against individual Chinese occurred during this period. One particularly ugly incident took place in Vulcan in 1918. "Several drunken cowboys entered [a] café...and ordered a meal. One cowboy complained [about] the meat sauce and poured it over the table. When the Chinese owner protested, the cowboy drew a knife and threatened to kill him. The restaurant owner reached for a gun behind the counter whereupon the cowboys also drew guns. In the ensuing battle, the Chinese owner was left unconscious with knife cuts across his face and the interior of his café demolished." Indicative of still lingering frontier oppression and blatant racist hostility, "local authorities merely ignored the incident and the cowboys were never brought to trial."[12]

During these times, too, Chinese were not permitted into the Banff Springs swimming pool, nor were Chinese girls allowed to train as nurses at hospitals in Calgary and Edmonton.

There were some citizens who defended the Chinese, however, and an authority on Alberta's ethnic relations has remarked in this respect: "many of those who defended them still had ambivalent feelings toward them. In areas where there were few Chinese and where people had direct contact with individual Chinese, attitudes were generally more favorable."[13] Some social reformers defended the Chinese against undue, harshly critical condemnations.

On a personal basis, individual Chinese were sometimes appreciated and even highly valued. In most cases this situation arose when farmers, housewives, and ranchers relied on the expertise of their hired Chinese cooks.

Newspaper articles which reflected favorably on the Chinese appeared from time to time. In 1913, for example, Alberta Supreme Court Judge, Justice Beck, stated that if some Chinese led immoral lives in Canada: "the Dominion Parliament [was] to be held responsible [as it had imposed] the poll tax on Chinese women of $500." He added that few Chinese could "afford to pay this sum for a prospective wife or go home to get married."[14]

Chinese contributions to charitable organizations were duly reported in newspapers; as were donations in support of the Allied cause during the Great War. (Alberta's Chinese residents contributed generously to the Canadian Patriotic Fund and subscribed to the Red Cross and Victory Bonds).

Labor's hostility toward Chinese was markedly less pronounced than was the case in B.C., but it certainly was prevalent. One authority has remarked that labor's anti-Chinese stance was caused by "much the same ethnocentrism as among the middle-class whites, since the Chinese in Alberta were concentrated in service occupations and thus did not pose direct threats to the economic position of labor."[15]

Yet, as early as 1914, officials of the Trades and Labour Council of Alberta proposed that the provincial government take effective measures to bar the entry of Chinese and all Asians into the province. This reflected the official program of the Trades and Labour Congress of Canada which, for many years, had demanded the total exclusion of Asian immigrants into Canada.

The employment of Chinese laborers by private companies occasionally created discontent in labor ranks. In 1920, for instance, the Alberta branch of the Brotherhood of Railway Carmen of America contended that the employment of Chinese by the Canadian National Railway between Edmonton and Calgary was causing unemployment in its ranks. The Railway Brotherhood accordingly submitted a resolution to the Trades and Labour Council of Calgary which stated: "Bar all Chinese from Alberta as we view with alarm the effect they will have on white workingmen."[16] Because the resolution conflicted with other acts then in effect, it was not voted on.

In 1921 Alberta's organized labor found another issue of contention. In the summer of that year, the Mackenzie Basin Fisheries Company constructed a large fish cannery on the shores of Lake Athabasca. In October the company announced that Chinese laborers from B.C. would be hired the following year to perform duties which whites regarded as too menial and unpleasant. Shortly thereafter, a letter to the editor was published in the *Edmonton Bulletin* condemning the proposal, and it came to the attention of the Calgary Trades and Labour Council. The council's secretary, J.E. Young, wrote two letters to the Hon. H. Greenfield, Premier of Alberta, expressing concern that the fish canning industry in Alberta would become the preserve of Chinese labor.

The provincial government asked for a statement from the company, "as already there [had] been a great deal of adverse criticism directed against [its] suggested policy."[17] The company replied that Chinese laborers would return to the coast at the end of the canning season, their transportation to be paid by the company; it was stressed that: "The greater part of this work is of a menial nature which experience has taught white help object doing. During the short period that we canned this season our white help did this work under protest and with the distinct understanding that they would not be asked to do it again."[18]

The company concluded its remarks by stating that if protesting parties would "undertake to supply...competent white help to efficiently do this work [it would] be pleased to consider any proposals."[19] After the provincial government sent a copy of this explanatory letter to the Calgary Trades and Labour Council, its secretary replied that the council requested the provincial government to "take every step possible to prevent the further influx of Oriental workers in [sic] this province."[20] Then, the matter was dropped.

Mention has been made of the existence of a so-called Chinese problem from time to time in Alberta. There is no evidence that a local Chinese problem or Chinese question arose in Medicine Hat or Edmonton. In Calgary and Lethbridge, however, several episodes indicated that Chinese were the objects of civic concern and discrimination.

In Calgary residents occasionally attempted to persuade the city to introduce and enforce restrictive measures directed against the Chinese community. In 1913, for instance, a group of citizens suggested that all Chinese residents be fingerprinted and photographed for ready identification. The incensed Chinese community held meetings and denounced the scheme as undemocratic; the proposal was dropped.

Three years later, a garage on the outskirts of Chinatown was purchased by Chinese residents, who converted it into a "Chinese concert hall."[21] A lobby of Calgary citizens opposed to the location of the hall soon formed and demanded that the city council pass a by-law prohibiting the hall's existence, but the council voted down the proposal.

In 1919 the location of Calgary's Chinatown—or, in other words, the question of segregating the Chinese community—was a matter of civic concern for a brief time. In July of that year, the *Albertan* reported: "There is talk of getting the almond-eyed sons of the far east to move to some sites to be selected somewhere in the neighborhood of Ninth avenue east, or around Langevin bridge, but if this is done it is liable to cause trouble in those districts."[22]

The city commissioners had previously written to the City Solicitor, Mr. Ford, later chief justice of Alberta, "asking him how the city [could] check any further growth of Chinatown."[23] Ford informed the commissioners that, while they could certainly enforce existing by-laws, they had no power under any by-law or any provision of the city charter "to prevent any class of residents locating in any portion of the city."[24] Accordingly, the possibility of Chinatown's relocation or constraint was dropped.

In Lethbridge at least one restrictive civic measure was directed against the Chinese population during the period being considered. In mid-1916 the Mah Tai Laundry opened on Fifth Street South, causing a controversy as to where Chinese laundries should be allowed to locate and under what conditions. The city council acted decisively and presumably had popular support for its actions.

A by-law was passed which designated two specific areas in South Lethbridge where Chinese laundries could operate. In North Lethbridge a

Chinese laundry could only conduct business on a lot "where consent [was] had of all the residents in all the blocks facing the site, as well as of the residents of the block in which a laundry [was] to be located."[25] The by-law was a shameful example of civic discrimination against Alberta's Chinese residents.

By the 1920s conditions were somewhat better in terms of the level of anti-Chinese sentiment. An authority has noted in this respect that: "The 1920s were generally a period of growing acceptance for the Chinese and Japanese in Alberta, despite the fact that [anti-Asian] sentiments were on the rise in British Columbia."[26] Prejudice and discrimination remained serious matters for the Chinese, but overt expressions of severe hostility toward them decreased somewhat.

Chinese Residents and Police Harassment, 1910-1925

From 1910 to 1925 and later, Chinese urban communities in Alberta—particularly in the case of Calgary—were subjected to a considerable amount of police activity which at times involved much intimidation and harassment.

In Edmonton a police raid was staged in July 1912 on a Chinese gambling joint located less than half-a-block from the police station. Five policemen broke down the doors at two o'clock in the morning. All those playing *fantan* or looking on, twelve in all, were arrested. Sixty sets of cards and a large amount of Chinese money were confiscated. It is not known if convictions were obtained.

In January 1913 three policemen staged an afternoon raid on a location on Namayo Avenue. Twenty men were playing a game of chance at the time: nine of them made good their escape; the remaining eleven were each subsequently fined fifteen dollars and costs. In March of the same year, six policemen raided a location and arrested thirty-two men who were playing *fantan* and stud poker.

In August 1913 nine policemen raided a gambling and opium joint on Rice Street. Eighteen Chinese were arrested, while a number managed to escape by fleeing through windows. A crowd of several hundred people observed the rather lively proceedings.

In June 1914 eight policemen staged a raid on a house on Namayo Avenue. Twenty-six men were arrested on various gambling charges. All gambling paraphernalia and some Chinese whisky were confiscated. "Chief of Detectives Kroning planned the raid on the alleged gambling joint with exceptional care. The sleuths walked in on the gamesters who refused to stop even after the officers were inside of the room."[27]

When one examines various actions of the Calgary police force as applied to Chinese residents, it becomes apparent that sheer animosity and a commitment to coerce the small Asian community into doing what the police dictated explains the stringent measures directed against the Chinese. The overall position of the Calgary police force from 1910 to 1925 was indicative of a prevailing state of serious cultural conflict between the Chinese community and the Anglo-Canadian majority.

Two social pursuits, gambling and using illegal drugs, provoked decisive action by Calgary's police officers. In 1909 Chinese indulgence in drugs was brought to the attention of Calgary's citizens in a feature article in the *Calgary Herald*, which described some aspects of the shadier side of life in Calgary's Chinatown, then situated at Tenth Avenue and First Street, South West. The reporter particularly emphasized the supposed prevalence of smoking opium in Chinatown. "In nearly every place that [we] went in the trip there was one or more Chinamen on each floor, lying on...opium beds [dragging] the poison fumes down into their lungs. In every place...the sickening smell of the dope was strong."[28]

The article stated that Calgary's police force had been "getting after the frequenters of the Chinese joints" in Chinatown; the reporter himself said he had observed a number of unused, abandoned *fantan* tables in several premises. As would become clearer with the passage of time, a pattern of police crack-downs on Chinese gamblers and drug users was beginning to emerge.

While Thomas Mackie was Calgary's chief of police, no serious confrontations arose between Chinese residents and the police force. In this respect Chief Mackie's fair-minded attitude was a strong contributory factor. In 1910 he remarked: "The Chinese in the city seem to be a harmless people, and they have not given the police much trouble....They have proven themselves to be law-abiding."[29] Succeeding chiefs of police did not hold such positive views about Chinese behavior. The general absence of police activity in Chinatown was possibly also due to the state of the police force under Mackie.

From 1910 to 1912 Chief Mackie's responsibilities, and the duties of his men, multiplied considerably. The number of policemen in the booming city soared from eighteen men in 1909 to seventy men in 1912. Despite the new recruits, Chief Mackie "could not possibly handle the number of complaints that reached his desk. But he tried."[30]

Serious internal and external problems also plagued the chief. For instance, in 1911 Calgary's commissioners gave him complete authority to reorganize the police force in order to rid the city "of some pestilential dives of the worst sort, which [were operating openly] and unabashed in the very heart of the city."[31]

The *Calgary Albertan* demanded that these "vicious hells" be closed down: "the proprietors...have assumed such a brazen effrontery that they are beginning to parade their vice in the open, to take a hand in the elections, and even to dictate to public affairs....Chief Mackie drove Big Ben Holmberg and his gang from the city, but Holmberg's gang was harmless compared with the keepers of the objectionable dives which are flourishing now....A worse condition of affairs could not exist in this or any other city."[32]

The strong editorial further alleged that the conscientious chief was being "handicapped by traitors in his staff who are worked by the dive-keepers."

Even safely assuming that Chinese gambling activities and drug indulgence existed in Calgary at this time, the police force clearly had other preoccupations—far more serious—which demanded considerable investigation and decisive action.

Chief Mackie did not totally overlook the Chinese community in the performance of his perceived duties. In January 1910 he ordered a raid on premises at First Street, South West: four policemen rushed into a room and, although several men escaped, twenty-nine others were arrested and charged with gambling illegally. The accused retained the services of the renowned Calgary lawyer, P.J. "Paddy" Nolan, who unsuccessfully contended that "only a friendly game among themselves was indulged in."[33]

Because of unrelenting and increasing pressure from all sides, in January 1912 Chief Mackie "decided that he could stand the heckling and pressure no longer and threw in the towel."[34] The city council deliberated a full month choosing his successor and decided on Alfred Cuddy, a former Toronto police inspector.

Social historian James Gray has concluded that: "[Alfred Cuddy was] everything his predecessors had not been. He was a 'professional' policeman in every sense of the word....Under Cuddy Calgary ceased to be the most wide-open city in Alberta. [However], the city remained a mild refuge for the gambling fraternity. Poker playing was still a popular male pastime and the police had great difficulty making gaming-house charges stick unless they had positive proof that a rake-off was being taken [by the house]."[35]

Shortly after Cuddy's appointment, a state of confrontation set in between the Calgary police force and the Chinese community. This situation prevailed until somewhat after the outbreak of the Great War in 1914. It appears that "the spark which ignited the blaze" was a mid-March raid on a Chinese residence on Tenth Avenue, South West. As a result of the raid, Detective-Sergeant Richardson arrested several men and charged them under provisions of the *Opium Act*.

At the ensuing trial, it became public knowledge that a significant drug problem existed in Calgary. Sergeant Richardson testified that there were numerous "hop joints" operating in the city. The *Herald* elaborated: "The police have information to the effect that several joints are running and have been running for some time. Should the prosecution be successful in the present instance it is likely that a rigorous campaign will be instituted to close out all 'joints'."[36] The "keeper" of the premises was convicted and subjected to a very heavy $250 fine.

Just a few weeks after the above-mentioned raid, Calgary's morality squad conducted a general raid in Chinatown. The new chief and twelve detectives raided the Canton Block on Centre Street, South East, and confiscated large amounts of opium and Chinese whisky. Twenty-four men were arrested, charged, and subsequently convicted of various offences.

Police Chief Cuddy rapidly intensified police pressure on the Chinese community. In a relatively brief span of time, many men were arrested and convicted of assorted offences. Considerable amounts of opium and liquor were confiscated in the course of police raids. To the undoubted joy of city of Calgary accountants, several thousands of dollars worth of fines were imposed and paid.

Many Chinese residents soon realized that Chief Cuddy was a formidable opponent to their chosen recreational pastimes. In an article entitled "War Is Declared on Chinatown," the *News-Telegram* commented on the determination of the Chinese to oppose Cuddy's restrictive measures: "...the Chinese will not give in without a struggle....Every case brought by the chief has been fought by the Chinamen. The best legal talent obtainable has been retained by them."

The article threw further light on the resolution of the community to oppose Cuddy's campaign of harassment: "According to one good authority a fund has been started among the big men in Chinese circles to 'buck' the chief, and as a result [Chinese] laborers in laundries and restaurants, even those who have no money themselves, have decided to appeal the convictions against them."[37] As mentioned, such a state of "war" prevailed for quite some time.

Chief Cuddy held strong convictions regarding Chinese gamblers and drug users. His comments in this regard appeared in the *News-Telegram*. "[The Chinese] have to obey the law....They [must] do as [whites] do. They can't sell Chinese whiskey and run gambling joints and opium joints for Chinamen in Calgary. As long as they are here they must live strictly to the law and we will keep after them until they do....We are going right ahead. We are not going to hound them, but they must obey the law and they might as well get that into their heads right now. If they won't they will keep coming up in court."[38]

Chinese did refuse to comply with the lines of appropriate behavior as determined by Cuddy; so, they continued to be hounded by the police.

In the course of police forays in 1913 and 1914, heavy iron axes were habitually employed to afford the quickest possible entry. The owners, or keepers, of gambling establishments responded as best they could under the law: to provide a measure of security to their patrons, Chinese gambling establishments were renovated into well-fortified premises.

The larger establishments resembled miniature fortresses. Frosted windows were installed to prevent watchful eyes from observing activities, and heavy iron bars were placed across all windows to obstruct the entry of any unwelcome intruders. Look-outs kept a keen watch on all entrance-ways: they manned stations at concealed peepholes with locking sliding panels.

When police raiders appeared, the look-out would pull a cord and a heavy iron door would automatically drop into place, much as a guillotine blade operates. On the other hand, a spring-operated, studded door might be induced to suddenly slam across an entrance-way. These so-called "emergency doors"—usually three in succession—were a definite deterrent to police incursions, and sometimes they served to prevent the police from laying any criminal charges.

On propitious occasions, fiercely determined police raiders would finally smash through all obstructions only to encounter a quiescent group of men calmly sitting in chairs or on sofas reading Chinese language newspapers or engaging in polite conversation.

The Calgary police force was extremely frustrated by the gambling establishments' defensive tactics; so, in 1913 Chief Cuddy ordered the immediate removal of all emergency doors in Chinatown. Any compliance was short-lived, if it occurred at all. The police effected a more or less successful raid in January 1914, after "scheming for weeks."[39] A door-keeper was grabbed by the throat, and the police squad rushed into the premises. Over thirty men evaded a hastily assembled police cordon, but nineteen others were arrested and charged.

Police actions in July 1914 led to an "upheaval" in a shocked China-town.[40] When detectives arrived at a suspected gambling location, they found their entrance—as had become customary—entirely blocked; but, when their commands to release emergency doors proved of no avail, the detectives smashed their way through the walls. The sensational episode astounded Chinatown's residents. Forty-one men were arrested and eventually convicted.

Commencing in mid-November 1914, Chief Cuddy and his morality squad carried out three successful raids on gambling locations within five weeks. Altogether, 114 Chinese were arrested and charged with committing various gambling offences. In his annual review of 1914, the chief appropriately remarked that Calgary's citizens should have noticed "the stringent manner in which the laws [had been] enforced against gambling, the principal trouble met with in this regard [having been] the Chinese."[41]

Chief Cuddy's abounding eagerness to apprehend Chinese law-breakers led at least once to his own court appearance. In May 1914 Cuddy and five detectives proceeded to the Chinese Masonic Temple at 107 Second Avenue, South East, hoping to arrest some gamblers that they had been informed were at that time right in the midst of a *fantan* game. The force acted with dispatch, "smashing doors and windows to effect an entrance,"[42] but the sole occupant proved to be a very frightened janitor.

Five prominent members of the Chinese Masonic Order sued the chief and the city of Calgary, demanding damages of $1 000 for alleged unlawful entry. The plaintiffs engaged A.A. McGillivray, a Calgary lawyer who was later elevated to the supreme court bench, but their action was dismissed by the Alberta Supreme Court. "In delivering judgment, Chief Justice Harvey stated that the police when armed with a warrant could legally force an entry into such places without knocking."[43]

Several appeals were entered against the Alberta decision, but they proved unsuccessful. The final appeal—to the Supreme Court of Canada—ended in dismissal of the Chinese Masons' action. The Chinese community was bitterly disappointed with the failure of the lawsuit.

Kim You, one of the plaintiffs, had earlier explained why the action had been undertaken. "We think that a great deal of indiscriminate smashing of property is liable to take place in raids if the police are not restricted to some extent."[44] Indeed, in coming years, with the general exception of the Great War period, police harassment and violence continued to be directed against Chinatown's gambling fraternity.

During the Great War the so-called Chinese question was of minimal proportions in Canada. As one Canadian historian has remarked: "Public agitation against [the Chinese and Japanese] was relatively light during the war years."[45] During the four-year duration of the war, public prejudices and hostility were directed primarily against Canada's German, Austrian, Hungarian, and Turkish populations, even to the extent of establishing a number of internment camps. In Calgary the years from 1914 to 1918 were peaceful ones between the Chinese community and the police force: raids on Chinatown premises came to a virtual standstill.

One year after the Armistice was signed, the familiar pre-war pattern of police harassment of recreation-minded frequenters of Chinatown re-emerged. Acting under orders issued by the new chief of police, David Ritchie, Inspector D. Richardson carried out the first post-war raid in Chinatown late in 1919. The routine raid surprised the gamblers concerned. All forty-one occupants of the gambling establishment were arrested, charged, and convicted of gambling offences, though all were assessed nominal fines.

Inspector Richardson became fiercely determined to force gamblers in Chinatown to adhere to the strict letter of the law. In early May 1920 Richardson and his detective department apprehended thirty gamblers "after an early morning raid" in Chinatown.[46]

A few weeks later Richardson struck again, demonstrating his acquired tactical training. The *Calgary Albertan* reported the incident: "Twenty-one Chinamen were arrested when city detectives, led by Inspector D. Richardson, invaded the Chinese Masonic Temple last evening. Five tables of *fantan* were in progress when the detectives battered down the doors, and before [the startled Chinese] could offer resistance, they were led out of the room, bundled into the patrol wagons, and taken to police headquarters."[47]

Richardson did not undertake any similar exploits until early in 1921. The most probable reason for this was that serious criminal cases arising from Chinese factional disputes were being heard in court and the docket was full.

In February 1921 Richardson (who had just been appointed a detective-inspector) decided to effect an all-out blow against the Chinese gambling fraternity. He planned and personally commanded a remarkable general raid which was quite unprecedented in scope in Calgary's police annals.

The formidable undertaking was described by the *Albertan* the next day. "One hundred Chinamen were placed under arrest, when the entire detective department of the city police force...raided three alleged gambling joints at a late hour last evening. The Chinamen were taken by surprise and although several attempted to put up a fight, the wicked 'billies' in the hands of the police cooled their ardor to a great extent."

The article also provided some details of the measures employed to successfully carry out the general raid. "The three raids were conducted at the same time. One man was detailed to enter each of the 'joints' by the front door, while the remainder took up their stations in the alleyway. While the policemen entered the front, the Chinamen attempted to escape by the back, and six actually reached the street before the officers, using their 'billies' freely, brought them back....The police patrol [had] to make ten trips before the last man was lodged behind the bars."[48]

The spectacular police foray ended on a sour note for the force, however, when all the accused were acquitted in police court. In dismissing the 100 men who filled his courtroom, Magistrate Sanders "warned them that it was because of insufficient evidence and not because they [were] allowed to gamble"[49] that they were being discharged.

During the next two months, Detective-Inspector Richardson demonstrated his continuing determination to quash gambling in Chinatown. In mid-March Richardson and axe-wielding members of his detective department conducted two successful raids on the same evening. Forty-two Chinese were arrested and arraigned on charges relating to drug use and gambling.

Just one month later, a crowd of over 500 citizens closely observed "the latter part [of another Chinatown raid], being attracted to the scene by the clanging of the police patrol."[50] In the course of the Sunday afternoon melee, "the police officers managed to corral [all Chinese gamblers in the premises] without losing one of them."[51] The raiding party also made their distaste with Chinese gambling most evident, "and in an effort to stop the gambling at this particular place, the gaming tables and all the paraphernalia were destroyed, together with the false doors and peepholes."[52]

It is significant that, from the spring of 1921 to the end of 1924, police raids in Chinatown virtually came to a halt. There are several probable explanations of this. In the first place, gambling was never a major issue of public concern in Alberta, although on occasion it became a topic of local concern. During the years from 1916 to 1923, moreover, the Alberta public was primarily concerned with enforcing (or evading) Prohibition, which was in effect during those years.

A final factor accounting for the absence of Chinatown raids was almost certainly the importance ascribed by the police to combatting the drug traffic. Following the end of the Great War, drug use and abuse rapidly increased throughout Canada. Calgary's police force regarded the drug problem as a serious menace and, increasingly, the police took measures against its existence and proliferation in the city. By 1923 the force had achieved a great deal in the battle against drugs, but continued enforcement of the *Opium* and *Narcotics Act* remained a police priority.

Regarding the police raids from 1919 to 1921, it should be realized that the temper of the post-war era was roughly in tune with the often violent police expeditions and methods of apprehension in Chinatown. James H. Gray has remarked that the early post-war years were marked by "disturbed and discouraging conditions," and Canadian society faced the problems of "social upheaval, witch-hunting, and clouds of uncertainty."[53]

Finally, the effectiveness and discipline of the police raids from 1919 to 1921 deserve comment. Although the morality squads of chiefs Mackie and Cuddy were often reasonably successful in apprehending Chinese gamblers, Chief Ritchie's plain-clothes squad essentially operated as a military unit when carrying out its well-organized, highly successful raids on Chinatown locations. Chief Ritchie and Inspector Richardson utilized tactical procedures and a paramilitary approach in the course of their Chinatown enterprises. This was a reflection of their many years of police work and accumulated related experience, as well as a reflection of the troubled post-war era.

The *Chinese Exclusion Act*

In the immediate post-war years, agitation against the Chinese in B.C. was particularly strong and, apart from the general hostility of provincial politicians, Chinese were confronted by "unfriendly business organizations, [as well as] organized trade unions [and unemployed] militant returned men."[54] Indeed, "Armistice Day had hardly drifted into history when a great new wave of anti-Orientalism swept the province, strengthened by veterans' organizations and the ever-growing power of labor unions."[55] The fact that Chinese had made significant inroads during the war in controlling the wholesale and retail trade in produce exacerbated the animosity of many British Columbians.

Because of "an unrelenting tide of anti-Asian sentiment emanating from British Columbia,"[56] the federal government took decisive measures to curtail immigration from China. Charles Stewart, the acting minister of immigration and a former Alberta premier, introduced a bill on 2 March 1923, which to all intents proposed total exclusion of Chinese. A few minor amendments were approved by the House of Commons, which passed the bill on 4 May 1923. Although the bill "allowed consuls, merchants and students into the country [it was, in effect,] an exclusion act."[57]

The *Chinese Exclusion Act*—as the *Chinese Immigration Act* has come to be known—was a major victory for B.C.'s anti-Asian population and organized labor, which had a long record of anti-Asian positions behind it by 1923. Ironically, the success of these groups was not immediately recognized: the *Act* was initially regarded as merely another restrictive action against Chinese immigration and not as the extreme measure it actually proved to be.

Passage of the *Act* did not proceed in an entirely smooth manner; numerous public objections to its various provisions arose. Those who were extremely anti-Asian protested the eligibility of students and merchants to enter Canada, while the Chinese and those in sympathy with their cause attacked the bill itself. The Chinese population strongly vented their emotions and convictions when news of the impending bill became public knowledge.

A scholar who specialized in Chinese-Canadian history, Cheng Tien-fang, has remarked that: "telegrams were sent by the Chinese in all parts of Canada to the Chinese minister at London and the consul general at Ottawa, asking them to protest. They did protest but to no avail....Due to the unsettled political conditions in China, the [Chinese republican] government could hardly do anything....the Chinese in Canada made a hard struggle against the passage of the bill."

In order to oppose the proposed racist legislation, co-ordinated organization and action were absolute necessities. As Mr. Cheng continued: "A Chinese Association in Canada was organized for the purpose of doing cooperative work and presenting a united front....A delegation was sent by the Chinese Association to Ottawa to present their case before Parliament. But as the bill had already been passed in the House, they concentrated their efforts on the Senate."[58]

The Chinese Association sent a number of petitions to the Canadian Senate, "setting forth all the objectionable points in the bill for its consideration."[59] A major objection of Chinese was that "the exclusion of wives and children of those Chinese already in Canada was unreasonable, unjust, and against the morality and well-being of society."[60]

A special committee of the Senate heard the representations of the Chinese Association, as well as the views of numerous supporters of the Chinese cause. Aside from six minor amendments, the Senate passed the *Act* intact, and the House of Commons accepted the amendments. The *Act* was given royal assent on 30 June, and it came into force the following day.

Chinese residents in Alberta were as alarmed about the *Act* as the rest of the Chinese population in Canada. Following passage of the racist act, a deputation of prominent Chinese leaders gathered in Ottawa in protest. Ho Lem went as the representative of Calgary's community. The protest was to no avail.

In Calgary several letters to the editor by prominent men upheld the Chinese stand. Frank Ho Lem, eldest son of the Calgary representative and a highly regarded Calgarian, felt that it was time "in the face of all these knockings"[61] for the Chinese viewpoint to be heard. He added: "I am anxious to see that the people in Canada should remain firm in their friendly relations with the Chinese and not be misled by the prejudiced appeals of the B.C. ministers. Most of the Chinese in this country are good, industrious and honest."[62]

Thomas M. Whaun of Vancouver, later a significant Chinese community figure in that city, expressed his convictions in writing to the *Herald*. He denounced the proposed parliamentary measure in "an attempt to prove the injustice and the harmful effects consequential of the said act."[63]

All Chinese Canadians were required by law to register by 30 June 1924 that they were residents; they faced dire consequences if they did not comply: a $500 fine; one year's imprisonment; or both. To help enforce the intent of the *Act*, provisions in it allowed immigration officers to arrest anyone under suspicion without warrant. Moreover, deportation without any right of appeal was permitted.

Interlude

Immigration Resumes; Communities Are Transformed

Fundamental community change over the last forty-five years or so can only be fully appreciated when the more important consequences of immigration policy are taken into account. Accordingly, much of the material in Chapters Six and Seven—both of which concern the period 1925 to the present—will be put into clearer focus after the course of post-1924 Canadian immigration policy toward the Chinese is outlined.

Passage of the *Chinese Immigration Act* of 1923 created great concern and dismay among the country's Chinese communities, which repeatedly urged the federal government to repeal its discriminatory legislation. Beginning in 1924, various Chinese Benevolent Associations (CBAs) sponsored an annual Humiliation Day, observed bitterly and sadly by Canadian Chinese every July 1st—Dominion Day (Canada Day)—for many years.

In another initiative, the Vancouver CBA and Victoria's Chinese Consolidated Benevolent Association made representations to the Republic of China's delegates at the international conference of the Institute of Pacific Relations held in Banff in 1933, requesting assistance in publicizing the issue.

China's status as an ally during the Second World War created considerable sympathy in Canada for China and its people. Madame Chiang

Kai-shek and other prominent Chinese representatives visited Canada during the war years.

During the late 1930s and early 1940s, several articulate Chinese-Canadian leaders emerged who worked very well with their white counterparts in organizing fund-raising activities for Canada's war effort. They also argued convincingly for equal treatment of Chinese in terms of immigration policy. E.C. Mark in Toronto and Foon Sien in Vancouver, in particular, did a great deal in this regard and received much public attention.

The combination of the United States repealing its *Chinese Exclusion Act* in 1944 and Canada upgrading diplomatic representation with China to embassy level in 1943 also helped move the Canadian government toward repealing the 1923 act.

The Committee for the Repeal of the Chinese Immigration Act was organized in late 1946; its leadership was eighty per cent non-Chinese. Several important newspapers vigorously supported repeal of the *Act*, which finally occurred in May 1947; however, this did not usher in a time of equal treatment of prospective Chinese immigrants.

There still existed in law a 1930 order-in-council, P.C. 2115, allowing Canadian citizens of Asian origin—excluding the Chinese, when it was promulgated—to bring their wives and unmarried children under eighteen years of age into Canada. The Canadian government decided to let stand this order-in-council and apply it to the Chinese (and other Asians). Other immigrant groups only had to be residents in Canada in order to bring wives and children into the country; they did not also have to be citizens. "For the Chinese this policy was hard to accept since Canada seemed to be opening her doors widely to immigrants from Europe and especially refugees from Eastern Europe."[1]

Prime Minister Mackenzie King stated clearly in 1947 that the government was opposed to large-scale immigration from Asia, because it would substantially alter the composition of Canada's population. This viewpoint would shape government policy for years. An increase in the age of admissible dependent Chinese children was made in 1950, but discrimination on racial grounds continued.

Although a new immigration act was passed in 1952 and became law in 1953, it had no real impact on Chinese immigration. The *Act* permitted prohibition or limitation of persons by reason of the following: nationality or ethnic group; "peculiar customs, habits, modes of life;" "unsuitability having regard to the climatic, economic, social, industrial, educational, labor, health or other conditions;" or "probable inability to become readily assimilated."[2] These provisos clearly demonstrated that no revolution had yet taken place in terms of the federal government's viewpoint toward Asian immigration.

One reaction to the government's stubborn discriminatory posture was traffic in illegal immigrants from Hong Kong—particularly after the tremendous turmoil in China during the late 1940s, when the Nationalists and Communists were engaged in a terrible civil war. In 1959 the Hong Kong police cracked down on a large illegal immigration ring which operated in several countries, including Canada.

The Royal Canadian Mounted Police conducted an investigation into the Canadian end of the operation. On 24 May 1960 it conducted a series of raids on Chinese homes, businesses, and organizations in cities throughout Canada, including Edmonton and Calgary. Documents were seized and twenty-eight people arrested, twenty-four of whom were Chinese. The paramilitary way the raids were conducted led to considerable outrage and condemnation from Chinese-Canadian community leaders and other Canadian leaders. Eleven Chinese and one non-Chinese were later convicted of various offences.

The government did not intend to prosecute or deport people already in the country. In 1962 amnesty was offered to illegal immigrants of "'good moral character'"[3] through the Chinese Adjustment Statement Program. By 1973, when the program was discontinued, over 12 000 people had changed their status.

Concurrent with the adjustment program, the Diefenbaker government changed various immigration regulations and came closer to officially abolishing racial and national preferences. Chinese were permitted to apply as independent immigrants through a 1962 order-in-council, but it contained a clause permitting a wider range of sponsorship for those of European and American origin. Asians were still permitted to sponsor only their immediate family, rather than their extended family.

Finally, in 1967, the revision of immigration regulations begun in 1962 was completed. The last vestiges of overt discrimination were eliminated by the establishment of a point system. Criteria for assessing potential immigrants were based on the potential contributions they could make to the Canadian economy and stressed a good education and skills in demand in the labor market. Chinese were at long last on an equal footing with all other potential immigrants.

In the late 1970s and early 1980s, there was an initially-unexpected influx of Chinese into Canada. The unique appearance of many thousands of desperate "boat people" on the high seas happened seemingly out of nowhere and soon—partly because of severe and tragic circumstances—captured world attention. How had such an unprecedented and strange situation developed, the world asked?

Vietnam was under Chinese domination from 111 B.C. to 939 A.D. Later attempts by China to reconquer the country were unsuccessful but confirmed the Vietnamese belief that there was a very real northern threat to their national survival.

The major influx of Chinese to Vietnam occurred after 1860, during the French colonial period. Chinese traders and small businessmen soon became commercially dominant in the country, though Chinese wielded little political power. Rapid economic growth in Vietnam from 1921 to 1931 attracted many Chinese immigrants; more arrived in 1937 after the outbreak of the Sino-Japanese War. When Saigon fell in early 1975, there were roughly 2.5 million ethnic Chinese in Vietnam, most of whom were urban dwellers.

From the outset, the Vietnamese Chinese were essentially a separate and distinct community. The web of associations they formed—based on district of origin, kinship, or commercial ties—helped promote distinctiveness. Colonial administrators allowed leaders of these organizations some independence in managing affairs of the Chinese community. This separation from the rest of Vietnamese society complicated the position of Chinese in the post-independence era.

In 1956 most Chinese automatically became Vietnamese citizens because all Vietnamese-born Chinese were naturalized by decree. Another 1956 decree prohibited Chinese immigrants from engaging in eleven categories of business in which Chinese were then heavily concentrated.

Despite "numerous hardships, [the Chinese] contributed enormously to the economic growth of Vietnam. Though they played an important role in the economy, they were not interested in politics and few [held] public offices."[4]

After the first wave of Vietnamese left with the American evacuation of Saigon, there was a small but steady trickle of boat people from Vietnam. This became a flood in 1978 and a torrent in 1979—over 150 000 during the first six months. The representation of ethnic Chinese in this exodus was far beyond their proportion of the Vietnamese population: they accounted for about seventy to eighty per cent of refugees and came from both the south and the north.

Refugees from the south were largely motivated by economic reasons and fear of the future. The government nationalized commerce in March 1978, effectively cutting off the majority of Chinese from their livelihood. Many feared being sent to the New Economic Zones, where collective farms were being hacked out of the bush. Currency reform and widespread crop failures augmented serious economic hardship; conflict with Kampuchea (Cambodia) heightened the prevailing instability of Vietnamese society.

The exodus of Chinese from south Vietnam seems to have had government approval. Although Hanoi denied involvement in refugee traffic, many refugees claimed they were granted permission to leave in exchange for gold. It is clear that large vessels—such as the *Hai Hong*, which had 2 500 on board—could not have left without official complicity.

Chinese from north Vietnam did not suffer such extreme dislocation, since they had been living under a socialist system for many years. Nonetheless, the government wanted to rid itself of a potential fifth column, as relations with China worsened. Many Chinese took the overland route into China before the border was closed. After China invaded Vietnam in February 1979, many north Vietnamese of Chinese extraction (Hoa) were demoted or lost their jobs altogether. Public meetings of Hoa were organized by the government: they were told they could either leave Vietnam or be sent to the New Economic Zones in the interior.

Neighboring countries were unwilling to absorb the huge number of refugees arriving on their shores. Some tended to see the exodus of large numbers of Hoa as an attempt by the Vietnamese government to destabilize them by intensifying already existing racial tensions. Several countries turned away the Hai Hong, and Malaysia refused to allow those aboard to disembark. The international community was forced to step in and guarantee homes to the refugees. Canada offered to take 600 from the vessel.

Public sentiment lagged well behind government policy regarding the number of Southeast Asian refugees to be admitted into Canada. The government made special provisions for the boat people as a designated class of immigrants, because they could not be classified as refugees under the United Nations' definition; provisions for private sponsorship of refugees were widely publicized.

Canadian officials worked hard to process applications from boat people held in camps in various countries to which they had escaped. In Malaysia, officers tended to choose Chinese with large families because a quota was in effect based on families rather than individuals; also, families were easier to place with private sponsors. Canada accepted a disproportionate number of refugees from north Vietnam, because the United States would not admit them.

Canadian immigration policy depended on co-operation of the provinces in accepting the boat people. Alberta accepted the third largest number of refugees (after Quebec and Ontario); this represented a sizeable increase in the usual percentage of immigrants settling there. Moreover, Alberta's prosperous economy attracted refugees from other provinces looking for jobs. By the end of 1984, over 22 000 Southeast Asians had settled in Alberta; about 10 000 were Vietnamese Chinese.

Because of private sponsorship, refugees were spread out across the province, rather than being concentrated in Calgary and Edmonton. Although these two cities accounted for nearly seventy per cent of the influx in 1979 and 1980, smaller centres took substantial numbers: Lethbridge, 337; Red Deer, 185; Vegreville, 89; and Lloydminster, 56; to name a few examples. Some people isolated in towns later moved to cities, to be closer to fellow refugees.

Despite well-meaning attempts by private sponsors to assist them in getting settled, refugees initially had a difficult time adjusting to life in Alberta. The Vietnamese Chinese had an even more difficult time than other Vietnamese because there was no established Hoa community in the province ready to lend a helping hand. The Hoa felt different from other Chinese after generations of living in Vietnam.

Nonetheless, the Alberta Chinese community was instrumental in providing much-needed services to the newcomers. In Calgary the Chinese Public School Board spearheaded the formation of the Calgary Refugee Advisory Council (CRAC) to create a cultural home for the refugees. CRAC opened an orientation and language-training centre, the Calgary Centre for Indochinese Refugees, in May 1980.

In Edmonton similar organizations were established, such as the Edmonton Area Refugee Services and Community Aid to Refugees Today. Smaller communities also organized to extend aid: for example, Lethbridge, Medicine Hat, and Red Deer provided English as a Second

Language (ESL) classes, translation assistance, and other services. Chinese churches provided volunteers to assist with settlement.

Chinese refugees encountered very onerous difficulties upon arrival. The language barrier was the most fundamental, because a good working knowledge of English was essential to obtain a well-paying job. Most refugees took marginal jobs and tried to learn English at night. Many arrivals had been engaged in small-scale entrepreneurship and had received little formal education. Even skilled workers and professionals tended to take unskilled jobs, while improving their fluency or obtaining recertification.

The serious recession which began in Alberta in 1981 hit refugee workers hard and led to unemployment levels estimated at thirty to forty per cent of adult Indochinese. The need to help relatives still in Vietnam made it very difficult to save money; the Vietnamese Chinese, however, are very future-oriented and strive to consolidate their economic position.

In addition to economic hardships, the newcomers had to endure serious social and cultural dislocation. At the very least, refugees suffer from anxiety and emotional stress similar to bereavement; more severe psychological problems can also occur. Indochinese refugees were totally unaware of Canadian cultural expectations.

Those who were government-sponsored, rather than privately sponsored, often were unaware at first of the various services available to them. Their feelings of dislocation were intensified by the Canadian tendency to view all Indochinese refugees the same way, despite occupational differences and, in particular, ethnic and linguistic differences.

The creation of associations by these new immigrants was an understandable response to sociocultural upheaval and the loss of family many experienced. Vietnamese Chinese associations have not expanded as much as those of the Vietnamese. This may be because the Chinese have been settled in Alberta for a shorter period of time; it has also been suggested that they may have a somewhat weaker sense of collective solidarity. Nevertheless, the Vietnamese Chinese Association was formed in Edmonton in 1979, and the Calgary Indo-China Ethnic Chinese Association has been active for a number of years.

Post-war changes in Canadian immigration policy have had an enormous impact on the composition of Chinese communities. Many immigrants of the 1950s were wives and children who had been separated from their husbands and fathers by Canadian immigration laws. "This wave of family migration altered both the sex and age structures of the Chinese community in Canada, which hitherto, were characterized by an adult population."[5]

The Chinese population in Canada was ninety-five per cent older males in 1947. By 1961 the sex ratio showed a substantial improvement with 36 075 males to 22 122 females. By 1981 the sex ratio had equalized and, as a whole, the Chinese population was actually younger than the overall Canadian population.

Apart from balancing the sex ratio, the most dramatic change in the pattern of Chinese settlement has probably been the move to larger cities. There had always been a greater concentration of Chinese in the larger cities, such as Vancouver, Toronto, and Calgary. But, the scattering of Chinese throughout rural areas in many towns and villages was seriously reduced during the long exclusion period and somewhat later. Market gardening and hand laundries became unprofitable businesses in the post-war era, and a consolidation of population in Calgary and Edmonton affected Alberta's smaller cities.

No noticeable replenishment of Chinese in small towns and villages has occurred in recent years. More Chinese than before, however, have settled in the smaller cities during the last ten years or so.

There has been a significant influx of Chinese immigrants since the changes to immigration policy in 1967. Data from the 1981 census showed that of all Chinese then living in Canada only 1.1 per cent had immigrated prior to 1946! About 4.4 per cent had immigrated between 1946 and 1955; a further 8.1 per cent from 1956 to 1966; some 40.3 per cent arrived between 1967 and 1977; and a further 20.3 per cent from 1978 to 1981. Altogether, over 60 per cent of Chinese immigrated during the period after 1967. A further 25 per cent were Canadian-born.

In 1921, a few years before passage of the *Chinese Exclusion Act*, there were 3 581 Chinese in Alberta. In 1941, six years before repeal of the *Act*, the number had dropped to 3 122. In 1961 there were 6 937 Chinese in the province and, by 1981, the figure stood at roughly 36 770 (no exact figure is available for 1981 because, that year, ethnic origin was not a consider-ation in the census-taking).

There has also been a dramatic shift in country of origin. The point system allowed Chinese families from South America, southern Africa, the Caribbean, and Southeast Asia to come to Canada. "During the peak period of immigration, 1972-1978, the overwhelming majority, about 77 per cent, came from Hong Kong...."[6]

The emphasis on education and skills as qualifications for immigrants has also changed the composition of Chinese communities in Canada. "The typical Chinese migrant before 1923 was rural-born, poorly educated, and without a knowledge of English."[7] This general situation persisted into the 1950s but, by the early 1960s, Chinese arrivals included many educated immigrants, including professionals, and students who later made Canada their home. Then, "after 1967 urban, well-educated, English-speaking Chinese came, especially from Hong Kong but also from such centres as Manila, Singapore, Johannesburg, and Lima."[8]

Because of various factors directly related to unfolding patterns of Chinese immigration, Chinese communities since 1947—on both an individual and a group basis—have been fundamentally altered. An ongoing process of social, economic, and cultural change in communities has been in place for forty-five years or so. The overall process of change will undoubtedly continue for many years, though on a scaled-down basis. Certainly, the most dramatic changes occurred during the decades of the 1950s, 1960s, and 1970s.

6

Community Developments in Lethbridge and Calgary

Lethbridge: Community Developments After 1925

By 1940 there were about 100 members of the Lethbridge Chinese Freemasons. As members died or returned to China, the membership steadily declined. By 1972 only about twenty members belonged. The society now has only a handful of members and is inactive. During the last forty years or so, the society has essentially been a fraternal one meeting social needs.

The Chinese National League in Lethbridge was very active from 1937 to 1945 when funds were collected to assist China's war effort against Japan. Regular meetings were held at least once a month; emergency meetings would be called between these.

The Lethbridge league "sent out people to see the restaurant-keepers, laundry-keepers, whoever, in the small towns for donations in the Chinese war effort. As long as you were Chinese you were in it, whether you were a Chinese Nationalist League member or not. We all had relatives over there."[1] Naturally, funds were actively solicited in the city, too. Interestingly, donations were sought on an individual basis, rather than through arranging lotteries, dinners, raffles, and the like.

In Calgary the National League formed an anti-Japanese movement for the whole of Alberta. The organization's leaders insisted that Lethbridge Chinese send all war-effort contributions through them. Previously, the

Lethbridge Freemasons had sent all the money they had collected to Nanking. The community became split about what to do and, finally, the Chinese consul in Vancouver convened a meeting in Lethbridge. A majority voted to continue sending money through the Freemasons and this settled matters.

Money collected by the Lethbridge Freemasons would be sent to New York, where it was wired to the Bank of China, a government bank. Also, Madame Chiang Kai-shek had an orphanage, and money was sent directly to her for this purpose.

On V-J Day the Freemasons and the National League joined together to celebrate the victory. The league put on a big fireworks display in Chinatown. Speeches were made and banquets held. The whole community participated and, from then on, relations between the two groups became much smoother.

In striking contrast to fifty years ago, when there were several hundred members, the National League now has less than thirty members, most of whom are inactive. Very few meetings are held and, when they are, just a few executives show up.

Moreover, in terms of its functional status, as a longtime member stated, it is "not a political organization anymore. The Nationalists have Taiwan. There's very little political action as a result, and the National League now has a different complexion."[2] The hall is being operated almost solely for the use of members living there; their rent of eighty dollars a month each provides sufficient revenue for maintenance purposes.

Way Leong has been mentioned earlier. Owner of the Bow On Tong store and founder of the Leung clan association, he was the virtual spokesman for Chinatown and an excellent businessman.

During the Great Depression of the 1930s, James Leong (the eldest son of Way Leong) appealed to the city of Lethbridge for assistance to unemployed Chinese. As a result, each such person obtained $1.25 per week from the city. One could at least get enough food to live on with this amount. The Chinese community helped out its members as best it could.

Things were especially arduous for the market gardeners during the Great Depression. A retired market gardener referred to some who went broke. "They went away and left everything in the fields. They couldn't pay their rent or wages."[3] After World War Two things improved, when the market gardeners "started selling to the large outlets on a wholesale basis. Before then [virtually] all Chinese market gardeners sold door-to-door by horse and buggy."[4]

Most market gardens were located just to the south of Lethbridge, on land that is now occupied by city residences. Farmers and at least one landowner, a Mr. Dainty, rented out the plots. Some Chinese operated in partnerships, such as Joe How and his uncle. During the winter, the two men rented rooms in the city and found jobs; most other market gardeners did the same. The last Chinese market gardeners were Fred Yee and Leung Chung, who worked into the 1970s.

The market gardeners would load their wagons in the darkness of early morning. When dawn arrived they would proceed door-to-door selling their produce. They would sell all morning and finish about 1:00 or 2:00 p.m. "Their vegetables were nicely cleaned and displayed. They'd knock on doors, but usually kids would spot them and tell their mothers."[5]

When their vegetables had all been sold, they would customarily head to the Bow On Tong store in Chinatown for a few hours. There, they would play dominoes or cards; read the newspapers; drink tea; converse; and smoke tobacco in long water-pipes. They would park their horses and wagons outside. They did this every day except Sundays.

Customarily, when the men left the Bow On Tong, they would lie down in their wagons and go to sleep. Their horses would safely take them all the way home. They knew exactly where to go, where to stop for traffic, having made the trip a great many times. Every time, they went directly home. This state of affairs prevailed until the mid-1950s. Fred Yee was the last market gardener to use a horse and wagon, which he did until about 1960.

Years ago there were two benches in front of every building in Chinatown. On a summer's evening, all benches in existence would be filled; so, extra chairs would be placed alongside each bench. On Sundays restaurant workers and others would congregate at the Bow On Tong and Kwong On Lung stores for an outing and to pass the time of day in convivial companionship.

For many years Chinese in Lethbridge did not deem it necessary to sponsor instruction in Chinese culture for children in the locality. There were few families residing in the city before the 1940s. In 1947, however, Chinese exclusion from Canada ended, and immigration of Chinese into the country was relaxed in succeeding years. During this period, there were also a number of families in the city with young children. These two factors were undoubtedly related in terms of setting up formal instruction for Chinese youngsters.

Elders of the community—at long last—would have been able to perceive a future for the Chinese in Canada, and they demonstrated a definite concern that young people had little knowledge of the Chinese language and other components of their cultural heritage.

The Chinese National League took the initiative in founding a school. Lee Duck and Zeke Kwan were two of those who instigated the formation of the Chinese Public School. Classes began about 1950 and were first held in a partitioned area on the main floor of the league's headquarters; an annex housing a classroom was later built. Some twenty students attended during the four years the school operated.

The Freemasons started a school soon after the Nationalists did. Called the Chinese Community School, or the Dah Gung Yih Shyver, it operated on the upper floor of the Freemasons' building. A dozen or so Canadian-born children from three families attended, and the school operated for about four years.

The schools' main function was to instruct children to read and write Chinese. Traditional songs and dances and tai chi, a martial art, were also taught. Classes were held every weekday during the early evening hours and on Saturdays. The schools closed because of a perceived lack of interest, augmented by the strain of students having to also attend public school.

Lethbridge's Chinatown has served the wants and needs of hundreds of Chinese for many years. During its existence, it has been of considerable service to the so-called married bachelors, who could not afford—or were prohibited—to bring over wives and families. Chinatown premises have supplied housing; groceries; herbs; recreational facilities; employment; clubs; associations; restaurants; and fraternity for over eighty years.

Now, Lethbridge's Chinatown is but a ghost of its past. It is a living reminder—a microcosm—of what it has been but will never be again.

Calgary: Community Developments into the 1950s

As the Great Depression worsened, many Chinese in Calgary lost their jobs in the vulnerable service sector. Unemployed men from many towns and villages steadily drifted into the city. Chinatown's various associations just could not cope with the demands upon them. Then, too, there were a significant number of men ineligible to join the clan associations in existence. By 1931 there were about 1 000 Chinese in Calgary, making it easily the largest Chinese community in the province.

Late in 1931 Chinese began applying for relief. Unemployed single men were granted an allowance of only $1.12 per week; in contrast, single non-Chinese recipients received $2.50 per week. The arbitrarily unjust reasoning in this respect seems to have been the old discriminatory contention that Chinese could live on less money than whites. "Since no bed allowance was given, the Chinese were forced to room in the cold, damp basements of Chinatown. Those who were not given relief were compelled to live on handouts from [Chinese in] Calgary or smaller towns...."[6]

Chinese dissatisfaction with discrimination meted out to them grew. Their protests were totally ignored. In May 1936 Calgary Chinese on relief were told to go to a single men's relief camp six kilometres west of Coleman, Alberta. The men refused and, accordingly, about forty-eight of them were completely cut off provincial relief rolls. Communist Party of Canada officials in Calgary took up the men's cause and persuaded them to picket government offices. The men also congregated at city hall seeking civic relief. The mayor's response was to have police clear them out. In the course of other protests arrests were made.

The plight of the Chinese was desperate in the extreme. In the eight months preceding March 1937, three Calgary Chinese died from malnutrition. In response the city health officer, Dr. W.H. Hill, checked Chinese living quarters. Instead of proposing meaningful improvements for the dire situation confronting the needy, he proposed that several premises be closed down altogether, because of allegedly unhealthy living conditions. This the city did and twenty-eight single men suddenly became homeless in mid-winter. They were forced to sleep on floors at the Chinese Mission, where fifty-two men were already residing.

Early in 1937, at the instigation of the Communists, about eighty unemployed Chinese staged a lie-down protest on streetcar tracks, demanding $2.50 per week. Nothing resulted, except quarrelling between the province and the city as to who was responsible for the welfare of needy Chinese. Peaceful sit-down protests continued throughout January. Early in February a similar protest turned violent and thirteen Chinese were arrested.

The Chinese cause garnered support not only from the Communists, but also from the Co-operative Commonwealth Federation (CCF) and the Calgary Council of Women. These groups pressed the Chinese case for justice and, at long last, Premier William Aberhart's government raised the relief payments for single unemployed Chinese men to $2.12 per week—still less than that for whites, though.

To oppose blatant governmental racism, in an unprecedented act, "Caucasian groups, and not simply a few isolated individuals, rallied to protest differential treatment of the Chinese. Nevertheless, the story...is surely one of the sorriest chapters in Alberta social history."[7]

In 1937 a Pan-Alberta Anti-Japanese League was formed in Calgary. Branches of the league existed in Edmonton, High River, Medicine Hat, and elsewhere. Donations were solicited "to assist the Chinese war effort against the Japanese in China; to purchase airplanes; to help wounded Chinese soldiers; to buy raincoats and cotton dresses for the army; and to relieve the famine-stricken Chinese."[8] Even in the small town of Blairmore, funds were collected to assist Chinese refugees.

The league headquarters in Calgary was in constant touch with anti-Japanese organizations throughout Canada; close contact was also maintained with the Chinese National League, the Chinese government at Chungking, and the Chinese consulate-general. From 1937 to 1945 Calgary's Chinese alone raised over $200 000 for China relief.

In April 1939 Louie Kheong died in Calgary. As mentioned earlier, he founded the first Chinese store in the city and served as president of the Calgary branch of the Chinese Empire Reform Association. In effect, he was the patriarch of the local Chinese community. Referring to him just after his death, the *Calgary Herald* stated: "Many and varied were his contributions to the welfare of his fellow-countrymen and to the community which he organized."[9] At the time of his death, he was president of the Dart Coon Club of the Chinese Freemasons.

Over 350 Chinese and about 100 whites attended his funeral. Services were held in Chinese and English at the Chinese Mission. "Long strips of paper hung from the walls of the mission depicting in Chinese writing the tributes paid to Mr. Kheong and the services he had done for the community and Chinese elsewhere."[10] Letters of sympathy from Chinese organizations across Canada were received.

The Second World War years marked a watershed in Chinese-Canadian history. China and Canada were fellow Allied Powers, and this proved to be of considerable import. For example, Canadians were very sympathetic to the vast suffering of the Chinese population under Japanese occupation and aggression: by extension, this certainly had application to attitudes toward Chinese in Canada.

A variety of factors were in play during this pivotal period. China's finance minister and a brother-in-law of Chiang Kai-shek, T.V. Soong, visited Canada twice during the war. Madame Chiang Kai-shek, his sister, visited Canada once and spoke to a joint session of Parliament. Chinese war-relief efforts received favorable attention. Moreover, over 500 Canadian-born or naturalized Chinese served in the Canadian armed forces. Some men obtained commissions, such as Calgary's popular resident, Frank Ho Lem (a son of Ho Lem), who was the first Chinese-Canadian commissioned officer.

After the war, attitudes toward Canadian Chinese were much better. Overt racism had become extremely unpopular because of the Nazis' race doctrines, and in May 1947 the *Chinese Exclusion Act* was repealed. During the debate concerning possible repeal, participating Alberta members of Parliament favored its revocation.

The success of Canada's Chinese population was only partial, however. "Unlike whites, Chinese had to be Canadian citizens before they could sponsor their wives and children and it was impossible for any Chinese immigrants, other than wives or children, to enter Canada."[11] Despite the continuance of discrimination against Chinese on the federal level, a course had been set for increased tolerance: in succeeding years regulations governing Chinese immigration were relaxed.

Increasing acceptance and appreciation of the Chinese was demonstrated, for example, in a *Calgary Herald* editorial in 1952. "The extent to which the citizens of Chinese ancestry have been assimilated into [our] society accepting many of its forms while never losing touch with the greatness of their own culture is a pattern of successful immigration....We have a Chinese, the son of one of the community's leaders as president of the Junior Chamber of Commerce and all over the city there is evidence of Chinese enterprise and initiative. It is a bright addition to...Calgary's life."[12] Such an editorial would not have appeared before the Second World War.

About this time, Chinatown's restaurants gained in popularity among whites and became the city's first night-clubs. Many Calgarians made it a regular practice to have a midnight snack in Chinatown, after spending an evening elsewhere. Soon, though, many couples decided to spend the whole evening dining and dancing at Chinatown locations. The dance floors were small but no one minded. Patrons brought along alcohol in flasks or were served it from teapots. The police customarily overlooked such breachs of the law.

During the 1950s many Chinese left Chinatown (though only a small minority had ever lived there over the years) and bought or rented houses in residential districts. Various take-out Chinese food locations were established during this period, and regular restaurants were opened throughout the city.

Calgary: Chinatown's Survival and Expansion

Commencing in the mid-1960s, there were direct threats to the very existence of Chinatown. In 1965 it was proposed to build an extension to the Bow Trail which would sever Chinatown from east to west and effectively destroy the area. A few years later, city hall envisioned that there should be a twelve-lane parkway along the riverbank, with a large interchange at Centre Street. Then, in 1967 City Chief Commissioner J. Ivor Strong maintained that the Centre Street Bridge would have to be rebuilt within the decade—another serious menace to Chinatown.

As a direct result of the serious threats to Chinatown's very existence, the Sien Lok Society was founded in November 1968—through the diligent efforts of businessman Ray Lee, who was determined to save the district from being destroyed. The society was composed primarily of young businessmen and professionals and purported to represent the Chinese community as a whole.

In April 1969 the Sien Lok Society organized a nation-wide National Conference on Urban Renewal as it Affects Chinatown. Chinese representatives from across the country and some Chinese observers from the United States attended the gathering and discussed their own local situations and problems. The conference did a great deal to renew the dedication of many Calgary Chinese who continued to actively fight against threats to Chinatown's existence. (Also, the proceedings of the conference—the first of its type ever held in North America—prompted community action in several other Chinatowns).

The conference received favorable media attention in Calgary, and in coming months the local press paid much closer attention to concerns of the Chinese community. The *Calgary Herald*, for instance, assigned a first-rate staff reporter to conduct an in-depth study. He was given a free rein to take all the time required to research and write a special series of articles concerning the local Chinese community and Chinatown. The series was factual, well-researched, and sympathetic to Chinese concerns about Chinatown and the preservation of community life.

Overall, since the landmark conference, the Calgary press has maintained an active and fair-minded interest in Chinese community affairs, not least in relation to the preservation and development of Chinatown.

It appears now that were it not for the Sien Lok Society's diligent efforts in 1968, 1969 and later, Chinatown would undoubtedly have been subjected to demolition. If either the twelve-lane parkway and/or the new bridge had not succeeded in the destruction of much or all of Chinatown, some other large-scale project would have done so. During these and later years, "civic authorities, often in concert with their provincial and federal counterparts, were pressing for 'urban renewal', an important consequence of which would have been to eliminate Chinatowns."[13]

In August 1969 the United Calgary Chinese Association (UCCA) was established. Its founders were dissatisfied with the Sien Lok's alleged lack of consultation with some Chinese community leaders. (The UCCA, like the Sien Lok Society, is still in existence). Twenty associations initially joined it to make it a somewhat representative body, at least from the standpoint of presumed input from formally organized member groups. (Now, membership is solely on an individual basis).

Twin houses in Chinatown, Calgary, 1969.
Glenbow Archives, NA-2645-46.

Because of determined community efforts to save Chinatown—especially the campaign conducted by the Sien Lok Society—the city of Calgary and the province of Alberta announced that they would not take moves to destroy Chinatown; they even backed the upgrading and rehabilitation of Chinatown. In 1970 the Bow Trail extension was shelved, and in 1971 the city council voted to repair, rather than replace, the Centre Street Bridge.

The extension to the Bow Trail—the Downtown Penetrator—was revived by city hall in 1973. It would have gone right through the heart of Chinatown and destroyed it, had it been built. The Chinese community became very alarmed, and its leaders formed the Chinatown Development Task Force, headed by George Ho Lem. The task force received broad support from the Chinese community and successfully fought against implementation of the drastic proposal.

By 1973 there were twenty-six businesses in Chinatown: nine restaurants; six groceries; three gift and book stores; one physician; one drug store; one accountant; one insurance agent; one travel service; one bean cake shop; one beauty salon; and one rooming-house.

In January 1974 the city council officially designated Chinatown's boundaries. They ran from the riverbank to Fourth Avenue, South West, and from Second Street, South East, to Second Street, South West. The Chinese community was very well-disposed toward the designation.

In July 1974 the Chinatown Development Task Force officially opened an information office in Chinatown. The task force was set up early in the year to propose guidelines for Chinatown development. One of its main concerns was the provision of accommodation for Chinese living in substandard, antiquated housing.

In August 1974 the task force completed its design brief and presented it to the city of Calgary. It called for the revitalization and growth of Chinatown. Twenty-eight main recommendations were set out dealing with land use, community services, traffic circulation, municipal improvements, and suggestions about how to implement the recommendations. Commercial and residential development was to be encouraged and arcades and malls to be developed. The city officially approved the design brief in 1976.

In 1974, too, work began on a major federal government building located between First and Second Streets, South East, south of the riverbank. Some 180 Chinatown residents had to be relocated. The existence of this building dramatically stimulated development in Chinatown because hundreds of people worked there and were potential patrons of businesses in Chinatown—located immediately to the west of the massive structure. Among the initial projects was rehabilitation of the notable Flat Iron Block on Second Avenue, South East.

In 1976 Oi Kwan Place, a senior citizens' residence, was completed. The project was conceived by the Chinese United Church; then, a non-profit organization, the Oi Kwan Foundation, was established. (Oi Kwan means Love of Humanity). The eleven-storey building was constructed at a cost of $1.6 million; it consists of thirty-six single units and twenty double units. It is open to all senior citizens and rent is geared to income; there are rental subsidies. In brick relief on both sides of the building is inscribed "longevity" in Chinese characters.

As a successor to the Chinatown Development Task Force, the Chinatown Development Foundation came into being. Its concerns have been primarily to provide more housing facilities and to improve Chinatown. The foundation was set up as a non-profit charitable organization in order to qualify for Central Mortgage and Housing Corporation funding for housing projects.

In 1977 work began on an eighty-eight-unit, non-profit housing project on Second Avenue, South West. The building, Bowside Manor, was a joint project of the Lee Family Association, the Chinese Public School, and the Chinatown Development Foundation. The school has quarters on the main floor. By the time work was underway on the project, the total planned redevelopment in Chinatown amounted to some $10 million.

In 1978 construction began on a building owned by the Mah Society. It is a five-storey apartment and retail complex. At roughly the same time, various other businesses were started in Chinatown.

In 1983 a Chinatown development committee was formed which "brought together community and corporate interests which, with the guidance of the city's planning department, came to an agreement on development priorities for the community."[14] A compromise resulted: in essence, the developers were permitted greater building density and more land reclassification; the community was given free property, plus a fairly significant amount of money to help advance the cause of a long-desired cultural centre. Even rival groups in the community approved the plan, and all groups were pleased with the intention to create a cultural centre spanning Second Avenue at First Street, South West.

Chinese Public School, Calgary, 1966.
Demolished in 1977 to build Bowside Manor, where the school continues to function.
Glenbow Archives, NA-2645-48.

In 1984 city council passed a land use by-law which recognized what had already been agreed to by the major players in the development drama: major issues relating to land use classification and development needs were approved. Various parcels of land were subsequently reclassified.

The Wai Kwan Manor for senior citizens opened in 1985 in Chinatown. The $9 million structure contains 122 one-bedroom units and three suites for the handicapped. The Oi Kwan Foundation initiated the project.

By fall 1985 there were ninety-three businesses in Chinatown: eighteen restaurants; twelve groceries; five video shops; four beauty salons; five travelling services; four bakeries; five drug stores; and five dress shops. Outside Chinatown there were 113 Chinese restaurants, including take-out enterprises.

In January 1986 city council endorsed a complex blueprint for redevelopment, titled the Chinatown Area Redevelopment Plan. The plan reiterated what had been approved two years earlier, but there was more elaboration and new specifications. Among other items, guidelines called for a height restriction of forty-five metres on new buildings; an allowance to let sunlight hit the streets; heavy use of Chinese motifs; and a fund to help pay for the upgrading of sidewalks and other features.

The dramatic transformation of Chinatown—which began after the approval of the Chinatown design brief in 1976 and the essentially concurrent completion of the huge federal building—recommenced in the mid-1980s, after a lull during the Alberta recession, which began in the early 1980s. After approval of the Chinatown Area Redevelopment Plan in 1986, public improvements—such as some brick sidewalks and decorative lighting—were initiated. Immigrants from Hong Kong and other Pacific Rim countries have increasingly been investing in Chinatown in recent years. In addition to some significant building projects completed during the period 1987 through 1990, existing buildings in the district have been extensively renovated.

In several years the focal point of Calgary's ever more dynamic Chinatown will be the Calgary Chinese Cultural Centre. The organization undertaking the project is the Calgary Chinese Cultural Centre Association (CCCCA), which has a volunteer board of directors consisting of two aldermen, a senior administrator of the city of Calgary, and Chinese community leaders. A development permit was granted to the CCCCA in July 1987. The official sod-turning ceremony was held on 20 October 1990. It is anticipated that construction will be completed by about May of 1992.

The four-storey centre will cost about $7 million to build and will comprise 4 940 square metres (50 000 square feet). Land for the site was donated to the CCCCA by two major corporations and the city. Interestingly, the structure will be built in Chinatown right across the intersection of Second Avenue and First Street, South West—it is apparently unprecedented to erect a building across a Calgary street or intersection.

The building will feature meeting-halls, classrooms, a library and resource centre, sports facilities, and a museum/exhibition gallery. In addition, space will be rented to some twelve commercial enterprises: the revenue so generated will help to offset the centre's operating costs and will attract new businesses and their employees to Chinatown.

Modelled after the Temple of Heaven in Peking (Beijing), the building will blend traditional Chinese architecture and contemporary Canadian architecture. The roof will feature a circular pagoda-style structure with a gold-colored knob at its apex. Inside, beneath the pagoda, will be the Great Hall, which will extend over thirty-three metres (100 feet) skyward. "An ancient construction system of double rows of columns and cross beams will be incorporated. It was used in the Zou [Chou] dynasty from 1027 to 770 B.C."[15]

The structure's design is quite spectacular. In July 1987, when the project was formally approved by the city: "The architecture itself left planning commission members searching for superlatives."[16]

Upon completion, the architecturally unique centre will become an important tourist attraction. Moreover, it will dramatically symbolize both Chinese-Canadian cultural heritage in Alberta and—despite some continuing minor factionalism—the vital and deeply committed communal sentiments of Calgary's Chinese community.

Calgary: Organizations

Mention has already been made of Chinese clan associations, but some additional remarks are in order. All Calgary clan associations have their headquarters in Vancouver, though they are autonomous groups. Nearly all of them own or rent premises in Chinatown. Officers are elected annually and serve on a voluntary basis. To be admitted to a clan association, "prospective members have to be able to trace their ancestorship through a family tree, and furnish proof of it. Once this criterion is fulfilled, acceptance of a member depends upon the favorable vote of the association's members."[17] Admittance and membership fees are nominal.

Clan associations of today fulfil fewer functions than they did many years ago. The welfare aspect of their activities, for example, has been assumed by the state. Nonetheless, fraternal activities are still important. Picnics, meetings, tea parties, and banquets are held; also, some Chinese festivals are observed. A number of associations rent out rooms to members at very reasonable rates. In recent years some groups have moved into new premises. When a need exists, funeral costs of members are invariably covered by the association.

Clan members help each other with filling out government and other forms, translating, writing letters, and other matters. Many immigrants find it very helpful to join a clan association on their arrival. Because of this situation and the relatively large number of immigrants who have settled in Calgary during the last twenty years, a number of new clan associations have been established.

The three largest clan associations in the city are the Lee Association, the Wong Affinity Association, and the Mah Society. Despite a diminished overall role in comparison to earlier times—partly due to a general failure to involve the younger generations—there is still a very definite role being played by clan associations. Old-timers and newcomers alike still join and participate in the associations, which are clearly meeting significant wants and needs within the community. Immigrants often join clan associations soon after arriving in Calgary and obtain satisfactory employment through new contacts among the membership.

Mention has been made earlier of the Chinese Public School. During the Great Depression and at several other times, the school was closed because of insufficient funds, or the absence of a teacher or pupils. The school was officially registered in 1939. By 1950 some forty children attended. A school board, elected annually, administers matters. Being a private school, it is tax-exempt.

The primary purpose of the school remains to teach students how to speak, read, and write Chinese; however, other instruction—in history, geography, singing and dancing, for example—is also provided. Classes are held daily after regular school hours and on Saturdays. During recent years interest in the school has mushroomed. Over 600 children and adults attend weekend courses, making it one of the largest such schools in North America. In October 1985 the school opened a library featuring 6 000 Chinese-language books.

Registrations at the school quadrupled in the 1980s to 800 students. Helen Wu, who has served as president of the Calgary Chinese Public School Society, attributes this dramatic increase in interest to two factors: first, the influx of many hundreds of culturally aware immigrants; secondly, a growing concern among second- and third-generation Chinese that their children might well grow up knowing scarcely anything about Chinese language and culture. A goodly number of Canadian-born Chinese seriously regret their own lack of knowledge of written Chinese. The school tries to involve parents in encouraging their children to study diligently, especially in regard to language.

Originally non-denominational, the Chinese Mission became affiliated with the United Church of Canada in 1949. The mission was responsible for forming a Y.M.C.A. It established Canada's "first all-Chinese hockey team...in 1928 with Donald Dong as coach and Frank Ho Lem as manager. The Jun Gon (True Light) basketball team of five Chinese girls (they played full games without substitutes) was formed in 1929 with Calgary hoop star Madeline Piette as coach."[18]

In 1928 the mission formed a boys' group, the David Yui Hi-Y. Not long thereafter, in 1932, a co-ed group, the Chinese Young People's Society, was established. For some time the society put out a monthly magazine. A number of clubs were founded for the younger ones: with names like the Incognitos, Tiger Lilies, and King's Daughters.

A Mothers' Club was organized in 1932 under president Mrs. Lem Kwong. During the Great Depression of the 1930s, members fed jobless men who slept at the mission. A women's Mission Circle club was formed in 1934. Many unemployed Chinese men learned English at classes sponsored by the club during the 1930s; club members also organized a singing group, the Unemployed Men's Choir.

In 1936 the mission mortgage was burned. Not long thereafter, the church's women held their first fund-raising Chow Mein Tea, still a major annual event "on Calgary's social calendars, and in 1937 the girls of the Young People's Society staged the first of a long series of Chinese Fashion Shows that have grown in popularity."[19]

In 1953 a new church building and gymnasium were opened. Those who had raised funds were Ho Lem, Mah Yet, and C.H. Poon. The church became self-supporting in 1971. Plans are fully developed for a new building.

According to Reverend Paul Chan, who became minister of the Chinese United Church in 1980, the composition of the congregation has changed greatly since the late 1960s. Then, most members were old-timers; now, about seventy-five per cent of members are English-speaking and second- or third-generation. Some twenty-five per cent of members speak and understand only Chinese; so, every Sunday service is bilingual. The congregation consists of about 120 families.

Membership classes are held for immigrants before they can join the church. New converts to Christianity must attend church services for at least one year before they can become members; they must also attend classes, be baptized, understand the essence of the Bible, and be willing to support the church spiritually and financially.

There is Sunday School for children. For high school and university students, various spiritually-oriented functions are held, including Bible study and seminars; in the physical and social spheres, camping, hiking, games, barbecues, and social gatherings are organized. Rev. Chan is very concerned about young people who dissociate themselves from the church;

he fully recognizes the pervasive strength of secularism in its many guises in modern society.

The Chinese Pentecostal Church was founded by Reverend Clarence Stahl in 1959. Its first services were held in a rented Chinatown house. Since then it has moved twice. In 1963 a church was built at 127 Second Avenue, South East, in Chinatown. The church is self-supporting and is affiliated with the Pentecostal Assemblies of Canada. A board of deacons administers affairs. Over 200 members belong and services are conducted in Chinese. There are various groups in the church. Assistance is provided in immigration matters and with filling out various government forms.

In 1981 the Chinese Alliance Church was built in the community of Beddington Heights. The church cost $1.6 million and was a communal effort with congregation members donating their expertise and time. The church is notable for being the second solar-powered church built in North America.

A few other Chinese churches—all relatively new—operate in the city. Among them are the Chinese Gospel Church, the Chinese Baptist Church, and the Chinese Evangelical Free Church.

By the mid-1970s the Chinese cemetery on Macleod Trail was nearly full. The Chinese community asked that a special plot be set aside in Queen's Park Cemetery for Chinese burials. In 1976 the city's community services committee approved this measure. Because room is now running out at the latter location, new measures will have to be implemented in the next few years if Chinese are to continue to have special burial areas.

In the 1950s the Chinese Freemasons formally detached themselves from Nationalist China because of its alleged corruption. In the 1970s the Calgary Freemasons formally accepted the People's Republic of China as the legitimate government of the mainland.

The Freemasons are administered by a board of directors and a few officials. Elections are held annually and all positions are voluntary. The organization owns its premises in Chinatown. Those over age eighteen are eligible to join. There are several groups in the body, including an athletic one. Help is provided with translating documents, paying funeral expenses, and obtaining employment. The three basic principles of the organization are: "Save the country with loyalty," "Eliminate the evils with chivalry," and "Unity with righteousness." The Calgary branch is the most active Chinese Freemason group on the Canadian prairies.

During the Second World War, the Chinese National League was especially influential. "The Party was regarded as the 'savior' of the mother country, fighting against the Japanese invasion."[20] After the defeat of the Kuomintang in China, the organization began to slowly but steadily lose its influence and status. In 1954 the league opened a new building in Chinatown. Its membership and activities have dramatically declined during the last twenty years.

The organization is administered by seven executives who are elected annually. At the group's premises, accommodation is provided to members at a nominal rate. Banquets are held, movies are shown, and some services are provided to members.

The Sino-Canada Cultural Association was established in 1975 and has a membership of about 130 adults and children. The group has five primary objectives:

1. To establish and supervise the operation of a Calgary Chinese school to teach Mandarin, the official Chinese language, orally and in writing.
2. To promote cultural exchanges between The People's Republic of China and Canada.
3. To promote an understanding and appreciation of Chinese heritage and culture.
4. To encourage and assist members of the association in their understanding of Canadian society.
5. To promote friendship among members through educational and recreational group activities.

These objectives are achieved by conducting various activities. Chinese language classes are held; both Chinese and white children and adults attend. Classes in Chinese brush-painting and kung fu (or gung fu), a martial art, are offered to the general public. The association actively participates in Chinese festivals. A major undertaking of the group has been the presentation of a Sunday morning radio program on the university radio channel which plays Chinese music and offers instruction in Mandarin.

In 1981 the non-profit Calgary Chinese Community Broadcasting service began. Aired on Channel Ten cablevision, language films and news are highlighted.

The Calgary Indo-China Ethnic Chinese Association has been in existence for five years and has premises on Second Avenue, South West, in Chinatown. It has about 500 members and an elected executive. The association exists to familiarize its members with Canadian society and culture and to preserve Chinese cultural values. An annual dinner is held to which some 400 people are invited, including aldermen, local members of the provincial legislature, and the mayor.

The association's membership consists primarily of immigrants who have arrived during the last twelve years or so; the majority of members originated in Laos, Kampuchea (Cambodia), and Vietnam. Many who belong have much difficulty obtaining well-paying jobs, despite the fact that they arrive with skills which are in demand. A leading member of the association believes that this is primarily a result of people's marked tendency not to assert themselves sufficiently well because of their lack of familiarity with the English language.

The Calgary Chinese Cultural Society (CCCS) was formed in 1975 and was officially incorporated in 1979. A voluntary organization, it promotes Chinese cultural programs within the context of the objectives of Canadian multiculturalism. The society actively promotes friendship, sports, and cultural exchanges between Canada and China. The primary objectives of the society are:

1. To promote mutual understanding and cultural interaction between the Chinese community and fellow Canadians.
2. To promote the construction of a multi-purpose cultural and educational centre in Chinatown.
3. To contribute to charitable and community service work.
4. To promote cultural exchanges and friendship between Canada and China.

The CCCS sponsors cultural and sports events, tours to China, and English and Chinese classes. In August 1980 the society organized two days of local multicultural performances to celebrate Alberta's seventy-fifth anniversary as a province. The CCCS participated with other organizations in establishing a centre for Indo-Chinese refugees.

On its own, the society has hosted banquets for senior citizens; organized Chinese New Year banquets; and spearheaded the planning and construction of the community's cultural centre. The organization has had an active dance group and has hosted performers, athletes, and scholars from China. Representatives of the society have been well-received while touring China.

Membership in the CCCS is open to all those with an interest in cultural matters who share the society's objectives. According to Dr. (K.W.) Kok-Wah Chang, a founding member and former president of the CCCS, the large number of people (this was before the 1989 massacre in Tienanmen Square in Beijing) attending the National Day celebration—commemorating the official creation of the People's Republic of China—and Chinese New Year celebrations shows "very good support from the community."[21]

The Sien Lok Society endeavors to promote Chinese culture and to foster better relations between the Chinese community and the wider community. Fifteen years ago the society began raising funds and accumulated enough money to create Sien Lok Park, which is immediately behind Bowside Manor on Second Avenue, South West, in Chinatown on city-owned land.

In addition to all landscaping and related costs, the society purchased and installed furnishings: primarily playground equipment and a pagoda. In the late 1980s, the Sien Lok Society expanded the park. An oasis of tranquillity amidst a bustling downtown district, it remains an invaluable addition to Chinatown and considerably enhances the quality of life for area residents who make use of it.

Each summer the society sponsors a picnic held in Sien Lok Park; it is free of charge and open to all Chinese. Several scholarships are awarded to Chinese students at the local institutions of Mount Royal College and the Southern Alberta Institute of Technology. Social events are held for Chinese senior citizens, and there are visitation programs. A children's group, the Sien Lok Dancers, learns traditional folk dances and performs on various occasions.

The United Calgary Chinese Association (UCCA), discussed above, engages in social and cultural activities. The UCCA very faithfully observes traditional ceremonies, including sacrificial offerings at the Chinese cemetery in the spring and autumn of each year. Before the mid-autumn festival, a fine senior citizens' banquet is held. The UCCA also sponsors a Chinese New Year celebration. Membership in the group is open to all Chinese eighteen years of age and older who reside in Calgary.

In addition to organizations mentioned in this chapter or previous ones, there are also groups devoted to specific interests. For instance, there are university and college clubs; a bowling club; a golf club; several martial arts and athletic clubs; a curling club; and the Chinese Elderly Citizens' Association.

An increasing interest in traditional music should not be overlooked. Calgary's Wah Kiu Musical Society, for example, which performs Cantonese opera, has been affected by this recent upsurge of interest. Many Chinese organizations request special performances by the society's members, and several groups have asked the society for coaching. Arthur Lui, a member of the society, has explained the appeal of Cantonese opera. "'The Chinese language is involved along with movements and traditional music.' [The] performances have a special appeal because 'kindness, good and beauty are always expressed.'"[22]

Before 1979, "there was very little co-ordination of the different cultural groups. Then, the community held its first Spring Festival to celebrate the Chinese New Year."[23] At that festival, four organizations presented a joint performance. The event has expanded since then, and many groups participate. Such cultural co-operation and performances serve to enhance community cohesiveness and cultural identity.

Chinese cultural activities have become very significant and widely encompassing in Calgary. This mushrooming interest in Chinese cultural heritage has been expressed in various ways and will continue to evolve and mature.

7

Community Developments in Edmonton

For many years, Edmonton had far fewer Chinese residents than Calgary; so, it is not surprising that fewer articles concerning the more northerly community appeared in the press. Sufficient information exists, however, to outline the general formation and development of Edmonton's Chinese community from the outset to the present. Having already looked at the initial decades of settlement, this chapter deals with the post-1925 period.

Community Activities and Change: An Overview

Pioneer Bing K. Mah arrived in Edmonton from China late in 1923; eleven years of age, he undertook the long journey in order to join his father, one of several partners in a local restaurant venture begun in 1909. Father and son lived on the premises in rooms on the second floor, though Bing's father died in his forties in 1928.

Young Bing attended public school, finishing Grade Eight (he had previously attended school in the city of Canton). In Edmonton, he engaged in additional studies, too. He recalled: "I went to Chinese school during evenings. It was a privately-organized school. My father was the one who organized and promoted it, because our teacher had been his teacher in the Old Country. He came over here when he was fairly old and wasn't able to work much any more. So, he taught quite a number of us kids to speak, write, and read Chinese. We were very busy, what with regular school too, but we loved it. He taught us the Chinese classics. To me that was very, very interesting."[1]

As was the case throughout Canada, Chinese in Alberta were barred from most professions and would hardly ever be hired in the better-paying core labor sector. Bing Mah remembered well the situation faced by Edmonton Chinese when he was young. "In those days the employment opportunities for Chinese immigrants were very, very limited; so, they either set up a laundry or a café. They deserve a lot of credit, because they looked after themselves. They'd hire you as a second cook for twenty-five dollars a month, with accommodation and food included. Workers would live above the restaurants. Thank God, Chinese society stressed perseverance and fortitude. They were thrifty, hard workers: that's how they survived and some got ahead."[2]

By 1935 there were fifty Chinese laundries scattered about the city. Almost all of these enterprises used electric washers. Laundry work, however, remained very demanding and tiring labor for many years to come, despite the availability of new equipment—and only some launderers had the resources to make such purchases.

In 1935, too, there were about fifteen Chinese market gardens operating in Edmonton. Most were scattered about the outskirts, and the land was leased from the city. Hong Lee apparently had the best-known operation, gardening over twelve acres on the river flats next to the municipal golf course. He sold his products to local groceries and produce firms.

During the Second World War, local Chinese contributions to both the Canadian war effort and the Sino-Japanese War received excellent newspaper coverage, very favorable to the image of the Chinese and China. The Chinese Benevolent Association formed special committees for fundraising; a great deal of effort went into drives to raise money for Chinese refugees, armaments, and aid to orphans in China, as well as for Canadian War Bonds, airplanes, and so on.

In the post-war years, it became clear that there was a new respect for, and a greater sensitivity to, the local Chinese population. Items regarding the community, its leaders, and Chinatown were reported fairly, as was the changing composition of the Chinese population because of immigration reforms.

A sad event which attracted the attention of the city as a whole was the death in 1980 of the generally acknowledged leader of Edmonton's Chinese community, Henry Wah Hein Mah.

Mr. Mah first came to Canada in 1912. His wife was later prevented from immigrating to join him because of the regulations of the *Chinese Exclusion Act*. She was finally able to join her husband in the early 1950s. Mr. Mah stated in a 1976 interview that the head tax and exclusion laws were "most inhuman" and added: "It was a lonely time for me when I first came to Edmonton. I was never happy."[3]

Mr. Mah operated a café and started a number of businesses in Edmonton and northern Alberta. Over the years he served as president of the following: the Chinese Benevolent Association, the board of directors of the Chinese Elders' Mansion (for which he initiated the building campaign), and the Edmonton chapter of the Mah Society. He made a point of helping new Chinese immigrants and was honored by the Chinese community in 1976 for his contribution to the growth of Edmonton's Chinatown.

In 1982 a conference was held in the Chinese Elders' Mansion to discuss the Nanking Massacre. The Edmonton Committee Against Japanese Distortion of History reviewed actions planned across Canada to protest changes in Japanese high school textbooks that play down the heinous 1937 massacre. Committee members were also concerned about the Canadian people as a whole knowing about the massacre and sharing their concerns and determination to promote world peace.

Extensive celebrations were held in 1983 to commemorate the 125th anniversary of continuous Chinese settlement in Canada. The festivities began in May with a lion dance performed by members of the Alex Taylor Elementary School. The children led people up the stairs of the Provincial Museum to the Chinese Canadian Cultural Heritage Exhibition. The exhibition traced the history of Chinese Canadians with newspaper clippings and old photographs.

Mayor Cec Purves presided over a flag-raising ceremony at city hall, with many dignitaries present, to signify the official beginning of Chinese Canadian Week on 17 September. Highlights of the week included a fashion show and a picnic at Borden Park. At the end of the week, the grand finale began with a parade of Chinese groups from the Chinese Senior Citizens Home to the city market in Chinatown.

At the market a cultural presentation was held, headlining Elena Lee Ho of Edmonton's Jing Wah Sing Musical Association singing—in full opera costume—a song from a famous Cantonese opera. A book display at the Centennial Library, lectures, and films were featured after the official commemorative period.

Edmonton's Chinese community annually celebrates several traditional festivals and events. The most important holiday is Chinese New Year. For many years the community has presented excellent cultural shows and held other celebrations—to which all Edmontonians have been invited. In 1987, for instance, over 1 000 people attended a New Year's banquet at the Edmonton Convention Centre. It is a testament to Edmonton's multicultural mosaic that most of the city's ethnic groups were represented at this event. Guests were treated to traditional Chinese entertainment during the meal. Local Chinese performed dances in the street to celebrate the occasion.

The community also observes the Dragon Boat Festival. On this convivial occasion, families usually dine out and order various kinds of specialty foods. The Mid-Autumn Festival is celebrated in traditional manner.

Indicative of the vibrancy and vitality of the community, three weekly Chinese-language newspapers operate in the city. As recently as 1983, the community depended on Vancouver papers for news. Now, the *Canadian Chinese Times*, *Edmonton Chinese News*, and *Alberta Chinese Times* compete with one another for approximately 30 000 readers. All three publications avoid political stands on Asian problems; they concentrate on compiling and printing news reports from a variety of Canadian and Asian sources. They aim at a readership of all local Chinese Canadians, rather than a restricted readership from just one part of the available spectrum. All three papers present international news and report local events.

The first paper to appear, the *Edmonton Chinese News* (*ECN*), began operations in December 1983. It publishes in Calgary also, though editorial information in the two papers differs. Fifteen people—only one is full-time—work on the paper; six partners and some others volunteer their time. One of the partners, Raymond Ng, who has close ties to members of Edmonton's Chinese Catholic church, sees *ECN* as a "way to reach other people" within a community "separated in blocks."[4] The editor, Joseph Lo, formerly a journalist in Canton and an educator in Hong Kong, regards his writing for the *ECN* as a hobby.

The *Canadian Chinese Times* (*CCT*) started in the early 1980s in Calgary with only an agent in Edmonton and no local news. Publisher H.K. Willie Wong joined the company in 1984 and now operates independently of the Calgary paper. In April of 1986, he bought out the other partners and began to use full-color and print more local information. A typesetting business, which uses photo-typesetting machines, keeps the paper afloat financially. The *CCT* has a larger staff than its competitors—twenty-three employees, including five in the editorial section. The company is one of eight in the Asian Pacific Investment group, which has ties to Hong Kong.

The smallest and most recent paper is the *Alberta Chinese Times* (*ACT*) which first appeared in April 1986. Originally, there were eleven partners; now, there is just one owner, Mr. Kan Ki Chiu. Four of the five employees are relatives of Mr. Chiu. An immigrant from Kunming, China, he was born in North Vietnam and lived there until 1957; so, he has an advantage with the Vietnamese Chinese compared to his rivals. Mr. Chiu is also very active in local Chinese organizations.

The community has been increasingly well-served by the non-print media in recent years. Since late 1980 radio station CKER broadcasts the Four Seas Chinese radio program in the 9:00-10:30 p.m. time slot six days a week. In February 1986 a pay-TV channel, Chinavision, featuring programming in Cantonese and Mandarin, expanded to the Edmonton market from Toronto and Calgary. Most of the programming originates in Hong Kong, although there is some Canadian content.

Organizations

Mention has already been made of clan associations in Edmonton, but some additional comments are in order.

The Mah Society is the largest clan association in the city. Like all such organizations, the society stresses the importance of mutual assistance and solidarity. There are fifty-eight officers elected annually to the executive board. In 1982 the association opened a $330 000 building at 9643 - 101A Avenue in Chinatown. In conjunction with the opening, the Edmonton branch of the family association hosted a national convention of the Mah clan—there are over 50 000 Mahs in Canada. About 850 delegates attended the three-day event.

Administered by seventeen executives elected every second year, the Wong Benevolent Society is also a clan association. It has over 200 members of all ages, with most in the fifty- to sixty-year-old age group. One can become a member by paying a nominal membership fee. Most of the members are immigrants. The society is very active in observing Chinese festivals. As is the case with other such groups in Alberta and throughout North America, members are given assistance regarding various personal matters, such as obtaining suitable employment, finding adequate housing, filling out government forms, and so on.

The society owns a building along 96th Street in Chinatown and maintains its organizational premises there. Portions of the building are rented out; this serves as a source of revenue for the society. Surplus funds accrued by the group in this way are donated to various worthy causes. For example, a few years ago the society donated $5 000 toward the local Chinese elders' care centre and also donated $1 000 to a Toi-san (or Toi-shan) vocational training school in Guangdong which is attended by many Wongs.

In 1930 Reverend Dickman Fong arrived to organize a formal Chinese United Church. He conducted church services and Sunday School in his home until 1932, when church premises were rented on 96th Street. Thirty-one people were baptized from 1930 to 1933, and regular church attendance stood at about twenty people. Reverend Leung was in charge of the church from 1939 until 1953, when a church was constructed in Chinatown. Several other pastors have served at the church since then. At present there are over 100 members. A few groups are in existence, including a women's one. The United Church of Canada provides financial assistance, and the pastor and five elders administer affairs. Services are conducted in Chinese.

The Chinese Alliance Church was formed in 1969, with help from another Alliance church. In 1971 the congregation bought a building. Over the years most of the members have been students from Hong Kong. A Sunday School operates and there are several members' groups. Services are held in Chinese.

The Edmonton Chinese Baptist Church is located reasonably close to Chinatown. The church is affiliated with the Canadian Southern Baptist Convention. A number of services are provided to its nearly 200 members: principally, a Chinese language school, bible study groups, and family counselling. Although Sunday church services were first conducted in 1974, not until 1981 was there a physical church for the congregation; that year, the MacDonald Baptist Church building was purchased.

Approximately seventy-five children participate in the Baptists' Chinese language school. About eighty per cent are from non-Christian backgrounds and are not members of the church. Bible study groups for all ages meet regularly. About 100 children participate in Sunday School. There are youth, college, and career group meetings on Friday evenings and Saturday afternoons.

Edmonton's Chinese Catholic Church (or Parish) has a membership of 400 adults and over 150 children. The only Catholic Chinese church in the city, it is an integral and vital component of the community's spiritual life. In 1987 a church building was acquired along 98th Street, a few blocks from Chinatown. During the four previous years, a building was rented for church services.

The parish priest, Father Francisco Lau, was sent by his superior in Hong Kong to lead the congregation. Although he served for years as the only priest for the parish, Father Lau obtained an assistant in August 1990, when a fellow Salesian priest arrived as an immigrant from Hong Kong.

The new priest lives in a hostel which opened its doors in September 1990. The facility serves high school students originating from Macao, Hong Kong, Taiwan, and throughout Southeast Asia. Designed as a good place to live and study, the hostel will have nine students the first year; a maximum of eighteen students will eventually live there.

The membership of the congregation consists mostly of immigrants. There are a number of adult and children's groups which the membership may join. These groups have been established in order to provide companionship and Bible study. In one group approximately sixty children are instructed in Chinese language and culture. Not all of these children have parents associated with the church, so in this regard the congregation is, in effect, providing a service for the community as a whole.

The Chinese Benevolent Association was apparently formed in 1929, though the year usually cited is 1932. The association used to claim to represent Chinese in Edmonton, northern Alberta, the Yukon, and the North West Territories. "The Association is concerned with the welfare and interests of the Chinese, and attempts to arbitrate social conflicts and business disputes among themselves. It is responsible for the care of a Chinese cemetery at 97th Street and 124 Avenue. Before World War II it used to arrange for the deceased's bones and ashes to be shipped back to China."[5]

Over the years the association fought diligently for the equal treatment of Chinese as potential immigrants and, concomitantly, for the elimination of discriminatory immigration regulations. The organization has a president, three executive directors, and up to fifty officials: this results in a wide spectrum of representation from among the community. The association observes the Ching Ming festival and its founding day.

The Chinese National League obtained new premises on 96th Street in 1928. During the Second World War (as in Calgary), the organization was very popular. During the last twenty-five years, interest has declined severely and there are just a handful of members now; a few celebrations are observed.

The Freemasons' organization was founded in 1954. In 1968 new premises were bought. A close relationship is maintained with the Vancouver headquarters. The group upholds the following principles: all people are brothers; all members should observe the supreme mottos of loyalty and righteousness; world peace is to be promoted; all countries should respect the liberty, equality, and national independence of other people. The organization observes a number of celebrations each year.

The Chinese Dramatic Club was established about 1914. It was formed both to promote "Chinese opera and music, and to raise funds for the Kuomintang army. The Club was very active during the Second World War when many performances were staged to raise money for the war refugees and China's relief."[6] For ten years thereafter, the club was inactive, but it was revived and operates at present.

The Alberta Chinese Cultural Society (ACCS), founded in 1970, is a very involved group. The ACCS's objectives are to share Chinese culture with other Canadians; to preserve and revitalize Chinese culture among all the generations; to promote cultural exchanges between Canada and China; to encourage Chinese to become more active in Canadian social affairs; and to promote overall racial harmony. The society welcomes both Asian and non-Asian members.

The ACCS has been involved in sponsoring various cultural exhibitions and performances; participating in multicultural conferences; publishing Chinese magazines and newsletters; sponsoring English classes for Chinese Canadians; and many other activities. In 1985 the ACCS sponsored Chinese New Year celebrations in the Convention Centre. Included were dining and dancing, the traditional Lion Dance, and a singing contest. The society also sponsored a special display at the Provincial Museum.

The Gung Yick Society has been in existence for about twelve years and has two main objectives: to provide language instruction in Chinese and to help bridge the gap between Western society and Chinese society. In order to meet these objectives, the society conducts Chinese language classes; hosts performing groups from Taiwan or The People's Republic of China; sponsors art shows; and participates in festivals. The Chinese language classes are taught by volunteers and are attended by all age groups.

The society has a voting membership and an elected board of directors. Since the group's inception, the number of members steadily increased until about 1987; currently, there are about fifty members.

"Gung Yick" means "for the public good," and this society of Chinese-Canadian businessmen and professionals tries to ensure that recognition is given to the achievements of young Canadians of Chinese descent.

The Chinese Canadian National Council (CCNC) is a Canada-wide organization with its head office in Toronto. The Edmonton chapter was established in 1980, when the CCNC was organized. The chapter has about 150 members; most are middle-aged and have been in Canada for a number of years.

The primary objectives of the CCNC are to ensure that the human rights of Chinese Canadians are being observed and to teach Chinese Canadians how to adapt to Canadian living. In order to help meet these goals, the Edmonton chapter has a human rights committee which investigates—with the assistance of lawyers—any complaints from Chinese Canadians regarding human rights violations.

Members planned a number of events to correspond to the national association's celebration in 1983 of the 125th anniversary of continuous Chinese settlement in Canada. The branch published a bilingual (Chinese and English) booklet, *Our Chosen Land*, to coincide with this anniversary. In November 1986 members premiered a video they had produced, also titled "Our Chosen Land." It was made to educate both the general public and the Chinese community about various aspects of Chinese-Canadian cultural heritage and to demonstrate that Chinese have integrated well into Canadian society.

In 1980 an Edmonton chapter of the Toi Shan Society was organized, primarily by Bing K. Mah. In Canada the society was originally established in 1893 in Victoria to serve fellow immigrants from the county of Toi-san.

The fourth national convention of the society was held in Edmonton in September 1984. At that convention, delegates arrived from Calgary, Victoria, Vancouver, Winnipeg, and Toronto. The Edmonton chapter proposed that the society build a Chinese temple in the mountains of British Columbia to honor the Chinese laborers who helped construct the CPR.

Delegates were supplied with coolie hats in tribute to these pioneers, hundreds of whom lost their lives.

In 1982 the Chinese Kindergarten Association applied to the Edmonton Public School Board for approval of a Chinese-English bilingual school. Concerned parents wanted their children to have greater exposure to their heritage. By 1985 there were two schools in Edmonton (Meyonohk and Kildare elementary schools) which offered Mandarin bilingual programs. Of the fourteen students enrolled in the Meyonohk school's Grade Two bilingual class, one was white.

The Edmonton Chinese Bilingual Education Association promotes the value of learning Mandarin, which is used in Singapore, Malaysia, and Taiwan, as well as in mainland China. Not only does an understanding of the language give second-generation Chinese Canadians a greater appreciation of Chinese culture and traditions, but non-Chinese would find it easier to do business in much of the Far East.

Some other associations active in Edmonton include the Chinese Businessmen's Association (most members are owners of grocery stores) and the Edmonton Chinese Lions Club. The businessmen's group has, for example, attempted to persuade the city of Edmonton to curtail Sunday and evening shopping. The Chinese Lions Club works where the apparent need is greatest, but it is particularly concerned about helping the city's Chinese population. For example, the club has raised funds for special projects at the Alex Taylor Elementary School, which has a large percentage of Chinese-Canadian students.

In 1977 a charter was granted to the Chinatown Credit Union—the first such financial institution in the prairie provinces. A group of businessmen decided that there was a need for it, and many people joined during the first year of operations. It was relocated in 1983 to the main floor of the Mah Society Building on 101A Avenue in Chinatown. A major concern of the founders was to assist elders and new immigrants who were experiencing language difficulties.

The Chinese Library Association is an organization of Chinese students at The University of Alberta. Since 1969 it has built up a collection of thousands of Chinese-language publications relating to China.

Clearly, there is a substantial, dynamic, and diverse cultural and organizational life in Edmonton's Chinese community.

Chinatown

Edmonton's original Chinatown was bounded by Jasper Avenue to 102A Avenue and 95th to 97th Streets. It was located within a rather run-down central district, the Boyle Street area. The main Chinese business district was situated in two blocks along the west side of 97th Street from Jasper Avenue north to 102nd Avenue.

By 1973 about 261 Chinese lived in Chinatown; a majority of these residents were elders or newly arrived immigrants; their rent was on the low side. As of 1973, too, there were twenty-seven Chinese businesses in the area, and many Chinese community organizations had premises in Chinatown.

In the 1970s pressure for redevelopment mounted in regard to the east end of the downtown core. The major project approved and built was Canada Place. Because its east side fronted 97th Street between Jasper Avenue and 102nd Avenue, most Chinese business premises in the original Chinatown were torn down—all those on the west side of the two blocks mentioned. In consultation with the Chinese community, Edmonton's city council decided to relocate Chinatown farther east.

Traditionally, the Chinese community has not taken an active role in local issues and civic decision-making. Even when businesses were forced to relocate or dissolve because of the Canada Place project, little opposition was put forth by the Chinese community. If Edmonton follows the pattern of other Chinese communities in the country—as certainly appears to be the case—Chinese political expression in significant issues will be far more assertive.

Official Chinatown's new range essentially radiates from the intersection of 102nd Avenue and 96th Street. The effective boundaries of the district are: on the south, Jasper Avenue; on the west, 97th Street; on the north, 102 A Avenue; and on the east, 95th Street.

In 1977 the Chinese Elders' Mansion on 102nd Avenue was officially opened. This home for the aged cost $2.5 million and is managed by the Chinese Benevolent Association. The residence has twelve storeys with ninety-two self-contained suites, including some for the disabled. There is an adjoining one-storey wing for social activities. Features include a spacious lobby; a large lounge; dining-rooms; a library; four recreation halls; and a landscaped inner court. In functional, symbolic, and communal respects, the structure has significantly helped to rejuvenate Chinatown.

A Chinatown master plan was approved by city council in the summer of 1979. It called for redevelopment of a four-block area surrounding 96th Street. The council adopted a revised plan in 1981, seeking to create "a unique and colorful character area to highlight the cultural, recreational, educational and religious aspects of Chinese culture."[7]

The plan called for the establishment of relatively high-density residential and commercial structures in the area. Several cultural features were also envisaged, such as a Chinese entrance gate, a classical garden, and a traditional ceremonial square. Chinatown was also to receive a new streetscape accentuating Chinese architectural designs.

Not surprisingly, Chinatown features a variety of restaurants. Patrons have their choice of Szechwan (Sichuan), Cantonese, and Hunan cuisine. In December 1981 China Garden, purportedly the then-largest Chinese dining establishment in Alberta, was officially opened on 102nd Avenue: it has a seating capacity of over 500 people.

The Chinese Freemasons' Senior Citizens Home was built in 1982 on 102nd Avenue. The home provides accommodation for over thirty elderly Chinese. As mentioned before, in 1982 the Mah Society opened a new building in Chinatown. The structure also houses the Chinatown Credit Union, the *Alberta Chinese Times*, and the Toi Shan Society.

In October 1983, 250 members of Edmonton's Chinese community gathered in a vacant lot next to the Chinese Elders' Mansion. They had assembled to perform a traditional ground-breaking ceremony. Organizers of the event directed the setting off of firecrackers, the burning of incense, and the performance of a dragon dance: all designed to ward off any resident ghosts. The site in question was to be occupied by the $1.25 million Chinatown Multicultural Centre.

In February 1985 the centre was officially opened and, according to Kim Hung, president of the Chinese Benevolent Association, which was the driving force behind the centre: "It [was] a great day for Edmonton's Chinese community."[8] The 18 000 square-metre building provides cultural, recreational, and leisure activities for all ethno-cultural groups. The centre is managed by the Edmonton Chinatown Multicultural Society, and it also houses the Edmonton Bilingual Day Care Centre. In August 1985 the Taiwan Graduates' Alumni Association presented a fine statue of Dr. Sun Yat-sen to the centre.

The magnificent Chinatown Gate is located at 102nd Avenue (Harbin Road), just east of 97th Street. The gate was a co-operative effort of the people of the twinned cities of Edmonton and Harbin in Heilongjiang province, China. The traditional and distinctive style chosen for the gate symbolizes friendship.

Led by a dancing lion, Mayor Laurence Decore and Harbin Vice-Mayor Hong Qipong walked beneath the arches of the gate on 24 October 1987 to officially open it. Before delivering his speech, Mayor Decore performed a Chinese good luck ritual. He left the speakers' platform, approached the two stone lions—each mounted on a base directly underneath the flanking pedestrian arches—and placed a ball in each lion's mouth.

The Chinatown Gate was designed by a master architect from China, Yeung Zhi, who chose to implement a classical style. Under his personal direction, seventeen Chinese artisans, ranging in age from their twenties to their sixties, built the structure. They employed materials, tools, and techniques which had been used for many centuries constructing gates in their native China. At first the artisans had trouble adjusting to the equipment used in Canada, but they soon became accustomed to it.

The gate spans twenty-three metres across Harbin Road and is twelve metres high. It features three arches: two for pedestrians and one for vehicles. Supported by eight steel columns, it is painted an antique Chinese red.

The decorative nature of the gate is strikingly beautiful and artistically well-integrated. The base for each of the two groups of four columns which support the structure is made of granite. On top of each base, at attention, sits a hand-carved quartz lion, one a male and the other a female. At the head of the four main inner columns are capitals shaped like lotus flowers.

The lower roofs (atop the two flanking arches) feature complementary ornamental ridges. Above each arch is a relief-tiled frieze. The ridge of the central upper roof is covered with ornamental tiles, and upon the peak of the arch stretch two complete dragons (the dragon is the Chinese symbol of power); the central finial, or ornamental top, is a "pearl on lotus." Yeung Zhi derived these particular features of the upper roof—which symbolize power and beauty—from the throne of the emperor in the Imperial Palace at Peking (Beijing). Over 11 000 glazed, hand-crafted golden yellow tiles highlight the gate. At night concealed red and gold neon lights illuminate the imposing structure.

The streetscape setting features red lockstone sidewalks; two Chinese telephone booths; four street lamps with Chinese lanterns; and benches.

Funding of the gate was a joint effort of the city of Edmonton, the city of Harbin, the province of Alberta, and the Chinese Benevolent Association. The gate cost $564 000 to build.

"The Chinatown Gate is a cause for pride among the Chinese community," according to Ed Lam, a past-president of the Alberta Chinese Cultural Association. He added: "By undertaking the construction of the gate during this period of economic recession, the city of Edmonton has shown the Chinese community that it values the community's contribution to the city. People driving through the area will know when they see the gate that they are in Chinatown."[9]

The gate will increasingly serve as a major tourist attraction, and it will stand in perpetuity as a monument of friendship between Edmonton and her sister city, the capital of Heilongjiang province in China's northeastern reaches.

Early in 1988 Edmonton's city council decided to decorate the Canadian National Railway underpass on 97th Street near 107th Avenue with a Chinese motif. In a competition among three local artists, held to determine the winning design, the winner proposed to decorate the underpass by portraying a Far Eastern fan on a colored aluminum relief. One of the judges in the competition thought the fan motif reflected a subtle depiction of East Asia, appropriate to the 1980s.

This artistic undertaking actually symbolizes the migration of many Chinese businesses in the original Chinatown to the area in question. When their premises were demolished to make way for the immense Canada Place structure, these businessmen chose to not relocate in the planned new Chinatown for two reasons. Firstly, there was a marked scarcity of small commercial buildings suited to the traditional Chinese practice of storefront markets. Secondly, spaces that were available carried prohibitively high rents. Consequently, Chinese businessmen relocated farther north on 97th Street, where rents were more affordable.

This significant development has led to the creation of an extensive commercial Chinatown, nearly a kilometre north of the boundaries of Edmonton's official Chinatown. The latter, then, serves as the cultural and residential Chinatown for the Chinese community.

Buoyed by immigration from Hong Kong in the late 1960s and 1970s, north 97th Street has been transformed into a vibrant Chinese district. On Saturdays one can walk through the area along both sides of the street for about six blocks and observe a traditional Saturday market. Businesses—

many with meat hanging in their front windows and most with traditional good luck names—handle a brisk trade.

In 1988 a new Chinese United Church was completed along 96th Street in Chinatown. Attendance at the church has always been of modest proportions, and at present there are over 100 members. During the 1980s the church's congregation has grown, but slowly. The church holds services in Chinese and a Sunday School operates. There are several groups within the church. For example, during the week a prayer group and a Bible study group meet; a youth group meets once a month.

A few years ago then-alderman Lance White observed that large department stores and suburban shopping centres are anathema to Chinese elders; thus, the new Chinatown along 97th Street is reasonably appealing to them. "They prefer the meeting-place aspect of the Hong Kong type of market. The North American type of market, where you drive in, park your car, buy your goods, jump from shop to shop, go back to your car and leave, is far too impersonal for the older Chinese."[10]

As in other Canadian cities, Edmonton's Chinatowns primarily serve cultural and/or commercial needs, rather than residential purposes.

When it is built, the planned Chinese Ceremonial Square will probably be situated at the intersection of two roads. The corner of 96th Street and 102nd Avenue is a distinct possibility. The square will be patterned in handsome decorative brick.

Octagonal in shape, the square would be bounded by a 150-room hotel, a professional building, a supermarket complex, and a cultural centre. The last structure is now a reality. The other projects have been placed on hold. The Chinese community intends to use the square to celebrate special occasions, particularly Chinese New Year.

Classical in design, the planned Chinese Garden is intended to serve as an oasis of tranquillity amid the hustle and bustle of the downtown area. Designed according to China's Soochow garden tradition—in existence for over 2 500 years—the garden will contain rock mountains, pavilions, a water pond, a Tai Chi exercise court, and secluded areas for contemplation and meditation.

The Chinese community is taking additional steps to care for the aged. A 150-unit multi-care facility will be built both behind and adjacent to the Chinese Multicultural Centre. The complex will incorporate about sixty nursing beds in a facility to the rear of the centre and ninety senior citizens apartments in a building just east of the centre. The three structures will be interconnected.

The nursing facility is intended to fill a void that cannot be met by conventional health care facilities. Many elderly Chinese have trouble making themselves understood in hospitals where the vast majority of the staff speak only English. Accordingly, Chinese-speaking doctors and nurses will be hired. Meals will be geared toward the traditional Chinese diet.

The community has purchased all the required land, received city approval and provincial funding, and construction of the apartment building for the seniors has begun. Upon its completion, work will begin on the health care building.

8

The Chinese in Alberta to 1940: Themes and Conclusions

Migration and Early Settlement

The diaspora of the Chinese to Canada, the United States, and many other lands scattered throughout the world, was an exceptional and major migratory phenomenon which persisted from the mid-nineteenth century until 1930.

Chinese migrated to North America in large numbers for various reasons. Of greatest importance was the chaotic condition of the area from which virtually all Chinese emigrants originated. For generations, southeastern China—the provinces of Guangdong and Fujian, or Fukien—was in an almost perpetual state of social, economic, and administrative turmoil. The great majority of Chinese residents in the region were poor peasants with little or no chance of advancement; many were landless.

News of large-scale gold discoveries in California in 1849 and in British Columbia in 1858 circulated widely throughout Guangdong province, particularly in the Canton district. Resulting "gold fever"—intensified by grave dissatisfaction with the dire state of affairs in the area—initiated significant emigration to frontier lands of North America bordering the Pacific Ocean.

As a result of economic necessities, social pressures, and related factors, for over sixty years thousands of Chinese men—most in their late teens or early twenties—left their homeland, destined for Canada. The majority hoped to achieve a measure of prosperity within a relatively short period of time; then, they would return to their native villages to retire.

During their overseas stay in North America, Chinese men sent remittances, as best they could, to their wives and children—or to immediate family or clan members who relied upon such assistance. Indeed, oftentimes, these much-needed resources from far-distant lands proved absolutely crucial to the survival of the recipients.

With the completion of the Canadian Pacific Railway in 1885, thousands of Chinese laborers faced joblessness. They either returned to China or crowded into B.C.'s few Chinatowns. Some venturesome souls, however, headed eastward; they travelled through mountain ranges and entered southern Alberta. In coming decades these pioneers—the first Asian group to settle on the Canadian prairie—were joined by hundreds of other men, and a few women, from their native land.

By 1890 there was a Chinese presence in Lethbridge and Medicine Hat. Settlement of Chinese pioneers in these southern Alberta centres followed the same pattern as that which appeared in Calgary from 1885 on. Early in 1890 Lee Turn opened a laundry in Medicine Hat and was soon extremely busy. Two years later another Chinese laundry opened, as well as a Chinese restaurant. A small Chinatown took shape during succeeding years along a street on the fringe of the downtown core.

As of spring 1890 three Chinese laundries were operating in Lethbridge. In the next few years several Chinese restaurants were established in the bustling centre and a Chinatown sprang up along a downtown avenue.

Chinese pioneers did not reach Edmonton as early as Alberta's other centres. In July of 1892 Chung Gee arrived from Calgary, where anti-Chinese hostility was ominously high because of the smallpox outbreak; he opened the first Chinese laundry in Edmonton. Several other Chinese settled in the town that summer, during which time Wing Lee opened the second Chinese laundry. By the turn of the century a small Chinatown existed in the downtown area.

Frontier Oppression

Americans' reaction to Chinese settlement during the frontier era was particularly hostile and of serious proportions. Over the years, for example, numerous instances of mindless violence were perpetrated against Chinese miners, laborers, and other workers in the western states.

In Canada, overall, frontier reaction to the initial and subsequent periods of Chinese settlement was less virulent. Nonetheless, in B.C., as in California, widespread and pronounced anti-Chinese sentiment—with accompanying prejudice and harsh discrimination—developed at an early stage and flourished for a great many years.

In Alberta anti-Chinese agitation and overt hostile discrimination never approximated that which prevailed in the Pacific province or California. There were comparatively few Chinese residents in the province; moreover, a large militant working class simply did not exist. Nonetheless, Chinese in Alberta were widely regarded as undesirable and unassimilable residents. Anglo-Canadian antipathy toward, and contempt for, the Chinese were most obvious, ominous, and potentially explosive during the frontier era, which ended with the outbreak of the First World War.

Despite Alberta's numerically insignificant Chinese population, mere Chinese settlement and the readily observable Chinese presence in an Anglo-Canadian milieu led to hostility and violence toward the Asian settlers. Animosity and disaffection with the Chinese population were expressed in various ways. In 1892 and 1907, incidents of mob violence against Chinese occurred in Calgary and Lethbridge, respectively. In each case, had circumstances been slightly different, deaths might well have resulted.

Anti-Chinese sentiment in its various guises and forms—including overt malice, antipathy, and discrimination—was in evidence for decades in Alberta. In Lethbridge and Calgary, for example, determined attempts were made to segregate Chinese residents. Throughout the length and breadth of the province, reporters and editors habitually wrote about Chinese in derogatory, demeaning ways in news accounts or editorial comments. Few citizens publicly defended Chinese causes, and fears about a supposed Asian menace to Western civilization were common.

Frontier oppression of Chinese in Alberta was but one example of what has aptly been termed the Anti-Chinese Movement: a rather amorphous, but determinedly purposeful and powerful, movement which found solid support in the U.S. and, later, in Canada.

Chinese "Bachelor" Society

For many years Chinese residents of Alberta constituted what is most appropriately designated a "Bachelor" Society.

The majority of Chinese immigrants who arrived in Canada and the U.S. during the latter half of the nineteenth century and the early decades of the twentieth century came as sojourners. They had expectations of amassing a comparative fortune in North America and would then, they anticipated, return to their native villages as relatively prosperous and well-respected men. The foreseen sojourn was a major factor accounting for the predominantly male Chinese population in Alberta.

Other factors affected the sex-ratio imbalance in Chinese communities. Firstly, the presence of wives and children during the husbands' sojourn was not economically feasible for almost everyone. Although lack of appropriate training or education and language barriers were factors, it was primarily discrimination that, for decades, forced men into various menial jobs; ones too low-paying, by far, to properly support a family. The steep head tax was an insurmountable obstacle for nearly all men and, moreover, most did not want to expose their wives and children to prejudice and discrimination.

Finally, Chinese tradition did not favor a wife leaving her familial village, even to join her overseas husband. Cantonese custom dictated that a wife in these circumstances would move into her husband's parents' home where she would be welcomed.

The predominantly sojourning nature of Chinese settlement was the single most important determinant in Chinese community formation and development. Chinese sojourners saw no great benefit in changing their basic attitudes and life-styles so as to considerably adopt, or assimilate, the emphatically alien, very peculiar, Western society and culture: they trusted (or, at least, earnestly hoped) that their overseas stay would not be a long-term experience.

Additional factors contributed to confining most Chinese to retain their own traditions and customary ways of thinking, interacting, and behaving. From the initial years of settlement on, Chinese were made to understand that they were not welcome in Alberta: they would be tolerated because they were useful workers, but that was about all. First subjected to harsh frontier oppression and discrimination, the Asian immigrants then faced for decades both a state of uncompromising cultural conflict and concomitant, cruel subjugation in the form of institutional racism.

The partially imposed condition of sociocultural exclusiveness of Chinese urban communities was given concrete expression in Alberta's larger centres in the establishment of culturally-exclusive ethnic enclaves, or Chinatowns.

What has been dubbed Chinese "Bachelor" Society—a predominantly male, largely culturally-exclusive, community—was composed primarily of so-called "married bachelors." In all important respects, the men in question shared a common socio-economic and cultural heritage. Most of them also shared a primary objective: to retire in their native villages, under favorable circumstances, as soon as this became feasible.

The two factors of the anticipated sojourn and a seemingly indomitable cultural barrier promoted the perpetuation of a semi-autonomous Chinese "Bachelor" Society in Alberta. In effect, Alberta's larger Chinatowns became cultural enclaves which reflected some societal characteristics of Imperial China, many years after its formal demise in 1911.

In part, such exclusiveness was certainly a direct extension of the nature of Chinese immigration and settlement and was represented in the life-styles of Chinese residents; their celebration of traditional festivals; and even in their chosen "vices."

Although the Chinese response toward institutions such as the Chinese missions in Edmonton and Calgary and the Chinese Y.M.C.A.s was generally positive, participation in their activities was largely predicated upon practical considerations; such involvements did not imply that the Chinese *as a group* were actively attempting to be acculturated or assimilated into Alberta's predominantly Anglo-Canadian society.

Social Institutions, Political Organizations, and Factions

Of all ethnic groups in Canada, the Chinese have been unique in establishing a complicated network of associations and organizations. The primary explanation of this phenomenon is that Overseas Chinese communities reflected contemporary sociocultural relationships and self-governing arrangements in southeastern China: where there was a proliferation of various associations, organizations, and secret societies.

Chinese residents in Alberta—like those throughout North America—organized and utilized traditional social institutions, which proved to be of great value in various respects. These institutions were complemented by voluntary Chinese fraternal associations founded for political reasons. Accordingly, Chinese urban communities developed their own vital social and political components, and Chinese community life found expression in an intrinsically independent manner.

By 1910 the Chinese presence in Alberta's urban centres was secure. Chinese had clearly demonstrated that they were useful citizens performing essential services. In the larger centres, Chinese merchants played a moderately significant role in the world of small business. They and their employees had firmly established themselves in service-sector businesses that were of considerable value to the majority Anglo-Canadian population. Until the outbreak of war in 1914, Chinese immigrants continued to land at Vancouver and Victoria, and many joined fellow countrymen in Alberta's urban centres.

By 1910, too, the prerequisites for the formation of institutionalized Chinese communities—including the erection of relatively substantial Chinatowns—were present in Edmonton, Lethbridge, and Calgary. These prerequisites were: the tacit acceptance of the Chinese presence by the majority Anglo-Canadian population; a reasonably well-established and numerically significant Chinese population; Chinese ownership and/or occupation, in a more or less spatially distinct area, of enough property to create Chinatowns.

Accordingly, from 1910 to 1930, the organizational infrastructure of the three largest communities was created: various organizations were established on a formal basis, while others functioned informally but, nonetheless, effectively; and, occasionally, by common consent of community leaders, a group of some sort was formed on the spot to deal with what was then perceived as an emergency situation. Overall, Chinese community life in Alberta was substantially altered in many ways by institutionalization.

In forming the structure of their communities, Chinese adapted traditional institutions to the North American environment. Essentially, there were four traditional Chinese institutions transplanted to Alberta, as elsewhere in Canada and the United States. These were the *fong* (headquarters); the clan association (also referred to as the surname or family association); the *hui kuan* (mutual aid society); and the secret society.

During the Exclusion period, 1923 to 1947, social institutions and political organizations in Alberta retained their strength and vitality. In order to maintain a meaningful community life, Chinese relied increasingly on existing associations to meet their various wants and needs. The preeminence of the mercantile elite in these associations continued after 1923.

As no new competitors could legally enter Canada, the task of this small elite to enforce its dominance was not difficult.

One question which naturally arises is: What effect did oppression and discrimination have in the formation of Chinese organizations? Briefly put, there does not appear to be any causal connection between the oppression of Chinese and a vital Chinese organizational life. Chinese have settled in many countries of the world and, wherever substantial Chinese populations have come into existence, institutionalization like that in North America has occurred.

Moreover, the Japanese experience in North America—marked by intense anti-Japanese sentiment—did not result in a proliferation of organizations and associations; also, the Japanese have not been nearly as culturally exclusive as the Chinese. In fact, the Japanese in North America have formed very few social institutions or political organizations, and ties to fellow Japanese have been expressed primarily in "courtship and marriage and in recreational pursuits."[1]

In both its political and non-political manifestations, factionalism was a major feature of Chinese urban community life in Alberta to 1925 and later. It was, in one sense, a result of the intense ethnic group cohesiveness of Overseas Chinese in North America. Urban Chinese were very aware that their various interests—social, economic, and political—could be furthered through alliances with other Chinese seeking similar goals. Personal advancement in the Chinese community was frequently enhanced when an individual aligned himself to a faction which commanded respect and which was usually led by members of the merchant elite.

Therefore, both within and without formal associations, factions appeared, with the inevitable consequence of intra-community dissension. Accordingly, there were periodic contentions and struggles for community influence or organizational control between factions with somewhat different, or markedly opposing, viewpoints and objectives.

Chinese in Alberta had a very avid and deep-seated preoccupation with political developments in their homeland. Residents' differing sociocultural and political viewpoints led to factional divisions which, on occasion, were of very serious proportions. Within Alberta's communities, it was during the decade preceding, and that following, the overthrow of the Manchu dynasty that political tensions were most serious among groups of different persuasion.

Factionalism had extremely far-reaching implications for Alberta's communities. "Factionalism made certain that politics for the Chinese was entirely within the Chinese community, rather than in the relationships between Chinese individuals and the non-Chinese society."[2]

In Alberta, political factionalism was certainly a very serious and preoccupying feature of urban community life for many years. There were, however, other internal dissensions. Clan rivalries and periodic intra-community struggles relating to the control of gambling operations, for instance, also acted as internalizing impulses which reinforced ethnic group cohesiveness.

Factionalism and strong community cohesion assisted the perpetuation of the cultural heritage and traditions of Imperial China, even after that socio-political entity had long since ceased to exist. Moreover, factionalism and the institutionalization of community life greatly enhanced Chinese sociocultural exclusivity, both by promoting ethnic group consciousness and by considerably impeding any possible processes of acculturation.

General and Institutional Racism

Official racist measures directed against the Chinese in Canada originated years before Chinese pioneers first set foot on Alberta soil. In 1871, for example, an act was passed forbidding Chinese from voting in British Columbia's provincial elections; it was not enforced until 1875, however. In 1878, by unanimous vote, Chinese were barred from employment on all public works in B.C. In coming decades a host of anti-Chinese acts were introduced and passed in B.C.'s legislature.

From 1886 to 1923 every Chinese immigrant entering Canada was forced to pay a head tax. The amount was raised to the extortionate amount of $500 from $100 in 1904. No other ethnic group in the country has ever been subjected to such a humiliating tax.

The first head tax resulted from the proceedings of an 1885 royal commission investigating Chinese immigration. Evidence at that commission's hearings and that delivered at a 1902 royal commission, with largely the same mandate, revealed how the Chinese were perceived by industrialists and others in positions of authority and power. At the 1885 hearings, "the Chinese were commonly equated with no more than a piece of machinery or a horse, something with a use-value, to be maintained when other labor power was not available."[3]

Both commissions concluded that Chinese were neither desirable nor assimilable immigrants, but agreed that their labor had been essential in industries that could not obtain white workers. However, inasmuch as at the time of the commissions' proceedings, a large Chinese work-force was available in B.C.—along with a greater number of available white workers—the commissions concluded that there was less need for more Chinese arrivals. A head tax was recommended by each commission in order to restrict the number of Chinese immigrants entering Canada.

Capitalist entrepreneurs in Canada—notably those in B.C.—very cold-bloodedly appraised the Chinese as a source of cheap labor which could be readily exploited and manipulated. In B.C., in particular, industrialists of all sorts, including mine and cannery owners, hired Chinese at low wages. This created considerable resentment among white workers.

In this regard, the Calgary Trades and Labour Council wrote to the premier of Alberta a number of times in 1921, condemning a large northern Alberta fish cannery which intended to hire B.C. Chinese as workers. The issue ended with the council requesting the provincial government to restrict the entry of Chinese workers. Because most Chinese in Alberta were engaged in the service sector, however, provincial labor hostility against Chinese workers only surfaced from time to time.

Anti-Chinese elements in B.C.—particularly labor unions and unprincipled, self-serving politicians—were dissatisfied with the results of the burdensome head taxes: for them, too many Chinese were still entering the country. As a result of pressure from B.C., the 1923 *Chinese Immigration Act* (often referred to as the *Chinese Exclusion Act*) was passed. The enactment and enforcement of the flagrant, cruel legislation signified a restrictive victory for anti-Chinese elements.

Virtually the ultimate measure within the bounds of legal stricture had been implemented against Canada's numerically insignificant Chinese population. The *Chinese Exclusion Act* was the most blatant proof of the inability or unwillingness of Anglo-Canadians to come to terms with the presence of an industrious, low-profile ethnic population of Asian extraction.

The 1923 act was an extremely humiliating blow to the country's incensed Chinese community. At the time of passage, there were only about 41 000 Chinese residing in Canada, or about one-half of one per cent of the total Canadian population.

About 4 000 Chinese had made their home in Alberta by mid-1923, when the *Act* was passed. Ho Lem travelled to Ottawa representing Alberta's Chinese residents; all protestations against the recently-passed legislation were to no avail.

Alberta's Chinese community naturally hoped that the *Act* would be revoked before long and, accordingly, most Chinese residents remained in the province. The legislation remained in force, however, until 1947.

Many Chinese were separated from their wives and loved ones for many years, if not forever. Charlie Chew, for example, was married in China in 1925. In 1930, as he recounted: "I wrote to Ottawa requesting that my wife be allowed to enter Canada. Ottawa refused, so I had to travel all the way to China to have a child."[4] Not until 1988 would Mr. Chew again see his wife; after a fifty-three-year separation, she was finally permitted to join him.

In the 1930s came the civil war in China, the Sino-Japanese War, and consequent social and economic upheaval. Many sojourners' families suffered a great deal during this period but, still, they were absolutely barred from entering Canada until the late 1940s or 1950s.

As mentioned earlier, Chinese could not vote in provincial elections in B.C. from 1875 on; later, the B.C. legislature also banned all Chinese from exercising the municipal franchise. In Saskatchewan the *Elections Act* of 1908 disenfranchised the Chinese population there. For a time Alberta considered following suit, but decided against it because support was quite insufficient for such a severe move.

Chinese in B.C. and Saskatchewan lost the federal franchise, too, because federal voters' lists were drawn up from provincial ones. Professional associations in Canada made it obligatory that members be registered on provincial voting lists; accordingly, Chinese in these provinces were barred from participating in occupations including pharmacy, law, teaching, and chartered accountancy.

It is particularly revealing that, in regard to disenfranchisement, both naturalized citizens and native-born citizens lost the franchise, as well as immigrants previously regarded as eligible voters. Through this means, Canadian citizens of Chinese ancestry were barred from pursuing professional careers. As a result, Chinese were further confined to low-paying job categories.

Equally revealing, according to provisions of the 1923 *Chinese Exclusion Act*, all Canadian residents of Chinese descent, including Canadian citizens, had to register with the government and obtain a certificate to this effect—or face heavy fines and/or imprisonment up to one year. The *Act*, then, was not just restrictive in nature, it was blatantly racist: the Chinese were singled out as a people for exclusion, manipulation, and domination.

The *Chinese Exclusion Act* provided that only merchants, students, members of the diplomatic corps, and children born in Canada had any hope of being admitted as immigrants. It was stated in Section 10.2 of the *Act*: "The examination of [applicants seeking] entry to Canada shall be separated and apart from the public and in the presence of such persons only as the Controller shall permit."[5] Conducted without public scrutiny, this process readily lent itself to considerable abuse; this, however, was exactly what was sought: Section 10.2 was included to make it much easier to deny admission to eligible applicants.

The oral testimony of Fred Yee, who sought entry into Canada in the mid-1920s at age thirteen, supports this conclusion and also illustrates scandalous behavior on the part of immigration officers at the time. Mr. Yee told of white immigration officers purposefully grilling boys until they became confused and contradictory in their responses to questions.

Through such cruel and contrived means, Chinese were refused admission. "Because of that incessant questioning, your replies would sometimes be slightly different....If you said something wrong, they'd mark it down and you'd be out of luck. They kept on questioning...boys until they got nervous."[6] He added: "you had to [give] the immigration men...something [or] you had a hell of a time getting in....eight [other boys] were deported to China because they didn't bribe the immigration men....Those guys [sure] were crooked."[7]

Various instances of institutional racism occurred in Alberta at the municipal level. In Calgary and Edmonton, for example, young Chinese women were not permitted to train as nurses at local hospitals. In 1919 in Calgary, city commissioners sought to either relocate Chinatown or check its growth, but the city solicitor advised against such measures on legal grounds and no actions were taken.

The Lethbridge city council restricted Chinese premises to designated areas on several occasions. A 1909 by-law forbade Chinese laundries to operate in the central area of the city. Then, from 1911 to 1916, Chinese laundries were confined to a three-square-block area known as the Restricted Area. And, for a while certain humiliating conditions had to be met for Chinese laundries to operate legally in North Lethbridge.

During the period between World Wars One and Two, there was definite job discrimination against Chinese in Alberta. Mrs. Helen Mock, for example, completed high school in Calgary and then sought employment. Although she had taken a business course in high school, she could not obtain an office job. "I believe that there was definitely discrimination at that time against Chinese who were looking for jobs....I got a job in a knitting factory and worked for my own people."[8]

Born in Alberta, Frank Lung attended public school, then completed a course of studies which included accounting at business college. Subsequently, as he recalled: "I tried to obtain work in a bank. They wouldn't hire me, and I believe that they discriminated against me. So, I became a partner in a laundry [in] British Columbia."[9]

Mrs. Alice Louie-Byne was born in Canada. One of her sisters received training in nursing. "But, no one [in] Calgary would employ her in nursing because she was Chinese. She had to leave Calgary and went to work in a small town [at] a church hospital."[10] Mrs. Louie-Byne referred to her own bitter experience. "You could not get good jobs in those days if you were Chinese....I wanted to write a civil service examination to try to secure a government job. They would not let me do so....one had no opportunities....all doors were closed."[11]

Racist positions by the provincial government reached a nadir in the 1930s. During the initial few years of the Great Depression, many Alberta Chinese lost their jobs in the vulnerable service sector, where most worked; those in towns, drifted into the cities. Beginning in 1931, unemployed single Chinese were granted an allowance of just $1.12 per week from the province; their white counterparts, however, received $2.50 per week. The resulting plight of jobless single men became most desperate in Calgary, where Chinese community organizations simply could not cope with the very heavy demands upon them.

Requests to the provincial government for equal treatment were mercilessly ignored for years. From July 1936 to March 1937, at least three Chinese men in Calgary died from malnutrition.

Buck Doo Yee arrived in Calgary in 1914. For over thirty years he worked at Chinese laundries. During most of the 1930s he was jobless, though. He spoke of this period: "many Chinese Canadians in Alberta were unemployed and starved....as a result, many destitute and desperate Chinese in Calgary and elsewhere committed suicide. I only survived because of money sent to me by my brother in China."[12]

In 1936 and 1937 the Calgary Chinese community took various actions. In desperation, men picketed government offices; congregated at city hall demanding aid; and staged peaceful sit-down protests. Not until white groups with influence supported the Chinese cause, did the provincial government raise relief payments to $2.12 per week—still less than that received by whites.

During various periods, local police forces attempted to contain or quash certain Chinese recreational activities. From 1912 to 1914, harassing and irruptive raids on gambling operations were fairly common in Edmonton and Calgary. Things quieted down greatly during World War One.

From late 1919 to spring 1921, however, particularly well-organized raids were conducted in Calgary. But, these raids and those before the war were often overly violent and obsessively determined in nature.

Rampageous paramilitary assaults aimed at members of a law-abiding, generally peaceful people dramatically demonstrated that civic authorities were determined to "keep the Chinese in their place." The Chinese community was expected to conform to Anglo-Canadian standards of acceptable behavior—even if violent means proved necessary time and again to achieve this objective. Such authoritarian thought and its violent consequences vividly exemplified institutional racism at the municipal level.

For many long years, racist discrimination against the Chinese manifested itself in the socio-economic, political, and law-enforcement spheres of Canadian life. Restrictions on immigration—primarily in the form of head taxes—eventually made way for virtually complete exclusion. Crucial rights connected with citizenship, such as voting, were simply taken away or not allowed to exist in the first place. Limitations on eligibility to engage in particular occupations served to bar Chinese immigrants and their children from upward mobility: this confined most people to demanding, low-paying jobs in the service sector. And, the list goes on....

Government legislation formalized and legalized general racist discrimination against the Chinese, "and its practice was rationalized by an ideology stressing the superiority of white over non-white. It is on this basis that the term 'institutional racism' is appropriate...."[13] As elsewhere in Canada, the effects of institutional racism in Alberta were severe and, at times, devastating. During the Great Depression, the provincial government's racist policies were vile and deadly.

Cultural Conflict

As related throughout this study, a serious state of cultural conflict arose between Chinese and Anglo-Canadians in Alberta. The prevailing conflict situation was primarily a product of white racism and widespread Anglo-Canadian acceptance of white supremacist notions. The partially fabricated social distance between Chinese and supremacist-minded whites was, nonetheless, perpetuated by a wide spectrum of diverse areas of disagreement and misunderstanding between the majority population and the Chinese.

For decades in Alberta, there was far too little meaningful—and, hence, potentially mutually beneficial—social interaction, discourse, and overall communication between the Chinese and Anglo-Canadians. Even as white residents were extremely ignorant about Chinese community life and customs, likewise, most Chinese knew little about social, political, economic, cultural, and other features of the towns and cities within which they resided.

Many Chinese traditions and customs, leisure activities, cultural pursuits, and general social practices were barely—if at all—known to exist by white Albertans. Consequently, Chinese community life and personal behavior were neither understood nor appreciated by other residents. On the one hand, for many years most whites had absolutely no interest in Chinese culture and customary behavior. On the other hand, they did not approve of the Chinese presence in their midst and did nothing substantial to promote assimilation of the Chinese into mainstream Anglo-Canadian society.

Chinese in rural Alberta encountered various forms of antipathy and were customarily shunned when not manning their laundry or restaurant counters. Often, feelings of isolation and grim fatalism held sway among those few who lived and worked together in many hamlets and towns scattered throughout the province.

The lives of many rural Chinese were exacting and grinding. Charles Lee recollected his many years in a southern Alberta town. "Life in Crossfield was hard and tough....there weren't many Chinese there, and we were discriminated against. I felt that we [were] surrounded by ill-behaved people. Sometimes, I really couldn't tolerate things."[14]

Charlie Chew would have understood well the context of Mr. Lee's experiences and what he endured over a long span of time. In the small town of New Dayton, Mr. Chew and his father were subjected for decades to hostility, antipathy, and, on several occasions, violence.

In 1923 Charlie Chew and his father had their second café erected at New Dayton; accordingly, their first café, built in 1917-1918, they designated for operation by themselves as a rooming-house. Mr. Chew recounted that, during the night of the day they moved into the new building, "the [local] hotel manager set a match to the old empty building....we had no insurance [and] lost everything. It was not until many years later that my friends told me who had been the culprit, but by then it was too late."[15]

Mr. Chew attested that, during the years prior to World War Two, running a small-town Chinese café was exceedingly tough. He stated, for example: "drunks caused plenty of trouble....they'd get crazy-drunk. [In] 1935 a drunken guy jumped up on a table and started dancing....My father tried to stop him, but he slugged him in the face....my father lost an eye [from that]."[16] He summed up that era: "We Chinese had a great deal of trouble with whites years ago."[17]

An almost unbridgeable societal chasm developed early on between Alberta's Chinese and whites. Naturally, this worked to the detriment of both sides. Over time, ignorance and consequent suspicion inexorably fed upon each other, further entrenching a general state of cultural conflict and exacerbating existing tensions.

White bigots and racists delighted in pointing out and ridiculing various customs and practices of Chinese. Particularly obvious conventions were singled out for derision. In this respect, an obvious example was mentioned by Paul Dofoo. "My father came to Calgary in 1900. Some [people] made fun of his long hair, or queue, and a few years later he decided to have it cut short."[18]

Certain aspects of marriage were also considered fit topics for scornful comment. White racists, for example, would have derisively dismissed the circumstances relating to Mrs. Tenie Quan's marriage as archaic. Mrs. Quan recounted: "[In] 1938, I married and moved to Calgary [from Winnipeg]. A matchmaker, or go-between, arranged my marriage."[19]

As for the marriage between the parents of Violet George, a Chinese male and a white female, racists would have regarded it as a clear example of what they imagined to be a very serious threat: namely, miscegenation posed by the mere presence of Chinese men in white Canada.

Primarily because of prevailing prejudice and discrimination against them, Chinese became alienated; frustrated; distrustful; inward-looking;

and culturally cohesive. Few immigrants from China saw any point in becoming Westernized when white Albertans generally regarded them as unacceptable Canadian citizens and, disdainfully, tolerated them as residents in "their" white communities.

One group in Alberta frequently and cynically exploited the hostility toward Chinese residents: that group was comprised of politicians. Arthur Yee Mock related: "During every election...wiseacres claimed that all the Chinese made money here and took it back home to China. That burned me up....at times Chinese did not make enough money to eat, yet they were accused of taking away money...."[20]

From 1910 to 1925, in particular, some Anglo-Canadian groups in Alberta sought, for a variety of reasons, to restrict the Chinese in various ways. For example, on occasion, organized labor protested alleged Chinese encroachments in the composition of the Alberta labor force. As well, a few clergymen unsuccessfully promoted the idea of preventing Chinese employers from freely hiring white help by passing restrictive provincial legislation.

Anti-Chinese sentiment was worsened by occasional newspaper accounts about a supposed Chinese menace to Western civilization. Fears so aroused were sustained and aggravated by press reports which habitually featured an overwhelmingly negative stereotype of the Chinese. This odious stereotype was a formidable barrier that absolutely had to be breached and demolished to make way for wider understanding, greater tolerance, and eventual acceptance of the Chinese by the majority population in Alberta.

Employment, Business Operations, and Related Matters

Long, lingering decades passed before the Chinese were widely accepted as worthy residents and were granted full rights of citizenship. Before this transpired, however, they were subjected to debilitating and humiliating intolerance, antipathy, and discrimination.

In the occupational sphere, this entailed being prevented from virtually any access to well-paying jobs. Hostile white workers and labor bosses, in particular, saw to it that Chinese workers were confined to jobs in the marginal sector of the labor market. The other major result of overall job discrimination was that—of necessity—the Chinese established their own commercial enterprises and, overwhelmingly, hired fellow countrymen as workers.

For many years the hand laundry was the primary type of business established by Chinese in Alberta. Moreover, the Chinese hand laundry itself was a notable hallmark of Canadian prairie settlement. Before about 1940 the Chinese hand laundry was to be found in virtually every hamlet and town throughout the Alberta parkland and prairie.

Mr. June Jay Chang operated a laundry in High River for fifty-five years, usually with a partner. From 1914 until about 1944, as he related, "the laundry business was pretty good; we [often] had two people working for us at thirty dollars per month."[21] He stated that, despite having switched to steam laundry equipment, he retired in 1969 "because there was little demand for my services—most people [had] their own washers and dryers...."[22]

For over forty years, virtually all Chinese laundrymen had no choice but to work by hand. Buck Doo Yee worked in hand laundries in Alberta for decades. "Since there was no hot water, I had to boil water in order to clean clothes. I scrubbed all the clothes with my bare hands [so they] had far too much contact with soap and washing-soda. They always had blisters and bled."[23]

Ook Wah Yee settled in Calgary in 1912 at age twenty-five. He recalled: "Many Chinese...opened laundries during the early 1900s. [In Calgary] laundry owners had to pay a monthly business tax of twenty-five dollars. In small towns they only had to pay five dollars a month because the people living in the country were poor."[24] Mr. Yee stated that hand laundries served other than strictly commercial purposes. "Chinese laundries were frequently used as free accommodation for Chinese immigrants who could not afford to stay in hotels. It cost about one dollar a night then to stay in a hotel; later, two dollars; then, three dollars."[25]

Some Chinese businessmen opened dry-cleaning businesses which initially used gasoline as the solvent. Jimmy (Hon Men) Lee related that in Lethbridge during the 1930s: "A lot of cleaners burnt up....It was a dangerous business."[26] He explained: "Weather permitting, you'd hang things outside...to dry. [In] wintertime you'd hang things inside. You can well imagine what would happen when the fumes evaporated and hit your stove! Still, I don't recall anyone being killed."[27]

For many years restaurants rated second numerically to laundries in terms of Chinese businesses in Alberta. Work in restaurants (Chinese-

The Sam Wing Laundry in Bowden, Alberta, post-1912.
Glenbow Archives, NA-3976-4.

owned and otherwise), however, was the major source of employment for Chinese in the province.

Working at Chinese restaurants in prairie towns and cities before the Second World War, was no mean accomplishment, even if one possessed basically good health and stamina. Byng Lee remembered rising at 5:00 a.m. all year long, about 1918, to go to work at a fellow Lee's restaurant. He was not exactly enamored with the conditions of work: "it was a tough job and I hated it....There were no breaks; non-stop work seven days a week until 8:00 or 9:00 p.m. [At] that time everybody worked fifteen to eighteen hours a day. I made about thirty dollars per month."[28]

Charles Lee ran his own restaurant in Crossfield from 1917 until 1957. "I started working at 5:00 or 6:00 a.m. and closed the restaurant at midnight; the work was very routine."[29] As a rule, restaurant work for white employers was no less demanding. In about 1914, for example, Charlie Chew put

The interior of a Chinese restaurant, Lacombe, Alberta.
Glenbow Archives, ND-2-109.

in eighteen-hour days as a cook and kitchen helper for twenty dollars per month.

The grocery store was another type of service-sector business commonly engaged in by Chinese. Numerically, for many years it ranked third in terms of Chinese-owned types of business enterprises in Alberta. Paul Dofoo was born in Calgary in 1913, two years after his father opened a grocery store in Chinatown. He remarked: "The grocery business has always been competitive. Our store had living quarters at the back. Most of the time family members helped to run the store."[30] The Dofoo's grocery—like its competitors—operated seven days a week. Like Chinese-owned prairie restaurants, Chinese groceries opened early in the morning and closed late in the evening.

For many years Chinese owners of laundries, restaurants, and general stores or groceries provided invaluable services to hamlets and towns scattered throughout the Alberta parkland and prairie. In the cities similar-minded men also established these badly needed service-sector businesses, as well as rooming-houses, gift stores, and shops specializing in Chinese foods and other items of interest to the Chinese themselves.

From about 1900 into the 1930s, Chinese merchants and businessmen in Edmonton, Medicine Hat, Calgary, and Lethbridge played an important role in the service sector of local business. In Edmonton Chinese operated twenty-five of the fifty-six restaurants in 1920, and twenty-four of the sixty-two operating in 1924. In 1920 they ran thirty-one of Edmonton's thirty-nine laundries, and forty-seven of sixty-one in 1924. In Lethbridge during the period 1914 to 1924 (and likely for some years before and after) Chinese residents owned the majority of restaurants and laundries, and in 1924 owned over one-quarter of the grocery stores.

In Medicine Hat Chinese operated just under one-half of the restaurants from 1914 to 1924 and virtually all the laundries during the same period. In Calgary Chinese owned twenty-two of the sixty-five restaurants in 1911; the proportion stayed almost exactly the same until 1925, when they owned twenty-four of fifty-three restaurants; in 1911 Chinese owned twenty-eight of the thirty-one laundries; in 1915, sixty-one of sixty-seven; and in 1925, forty-two of forty-seven laundry operations.

On the outskirts of Alberta's larger centres and elsewhere in the province, many Chinese engaged in market gardening. Greenhouses were built and managed by Chinese in several locations, including Calgary and Lethbridge. As well, the reliable Chinese vegetable pedlar—with his fine array of fresh produce—came into existence and became a welcome institution of urban life in Alberta.

The most popular area for market gardening was in and around Lethbridge. While some sixty or more market gardeners operated at Lethbridge in 1914, by the mid-1920s only about thirty remained. A few of these went broke during the Great Depression. Jimmy (Hon Men) Lee stated: "Early in the morning they'd take their horse and buggy to town and go from door-to-door and sell their produce....[They] didn't sell much in Chinatown."[31] He added: "Some sold to wholesalers. Those fortunate enough sold in quantity."[32]

Fred Yee referred to positive changes in the industry centred in Lethbridge in the mid-1940s. "After the Second World War, market gardeners started selling to the large outlets on a wholesale basis. Before then, [virtually everyone had] sold door-to-door by horse and buggy."[33]

Market gardeners lived hard lives marked by toil, customarily meagre returns, isolation, and economic uncertainty. All work was done by hand, and the men usually lived in shacks on plots of five acres. Johnny Long related that: "For a whole year's work they might make $200 or $300. Most operated south of Lethbridge and rented land from the farmers. Just a few were in partnerships."[34] Mr. Long's appraisal of net income was supported by the testimony of long-time market gardener Fred Yee. "We market gardeners worked all day year-round and by the end of a year we'd be lucky to have each made $300."[35]

From frontier days on, many men who worked in Chinese restaurants in towns and cities were also partners in those enterprises. Partnerships were virtually the only way that low-paid Chinese workers, with very limited savings, could establish businesses and attempt, thereby, to have some say in directing the course of their lives.

By investing a small amount of money, a man could both create his own job and, hopefully, pave the way for a long-term livelihood. Moreover, by going into business for themselves—on a partnership basis, in this case—Chinese could avoid both exploitation by white employers and hostility from white workers, union bosses, and racists.

Because the profit margin of restaurants was small, often there was insufficient reason for men to remain long as partners. Besides, even when one was a partner, the work performed would be the same as that of a hired worker. So, there was frequent coming and going in what were very fluid, informal (usually word-of-mouth) partnership arrangements.

Security, though, was a strong enough incentive for some men to remain partners for a long time, should they be involved in a successful enterprise. For these men it was important "to secure a guaranteed place to work and live....The restaurants provided an economic refuge for the Chinese in a restrictive labor market."[36] Partnership in a restaurant served as "a refuge in economic hard times....During the Depression, the restaurants provided a means of survival for many Chinese."[37]

Throughout the duration of their working lives, a not insignificant number of men were variously engaged in partnership arrangements, operating their own businesses, and working as employees. Joe How, for example, went into partnership in market gardening with an uncle for a few years; then, he successively opened two groceries of his own; subsequently, he and two Chinese partners established an ultimately successful, large market gardening operation.

A very good example of men pursuing different kinds of working arrangements—which was the norm until recent decades—is provided by the career of Johnny Long. For a few years Mr. Long worked at various jobs for others; then, he started his own restaurant in a small town; after a while he rented it out and worked in a restaurant in Lethbridge; next, he sold the business and worked again in a Chinese restaurant; then, for three years he and a partner ran a restaurant in another small town, Vauxhall; in later years he established his own businesses there.

In addition to some market gardens and many restaurants, partnerships in Alberta also accounted for the appearance of general stores, laundries, rooming-houses, grocery stores, and other business ventures, including gambling operations. In relation to the financial and functional arrangements of *fantan* houses, Joe How recalled: "One man couldn't take the chance of operating a game....So, it was run by a pool of some twenty or twenty-five men, each contributing about twenty-five dollars. It took a lot of money to operate a game....one guy took care of it full-time."[38]

Frequently, kinship assistance—help from relatives or fellow clan members—was a crucial factor in determining the pattern of men's employment histories. Partnerships, for instance, were frequently formed on the basis of kinship ties. Even seemingly distant ties, such as a shared surname, would usually suffice to seal an arrangement between parties.

Naturally, partnerships of a close familial nature were common; for example: between father and son, as with Fred Yee and his father; between uncle and nephew, as between Joe How and his uncle, who engaged in market gardening together for three years; between or among brothers, as in the case of Joe How's father and two brothers, partners in businesses established successively in Calgary, Okotoks, and Lethbridge.

The number of Chinese partnerships in Alberta began to decline in the late 1940s when immigration regulations were passed permitting wives and children to enter Canada. With their arrival, additional labor was made available to men operating restaurants and other businesses, and many partnerships were dissolved.

The testimony of Kim Dong throws light on the considerable importance of kinship assistance in the job market. All of Mr. Dong's adult life (from 1912 into the 1970s) was spent in Canada, primarily in Alberta. In terms of employment, he experienced a general lack of opportunity and customary uncertainty as to how long he would retain positions.

He outlined the situation: "most Chinese employers only hired their relatives or people who had the same surname. Even if you were hired by an employer to whom you were not related, as soon as he found a relative to take your place, you would immediately be fired."[39] Because Chinese employers bearing his surname were very scarce in Alberta and beyond, Mr. Dong was subjected to frequent firings. In this regard he noted: "Thus, over the years, I moved around to many towns and cities."[40]

As a general pattern, the lives of a majority of Chinese in Alberta were much the same as that of Kim Dong. This is hardly surprising. Chinese immigrants who arrived in Canada before 1923 shared a common background in virtually all important respects and—given what they encountered in Canada—their lives strongly tended to follow a similar course.

Impelled by socio-economic turmoil and severe poverty in Guangdong province, young men in their teens and twenties emigrated to Canada. Most arrived as sojourners: they looked forward to saving enough money to retire in their native villages; in the meantime, they would send remittances home to relatives. Only a handful arrived with any marketable skills acquired through work experience or vocational training; most had received minimal education and knew no English.

Work had to be found soon after arrival, not the least inducement being to begin paying back loans incurred to meet the extortionate head tax. Because hostile white workers, backed by bigoted labor bosses, made it very hard for Chinese to obtain positions in the core labor market, most arrivals in Alberta had no choice but to look to the marginal labor sector. Jobs in this category included dishwashers, unskilled laborers, waiters, houseboys, laundry workers, hotel workers, store employees, and cooks.

Men engaged in these kinds of jobs were placed in an extremely unenviable position. They received very low pay; worked for extremely long hours, six or seven days a week; performed burdensome work of a menial nature; and had low social status. Most worked in laundries and restaurants, primarily the latter.

As Kim Dong explained earlier, there could easily be little or no security for hired workers at Chinese businesses. When a jobless relative appeared on the scene, for instance, a hired worker who was not closely related would be dismissed. Or, if a fellow clan member needed work, the employer would fire a hired worker without the same surname. Thus, kinship assistance frequently worked against the individual.

The various circumstances connected with marginal employment dictated that Chinese experienced considerable instability and insecurity in their working lives. High turnover rates were the norm. This meant that many workers—those in restaurants, in particular—were forced to be very mobile: they had to move periodically from town to town on a regular basis in order to remain employed.

Such reoccurring disruption introduced very disturbing and unwholesome elements into the lives of many overworked, underpaid men. Toe You

Mah, for example, arrived in Canada in 1912 at age sixteen and moved to Alberta in 1917. After mentioning some of the Alberta towns and cities where he had lived over the years, he remarked: "I worked at hotels, restaurants and night-clubs for many years. At that time, the most I earned was eight dollars per week....All the jobs that I ever had were temporary, short, and had long working hours."[41] After twenty-six years of such demanding and unpredictable employment, Mr. Mah lost his health and was never able to work again.

The Chinese in Alberta were seriously restricted in terms of employment opportunities; stringently oppressed by discrimination; and subjected to general and institutional racism. After working for a few years in the province, many workers undoubtedly concluded that they had little chance of significantly improving their socio-economic standing. Nevertheless, they persevered in their various endeavors, demonstrating considerable self-discipline and industry in the process.

Undoubtedly, in the recesses of their minds, hopes were kept kindled that fortune might well smile on them someday. Perhaps they would choose just the very numbers to make a small fortune in a Chinese Lottery draw, or maybe a winning streak at *fantan* would bring them a relative measure of wealth—though highly exceptional, such things did happen, after all...

9

A New Era

Background to Change

A substantial change in the general public's attitude toward the Chinese occurred during, and soon after, the Second World War. The stage for this significant development was set during the 1930s. Initially, in 1931-1932, Japanese armies invaded and occupied Manchuria, in northeastern China. Then, in mid-1937 Japan launched a large-scale campaign, and the Sino-Japanese War began. After success in north China, Japanese armed forces advanced southward. China was plunged into crisis, forced to defend herself against the savage armed expansion of the invaders.

The Chinese war effort and the desperate state of affairs in China evoked considerable sympathy among the Canadian population. The calamitous situation galvanized Chinese communities throughout Canada to work together in common cause and aid China to the maximum extent possible.

In December 1941 the Japanese attacked Pearl Harbor, and the Second World War was extended into the Pacific. Canada and China became fellow Allied powers. Thereby, Chinese communities in Alberta and throughout Canada were placed in the position of supporting Canada's and China's joint causes. Throughout the duration of the Second World War, the war effort in China was given ample and very favorable coverage. Journalists in the various media of the day portrayed the Chinese people as courageous, admirable, self-sacrificing, determined, and heroic.

With the outbreak of the Sino-Japanese War, the Chinese government requested financial assistance from Chinese living overseas. During the eight years of warfare, the Overseas Chinese responded superbly—both in terms of direct monetary aid to the government and also in terms of assistance to relatives through remittances. The Chinese in Canada alone contributed about $5 million (roughly $125 per capita).

As mentioned in Chapters Six and Seven, Chinese communities in Alberta participated avidly in fund-raising to help China. In 1937 the Pan-Alberta Anti-Japanese League was formed, with headquarters in Calgary and branches in various towns and cities. From 1937 to 1945, the Chinese in Calgary alone raised over $200 000 for China relief.

Aid to China from Alberta was not solely monetary. Some Chinese residents travelled to China to devote themselves to its salvation. For example, Calgary residents Paul Dofoo and his brother—both Canadian-born—arrived in China in 1941. Paul Dofoo stated: "[We went] to see what service we could render to Nationalist China, then in deep peril. I worked as a technician in a studio for the Chinese Central Broadcasting Station. My brother worked in the electrical field."[1] Paul Dofoo stayed in China until 1949; his brother died in Chungking.

In addition to supporting China's struggle, Chinese individuals and communities contributed much to the Canadian war effort. For example, a total of $10 million in Canadian Victory Bonds was purchased by Canadian Chinese. Moreover, over 500 Canadian-born or naturalized Chinese served in Canada's armed forces; some obtained commissions. A significant proportion served in Asia, and among them was "an elite corps of Chinese-Canadian commandos...."[2] Various Alberta residents, such as Frank Lung, joined the armed forces but were not sent overseas; others, like Mrs. Alice Louie-Byne's brother, lost their lives fighting beside fellow Canadians in Europe.

During and after the war, Chinese community leaders argued convincingly for equal treatment of the Chinese in terms of immigration policy and citizenship rights. Watts D. Lee served for nine months as an undercover intelligence officer in Japanese-occupied Singapore. He expressed succinctly the prevailing community viewpoint. "The Chinese felt that they went to fight in the war, too, and it should not be that they were still denied rights and privileges."[3]

In the immediate post-war period, it became clear that attitudes toward the Chinese in Canada had improved significantly. The image and status of the Chinese had been enhanced a great deal. In addition, overt racism and discrimination had become extremely unpopular because of the horrifying measures taken against Jews by the Nazis, who had espoused perverse racial doctrines.

To the mind of virtually all Chinese, the end of the war ushered in an altogether new era. Charlie Chew, who arrived in Canada in 1913 at age seventeen, remarked: "The feelings against Chinese disappeared very suddenly after World War Two. I can't understand why whites were so against us. It was to Canada's benefit that everyone co-operate, but that's not the way it was for a long time."[4]

In 1947 the *Canadian Citizenship Act* was passed, permitting Chinese—at long last—to have equal opportunities to become citizens and, thereby, to send for their wives and children outside Canada. During prior debate regarding repeal of the *Chinese Exclusion Act*, participating Alberta members of Parliament favored its revocation. Many families were reunited and, after some years, the sex-ratio imbalance among Chinese was ameliorated.

Other relatives of Chinese Canadians became eligible to enter the country in 1957, and in 1967 new regulations were enacted which did not stress one's country of origin. Indeed, in 1967 the last vestiges of overt discrimination were eliminated by the establishment of a "point system" for assessing the eligibility of all potential immigrants.

As immigration reform proceeded, some community members in Calgary and Edmonton became well-known locally and beyond for their achievements. These included sons of Ho Lem in Calgary, and the football great, fullback Normie (Norman) Kwong, "The China Clipper." These leading lights of Alberta's Chinese citizenry contributed a great deal beyond what was directly related to their fine careers: they were very worthy representatives of the Chinese-Canadian people and were perceived as such.

Born in Calgary in 1918, George Ho Lem Sr. attended public school, Chinese School, and joined Chinese Mission youth groups. His eldest brother, Frank, a popular city resident, was a champion marksman and became the first Chinese commissioned officer in the Canadian Army during World War Two. Charles, an older brother, was the first Chinese president of the Kiwanis Club in Calgary. David, next-oldest brother to George, was elected president of the Calgary Junior Chamber of Commerce; later, he was elected international vice-president; he engaged in considerable work with service clubs and other worthy groups, including charitable foundations, over the years.

In post-war years the best-known of Ho Lem's five sons has been George Sr. He and David set up a flourishing laundry/dry-cleaning business at Dawson Creek, B.C., in the 1940s when the Alaska Highway was built; a few years later, the two launched the highly-successful Rosedale Cleaners in Calgary, which they ran for nearly thirty years.

In 1959, after serving as president of the Junior Chamber of Commerce, George was approached by supporters and urged to run as alderman that year. He did, polling more votes than those of the thirteen other eligible city-wide candidates combined, including the mayor! Re-elected twice, he was the first Chinese-Canadian alderman of a large city.

Elected in 1971 as a Social Credit MLA (member of the legislative assembly), he subsequently headed the much-divided twenty-five-member Opposition caucus, astutely keeping it intact; he was the first Chinese MLA in the province. Though defeated along with most fellow Socreds in 1975, he did not abandon politics and managed, or headed fund-raising for, several other people's successful municipal or provincial campaigns.

The achievements of the Chinatown Development Task Force, which George established in 1973 and headed as chairman, have been outlined in Chapter Six. He has had many other involvements with societies, foundations, official boards, and the like, over many years. A man with numerous friends and contacts, supporters, and invaluable connections of all sorts, he has been a formidable force in community affairs since the early 1960s. For almost twenty years, George Ho Lem was the predominant leader of the Chinese community in Calgary. (Officially, he is now retired).

Normie Kwong is virtually a household name in Alberta and among all Canadian football fans. Dubbed "The China Clipper," the former star fullback is one of the country's all-time great football players. He is a member of the Alberta Sports Hall of fame, as well as the Canadian Football Hall of Fame.

Born (1929) and raised in Calgary, Kwong was the son of Mr. and Mrs. Charles L. Kwong. After playing for the Calgary Stampeders for several years—he was, from the onset, extremely popular with Calgary fans—Kwong was traded to Edmonton in 1952 for Reg Clarkson, who was unwell most of his sole year with Calgary: one of the most terrible trades in Canadian football, all agree.

Normie Kwong, "The China Clipper."
Glenbow Archives, PA2807-2189 (a).

Kwong was an immediate hit with the Edmonton fans, and deservedly so: during the next decade, he won many awards. He was the outstanding Canadian player twice (Schenley Award, 1955-1956); Canada's outstanding male athlete of 1955—in an official Canadian Press year-end poll of sports editors and sportscasters; Canadian Football League all-star, five times. From 1950 to 1961, he averaged 5.2 yards per carry, gained over 9 000 yards, and scored 74 touchdowns. Kwong is presently part-owner of the Calgary Flames and general manager of the Calgary Stampeders.

The respect and esteem generated over many years by Normie Kwong and the Ho Lem brothers considerably enhanced the image of Chinese-Canadian residents. This was of particular significance during the 1950s and 1960s, when, with post-war tolerance and general acceptance, Chinese became very well-regarded in Alberta—no small credit owing to "The China Clipper" and the dynamic, community-minded sons of pioneer Ho Lem.

Contemporary Immigrants: The Personal Side

The influx of immigrants since 1967 has been largely due to Canada's attractiveness as a place to live, rather than because Chinese were forced out of their countries of origin. Canada's comparatively high standard of living, political stability, and fine educational system have served very well in attracting newcomers. Immigrants of Chinese descent have arrived from a wide variety of lands, including Peru, the Caribbean, and South Africa; but, for the most part, they have originated from Hong Kong and Southeast Asia, especially the Philippines, Malaysia, and Singapore.

In relation to Canada's socio-economic, political, and educational attractiveness, it is of interest that, of the nineteen contemporary immigrants interviewed for this study, eight came to Canada as students and remained here. One of these, Hornby Jear, was attending the University of British Columbia on a Kuomintang provincial government scholarship in 1949 when the Communists gained control of China; remaining in Canada was the only sensible course of action for him.

The other contemporary immigrants interviewed also settled in Canada for reasons related directly or implicitly to the attractive features of Canada. Dr. K.W. Chang had no intention whatsoever of residing permanently in Canada, but he and his wife liked Alberta too much to leave. It was with the intention of practising as a psychologist in Alberta that Michael Ho emigrated from Hong Kong with his wife; professional reasons, then, appear to have been predominant in his decision to relocate. Mrs. Virginia Lui and her husband have operated a restaurant together since their arrival in 1973, so economic considerations apparently prompted their move to Canada.

Canada's political stability and geography attracted Paul Tse, who settled in Alberta in 1975. "...Hong Kong is over-populated, and I wanted to live where there was much land and where peace prevailed, because I enjoy a peaceful life."[5] Peter Ng arrived in Alberta with his wife in 1976. The decision to emigrate was adventurous in nature; as he related: "I wanted to go to Canada to find something challenging for my life."[6]

Kinship assistance and maintaining family togetherness have also been important in the decision-making process of many contemporary Chinese immigrants. In 1981, for instance, Johnnie Chui visited with family members in Alberta. A sister of his had migrated to Alberta in the mid-1970s and had sponsored their parents as immigrants. The parents arrived and were soon operating a Chinese restaurant in a small town. Johnnie Chui remarked of his visit: "I could see that Calgary had much potential for all sorts of trades and businesses. My mother wanted me to migrate, too, so I returned to Hong Kong to apply to emigrate to Canada."[7] He arrived in Alberta the next year.

Family considerations certainly played a major role in the decision of Ng Yuk Sum to emigrate to Canada. Born and raised in the county of Toi-san, he moved to Hong Kong in 1953 at age twenty-two. In 1954 he successfully applied to enter Canada as an immigrant. He recounted: "...I settled in the town of Gleichen, Alberta, where my grandfather was running a café. He had arrived there in 1950. In 1958 I applied for my family to join me....My wife brought over my son Tony and my daughter Peggy."[8]

A few years later Mr. Ng began operating the café himself, when his grandfather died. Subsequently, he did remarkably well in real estate investments and other ventures. Then, as he related: "In 1969 I brought to Canada my brother's family, my nephew's family, and my mother from Hong Kong under my sponsorship. Altogether, I arranged for fifteen people to emigrate to Canada. I do my best to assist my relatives...."[9]

Chinese in certain countries have been forced to consider migration as a solution to their long-term problems. A relatively significant number of those who decided to emigrate have made Canada their new home.

One such emigrant was Mrs. Agatha Lim. Born and raised in Sarawak, East Malaysia, she taught school there for ten years. In 1963 Sarawak became virtually independent within Malaysia and, before long, Muslim was officially designated Sarawak's national religion and Malay its national language. Mrs. Lim and her husband did not agree with the latter measure, because, as she stated: "...Malay is not an international language and English is. So, we decided to pick another Commonwealth country with the same general background as Malaysia."[10] Like many other ethnic Chinese from Sarawak and elsewhere in Malaysia, the Lims chose to emigrate to Canada. They and their four children arrived in 1971.

Two other contemporary immigrants chose to leave their homelands in response to long-standing difficulties. Born and raised in Manila, Philippines, Joe (José) Khu started an importing business in his home city in 1945; later, he expanded into other commercial ventures. Then, as he explained: "In 1973 I left the business to my brother and migrated to Canada with my family. The economy and politics in the Philippines had been gradually deteriorating. So, I decided to move...."[11]

Khuu Biuh Phu was born and raised in Vietnam, the son of Chinese parents who had left China when very young. A businessman for many years, he provided for himself, his wife, and ten children. After the fall of South Vietnam, as he stated: "I decided to leave Vietnam, which was in utter turmoil. We gathered together 228 friends and relatives and, using a wooden fishing boat, we sailed to Malaysia....I served as captain."[12] Through Canadian federal assistance, the Khuus entered Canada and settled in Alberta in 1979.

In regard to long-term difficulties stimulating Overseas Chinese migration to Canada, the situation in Hong Kong is of fundamental importance. Certainly, many immigrants who have left Hong Kong for Canada over the years have done so for personal reasons, such as maintaining family togetherness, seeking better economic opportunities, or advancing educational qualifications; but, there is another side, too, and both require attention.

In this respect, 1967 was not only notable for the removal of the last minor remnants of discrimination against Chinese immigrating to Canada. During the summer of 1967, Hong Kong experienced a bitter taste of the cataclysmic Great Proletarian Cultural Revolution convulsing China. The colony was afflicted for several months by strikes, mass demonstrations, and bombings; martial law was imposed. Many Chinese became apprehensive about their future and that of their children; they looked to a more open Canada as an attractive alternative in which to reside, either soon or in years to come.

From 1962 on—when immigration restrictions affecting the Chinese were relaxed significantly—more Hong Kong residents were enabled to reside in Canada. Before 1962, Chinese immigrants were nearly all close relatives of Canadian citizens; but, after 1962, Chinese also could and did enter as unsponsored migrants, admitted because they had skills to contribute to the country's economic well-being. A relatively large number of Hong Kong residents arrived from 1962 to 1967; after 1967 a greater number arrived, including many students.

Obtaining a post-secondary education in Hong Kong has been extremely difficult for decades. It has been impossible for the great majority of eligible young people to attend university locally, because only a small percentage of applicants could be enrolled at the colony's two universities. Accordingly, "the educational system [has been] extremely competitive and the strain on pupils and parents alike [has been] substantial. The less pressured, more open system in Canada [facilitated many people's] decision to migrate."[13]

Moreover, of strict necessity, many students successfully applied to Canadian universities, colleges, and technical institutes and came by themselves to Canada. A significant number of these young people decided to remain in Canada.

Tony Leong, for example, arrived in Canada in 1968 and completed courses in drafting and business management. Dr. Stephen Tse came to Canada in 1969 at age twenty-two and completed a dentistry program. Dr. Nicholas Choi arrived in Alberta in 1972 at age twenty; he obtained a bachelor of science degree, before pursuing a chiropractic career. Dr. Patrick Lai came to Alberta in 1971 at age nineteen; after earning a Ph.D. in physiology, he attended medical school and now works as a general practitioner. Vincent Lau arrived in the mid-1970s and earned a university degree in engineering.

Immigration from Hong Kong

During the 1970s and 1980s, Chinese communities in Edmonton and Calgary experienced significant growth, primarily because of emigrants from Hong Kong. These contemporary arrivals were completely unlike those who had arrived 50 to 100 years previously. Through feature films and television, most people were already familiar with the popular culture and general life-styles of North Americans. A significant number had been partially or fully educated in English. Moreover, they were accustomed to the often rigorous demands of urban life. As a result, they have generally adapted very well to their new situation.

Two developments, in particular, have dramatically altered Hong Kong residents' attitudes toward emigration. In 1982 Prime Minister Thatcher made it public that her government would be giving in to Peking's demands for return of the colony *in toto*. News of this unexpected development struck the Hong Kong psyche with an impact and suddenness not unlike the typhoons which seemingly appear from nowhere and badly batter Hong Kong. (Subsequently, in 1984 Britain signed an agreement with the People's Republic whereby Hong Kong Island and Kowloon would also be returned to Chinese control when the New Territories' lease expired in July 1997).

Thatcher's announcement created great distress among the colony's residents and, of those who emigrated because of the new development, many headed to Canada. An authority on Hong Kong emigration wrote in 1989: "The panic of 1982-83...subsided, but the surge of interest in Canada that began in those years has hardly subsided at all."[14]

The second development concerned a news item that circled the globe on 5 June 1989. The previous evening, hard-line leaders in Peking had let loose tanks and troops to slaughter hundreds of unarmed students demanding democratic reforms and the resignations of leading government figures. The above-mentioned authority also wrote in 1989: "...fear and desperation—not greed—is the engine driving the Hong Kong exodus. That fear and desperation has now increased a hundredfold [because of the massacre] and so the drive to get to Canada and safety will increase in kind."[15]

Applications to enter Canada rose twenty-five per cent in 1989; most of the increase followed the events of 4 June. The Canadian High Commission in the colony expects no decrease whatsoever in demand for Canadian visas.

Hong Kong emigrants rank Canada first as their preferred country of destination. From 1987 through 1989 alone, fully 22 000 people a year—half of all those leaving the colony—have headed to Canada. About 5 300 of these immigrants have settled in Alberta during this period, bringing with them $130 million, which has been invested and has created many new jobs.

For the past twelve years, the Alberta government has been very active in Hong Kong, trying to persuade promising entrepreneurs to settle in Alberta. The impetus for this originated in 1979 when the federal government set out to recruit many more "business immigrants." As the recession of the 1980s gripped Canada, this aspect of immigration policy received much greater emphasis, and the number of business immigrants nearly doubled from 1979 to 1984.

Currently, business immigrants fall into three categories: self-employed businessmen, entrepreneurs, and investors; the latter category was added in 1986. To obtain visas, those in the Investor Program must have savings of at least $500 000 and agree to invest a large specified amount in a particular province. In the case of Alberta, the investment must be at least $250 000.

Those applying as entrepreneurs must submit a detailed proposal outlining their prospective business. An entrepreneur with business experience but no specific proposal, however, can submit a general plan and be granted a conditional visa; then he or she has two years to buy a business or establish an enterprise which employs at least one Canadian.

In 1988, 1 000 Hong Kong business immigrants entered Canada. About 200 of these immigrants were destined for Alberta, and over half went to Calgary. In 1989, of all Hong Kong immigrants who came to Alberta, business immigrants accounted for seventeen per cent of the arrivals.

The Cosmopolitan Component of Communities

The various Overseas Chinese immigrant groups which have settled in Alberta come from diverse sociocultural backgrounds. Chinese from Peru, say, have had a unique experience in adapting traditional Chinese culture to the society and culture of Peru; the same applies to Chinese from Jamaica, Johannesburg, Manila or Malaysia. Each specific group has experienced its own particular difficulties in adapting to foreign ways and, often, in choosing means to confront or dilute opposition to their very presence.

Though all groups share at least some sociocultural features, such as traditional festivals, veneration of elders, and the same written language, for example, the history and cultural heritage of every Overseas Chinese community is distinct. This diversity and variety of "cultural baggage" has served to enrich and invigorate Alberta's Chinese communities, rather than dilute their vitality or obscure their image. A definite cosmopolitan component has been added to what existed previously.

The broad diversity of Chinese organizations active in Alberta reflects both the differing backgrounds of members of the Chinese community and the many interests being served. Clan and locality associations have continued to operate since pioneer days and retain significance, though less than before the 1950s; moreover, interestingly, a goodly number of just such associations have been founded in Calgary and Edmonton during the last fifteen years.

Also, an ample number of relatively new organizations are meeting very real wants and needs. Some of these are outward-looking and are attempting to create greater mutual understanding between the Chinese community and Alberta society as a whole. There are other organizations which have been formed for quite specific purposes, such as: promoting bilingual education (English and Chinese); engaging in sports; performing community service; preserving traditional Chinese culture; advancing business owners' interests; and so on.

Well-educated professionals, in particular (both immigrants and second- or third-generation Canadian Chinese), have established new organizations, especially during the last twenty years. New community leaders have chosen to become involved in Canadian social, political, and cultural concerns, rather than become mired in the politics of China and Taiwan. On the other hand, important groups have been formed to preserve Chinese tradition and culture.

The formation and functioning of these groups, confined primarily to Edmonton and Calgary, exemplifies the rich infusion of Chinese culture into Alberta since 1967. Also, service organizations have been set up by the younger, better-educated portion of the community to help older residents and newcomers cope with urban life.

In respect to contemporary community leaders, several interviewees should be mentioned. Dr. K.W. Chang, a professor of mathematics, is representative of the well-educated professionals, mentioned above. Born and raised in West Malaysia, he graduated from university in Australia. In 1975, he was a founding member of the Chinese Cultural Society in Calgary. "We sought to promote greater understanding of contemporary China....Our aim has been to foster a closer relationship between Canada and China through cultural pursuits."[16] Interestingly, Dr. Chang's parents were natives of China who emigrated to Malaysia in their teens. Dr. Chang has served as president of the society, as well as chairman of the board of the Calgary Chinese Public School.

Another contemporary leader who was interviewed is Joe (José) Khu, who was born and raised in Manila, Philippines. He attended university in Chentu (Chengdu), China, from 1940 to 1945. After a career in business in Manila, he came to Canada in 1973.

Mr. Khu stated of his community involvement: "I have been active in Chinese community service since 1975. Only last year I was elected president of the United Calgary Chinese Association....Before that, I was the vice-president."[17] This association is particularly concerned with preserving important traditional festivals and promoting respect for Chinese elders. He added: "I taught Mandarin at the Calgary Chinese [Public] School for seven years. I found it interesting and satisfying. It is my belief that we should preserve our Chinese culture as much as possible."[18]

Since the mid-1970s, Kim Hung has played a significant role in Edmonton's Chinese community, helping to identify gaps in community services and helping considerably to meet the needs perceived.

Born in Fukien (Fujian) province in 1951, he completed his secondary education in Hong Kong and earned his bachelor of science degree at the University of Alberta in 1975.

Founder and past-president of the University of Alberta's Chinese Library Association (1971-1974), he has served in a wide range of other positions. These include: founder and chairman of the Edmonton Chinese Community Services Centre (1978 to the present); secretary (English) to the Chinese Benevolent Association (CBA) of Edmonton (1980-1982); president, Chinese Graduates' Association of Alberta (1987-1990); president, Edmonton CBA, (1982-1991), with additional responsibilities for the Chinatown Multi-Level Care Facility Foundation.

A goodly number of post-1967 immigrants are involved, to at least some extent, in activities which preserve and promote Chinese culture.[19] Moreover, many Chinese Canadians of the second, third, and even fourth and fifth, generation are likewise involved in culturally oriented activities, some over a period of many years.[20]

Changes in Occupational Patterns

The life-styles and various activities of Chinese Canadians—as well as the nature of their communities—have experienced considerable changes in virtually all respects during the last forty to fifty years. In terms of employment and job opportunities, the situation today is dramatically different from that of the 1930s or early 1940s.

Occupationally, more opportunities emerged soon after the Second World War. The changing tenor of the times was likely best exemplified in early 1945, when British Columbia—the customary Canadian bastion of anti-Chinese sentiment—gave the right to vote to Chinese who had served Canada in the armed forces in either world war.

By 1947 all Chinese in B.C. were enfranchised provincially and restrictions from engaging in various professions had been lifted. Watts D. Lee remarked upon the new Canada-wide situation: "...after the war, Chinese started all sorts of businesses. Nationally, there were more professional people, such as lawyers, doctors, engineers, pharmacists, and accountants among the Chinese community."[21]

Over the last fifty years or so, Chinese Canadians, as a group, have experienced substantial upward mobility. An examination of occupational patterns and educational attainment reveals that much has changed for the better, though various concerns remain to be addressed.

Regarding occupations, much has changed. In 1931 fully 61 per cent of Chinese workers were engaged in the service sector: they worked as servants, cooks, waiters, janitors, laundry workers, and unskilled workers. In 1981 service occupations accounted for 24.5 per cent of workers: though the service sector continued to employ the largest number of Chinese workers, the percentage had dropped a dramatic 36.5 per cent. Whereas in 1931 less than 1 per cent of Chinese workers had professional occupations, in 1981 technical and professional fields accounted for 17.8 per cent of workers, a striking increase.

Census data for 1981 indicated other substantial increases in certain sectors of employment. In 1931 clerical and related occupations among Chinese were virtually non-existent but, in 1981, 18.5 per cent of Chinese engaged in this type of work. Though customarily restricted from most skilled jobs until the 1940s, by 1981 Chinese to the extent of 16.5 per cent engaged in processing, machining, and construction occupations.

Increasingly, Chinese in Alberta have been entering the fields of financial management, business administration, and related areas. In 1981, for example, 4.9 per cent of Chinese workers in Canada were employed in managerial, administrative, and related occupations; whereas for other Canadians the percentage stood at 6.4 per cent. With the admission of many Chinese business immigrants and others with business-related backgrounds, by the time the 1991 Census of Canada figures are compiled, Chinese residents of Alberta will almost certainly be much closer to other Canadians, percentage-wise, in these white-collar areas.

Chinatowns

Cosmopolitan Chinese immigration since 1967 has, to varying degrees, invigorated nearly all Chinatowns in larger Canadian centres, including those in Calgary and Edmonton. No longer isolated urban enclaves, they have become increasingly vital entities. The customarily important role assumed by voluntary organizations has been an integral component in the process of forming resurgent Chinese communities. Both old and new organizations alike have generously made—and continue to make—their own unique contributions to the still-evolving essence of the new Chinatowns in Edmonton and Calgary.

When two blocks on the western side of 97th Street were demolished a decade ago, much of Edmonton's original Chinatown business district was destroyed. It was decided to officially relocate Chinatown to a four-block area to the east, where some Chinese premises were already located.

Partly because of problems relating to relocating businesses and subsequent set-backs in development, resulting from the recession of the 1980s, Edmonton's official Chinatown is not nearly as developed as Calgary's. Its prospects for a very good future, however, are excellent. Significant community organizations, institutions, and businesses are located in the district. Construction of some of these premises has occurred in relatively recent years; more such projects, as well as strictly commercial enterprises, are scheduled to be built.

Edmonton's official Chinatown has specific boundaries: an extremely important factor in both preserving and developing the district. Moreover, the civic government and its planning department are fully committed to the objective of systematically developing a Chinatown that will eventually rank reasonably high in Canadian terms. Already, the strikingly beautiful and imposing Chinatown Gate spans the recognized entrance to Chinatown. In coming years, the planned Chinese Ceremonial Square and classical Chinese Garden will add an aesthetically rich dimension to Chinatown and downtown Edmonton itself.

Because of the demolition of most of the original Chinatown business district, small business operators were forced to look elsewhere for new sites for their enterprises. Within a few years, an unofficial, commercially oriented, Chinatown was created along about seven blocks on both sides of 97th Street. The dynamic new Chinatown begins some blocks north of the northern boundary of the official Chinatown.

Accordingly, it seems certain that two separate Chinatowns will continue to exist in Edmonton: one, a commercial centre; the other, a cultural, recreational, and residential centre.

From 1965 to 1974 it seemed likely that most of Calgary's Chinatown would be demolished. On three separate occasions, city hall proposed that major freeways be laid down through the district's core. Had any of the

Restaurants and stores in Calgary's Chinatown, 1967.
Glenbow Archives, NA-2645-52.

proposals indeed been implemented, Chinatown would have ceased to exist. Also, in 1967 a new Centre Street Bridge was recommended; had a new bridge been built, the result would have been much the same.

In 1968 businessman Ray Lee established the Sien Lok Society to save Chinatown. Determined efforts by the new group and the community as a whole, led to the province and the city agreeing by 1971 to leave Chinatown intact—for the time being.

In 1973 the third civic freeway proposal was made public. Accordingly, under the dynamic leadership of MLA George Ho Lem, community members formed the Chinatown Development Task Force. The group mustered considerable community support and successfully fought the proposal. In 1974 the city was persuaded to officially designate boundaries for Chinatown. The task force subsequently submitted a design brief, calling for the revitalization of Chinatown; it was officially approved in 1976.

In 1974 work began on the Harry Hays Building, a major federal government structure occupying a full block in Chinatown. Erection of this massive structure, with its hundreds of employees (i.e., potential customers), dramatically stimulated development in Chinatown. But, in the early 1980s, developers wanting to build office high-rises threatened the integrity and character of the distinctive district.

Guided by the city's planning department, a committee representing community and corporate interests reached an agreement on development priorities in 1983. The agreement was a compromise: developers were permitted some building density and land reclassification provisions not included in the approved design brief; the community was given some free land at Second Avenue and First Street, South West, in Chinatown and a large amount of money toward building a cultural centre.

Even rival Chinese groups approved the eventual plan, and all community groups were pleased with the much more attainable goal of finally building a cultural centre. In 1986 city council officially put its stamp of approval on the agreement, by endorsing a blueprint for redevelopment, titled the Chinatown Area Redevelopment Plan. Since then, about ten building projects have been completed, and at least three others—one a $45 million complex—are being financed.

As of June 1990, $4.5 million of a needed $6 million had been raised to build the Calgary Chinese Cultural Centre. The association in charge of the project held the official sod-turning ceremony in October 1990, and the centre is scheduled to be finished in the spring of 1992. Modelled after the Temple of Heaven in Peking, the magnificent building will blend traditional Chinese architecture and contemporary Canadian architecture. Upon completion, the centre will become a major tourist attraction and a great asset to Chinatown, the Chinese community, and Calgary itself.

Appendix

Table 1
Total Population, and Chinese Population in Calgary, 1881-1926

	Chinese Population			
Year	Female	Male	Total	Total Calgary
1881	0	0	0	75
1891	0	unknown	unknown	3 876
1901	0	63	63	4 091
1906	unknown	unknown	416	11 967
1911	3	482	485	43 704
1916	13	555	568	56 474
1921	39	649	688	63 305
1926	25	414	439	65 291

Sources: Canada, *Dominion Census, 1881-1921*; *Census of the Prairie Provinces, 1906-1926.*

Table 2
Total Population, and Chinese Population in
Medicine Hat and Lethbridge, 1911-1926

	Chinese Population			
Year	Female	Male	Total	Total Population
Medicine Hat				
1911	-	-	unknown	5 608
1916	0	91	91	9 272
1921	7	94	101	9 634
1926	-	-	unknown	9 536
Lethbridge				
1911	2	106	108	9 035
1916	1	97	98	9 436
1921	8	162	170	11 097
1926	4	108	112	10 735

Sources: Canada, *Dominion Census, 1911-1921; Census of the Prairie Provinces, 1916, 1926.*

Table 3
Chinese Population in Edmonton, 1899-1926

Year	Number	% of Population
1899	13	0.59
1911	130	0.52
1916	329	0.61
1921	518	0.88
1926	332	0.51

Source: *Our Chosen Land*, p. 60; *From China to Canada*, pp. 303, 306; *Chinatowns*, p. 92.

Table 4
Chinese Businesses in Calgary, 1902-1911

Type of Businesses		1902	1906	1911
Grocery Stores	Chinese	unavailable	7	unavailable
	Other	16	38	unavailable
	Total	16 or more	45	104
Restaurants	Chinese	3	7	22
	Other	2	12	43
	Total	5	19	65
Laundries	Chinese	10	17	28
	Other	3	6	3
	Total	13	23	31

Sources: *Gronlunds' 1902 Directory, Henderson's Alberta Directory* for 1906 and 1911. City of Calgary License Records for 1902, 1906 and 1911.

Note: In 1911 there were 104 grocery stores listed in the directory, and, of at least 3 or 4 Chinese groceries known to have existed, none was listed; also, the licence records for 1911 were obscure in this respect.

Table 5
Chinese Businesses in Calgary, 1915-1925

Type of Businesses		1915	1920	1925
	Chinese	13	7	6
Grocery Stores	Other	149	142	155
	Total	162	149	161
	Chinese	26	22	24
Restaurants	Other	37	42	29
	Total	63	64	53
	Chinese	61	34	42
Laundries	Other	6	4	5
	Total	67	38	47

Sources: *Henderson's Alberta Directory* for 1915, 1920 and 1925.

Table 6
Chinese Businesses in Edmonton, 1920-1924

Type of Businesses		1920	1924
	Chinese	2	10
Grocery Stores	Other	114	210
	Total	116	220
	Chinese	25	24
Restaurants	Other	31	38
	Total	56	62
	Chinese	31	47
Laundries	Other	8	14
	Total	39	61

Sources: *Wrigley's Alberta Directory*, 1920; *Henderson's Alberta Directory*, 1924.

Table 7
Chinese Businesses in Medicine Hat, 1914-1924

Type of Businesses		1914	1920	1924
	Chinese	0	2	1
Grocery Stores	Other	17	27	29
	Total	17	29	30
	Chinese	7	4	4
Restaurants	Other	9	6	7
	Total	16	10	11
	Chinese	1	7	6
Laundries	Other	1	1	1
	Total	2	8	7

Sources: *Henderson's Alberta Directory* for 1914 and 1924; *Wrigley's Alberta Directory* for 1920.

Table 8
Chinese Businesses in Lethbridge, 1914-1924

Type of Businesses		1914	1920	1924
	Chinese	1	7	9
Grocery Stores	Other	20	12	23
	Total	21	19	32
	Chinese	10	10	12
Restaurants	Other	5	4	11
	Total	15	14	23
	Chinese	8	5	6
Laundries	Other	1	1	2
	Total	9	6	8

Sources: *Henderson's Alberta Directory* for 1914 and 1924; *Wrigley's Alberta Directory* for 1920.

Chapter Notes

Chapter 1

1. Peter Caley, "Canada's Chinese Columbus," *The Beaver,* Spring, 1983, p. 9.
2. Fang Zhongpu, "Did Chinese Buddhists Reach America 1,000 Years Before Columbus?", *China Reconstructs*, August, 1980, p. 65.
3. Peter Caley, op cit., p. 6.
4. Ibid., p. 8.
5. Fang Zhongpu, op cit., p. 65.
6. Peter Caley, op cit., p. 9.
7. Fang Zhongpu, op cit., p. 66.
8. Ibid.
9. Anthony B. Chan, *Gold Mountain* (Vancouver: New Star Books, 1983), p. 23.
10. Molly Joel Coye, Jon Livingston, eds., *China Yesterday and Today* (New York: Bantam Books, 1975), p. 145.
11. Anthony B. Chan, op cit., p. 26.
12. Franz Schurmann, Orville Schell, eds., *Imperial China* (New York: Vintage Books, 1967), p. 131.
13. Ibid., p. 178.
14. Shih-shan Henry Tsai, *China and the Overseas Chinese in the United States, 1868-1911* (Fayetteville, Arkansas: University of Arkansas Press, 1983), p. 10.
15. Ibid.
16. Joe How, Interview.
17. Fred Yee, Interview.
18. Jin Tan and Patricia E. Roy, *The Chinese in Canada* (Ottawa: Canadian Historical Association, 1985), p. 3.
19. Edgar Wickberg, ed., *From China to Canada* (Toronto: McClelland and Stewart, 1982), p. 9.
20. Ibid., p. 6.
21. Ibid., p. 10.
22. Ibid.
23. Ibid.
24. Stanford M. Lyman, "Overseas Chinese in America and Indonesia," *The Asian in North America* (Santa Barbara: ABC-Clio, Inc., 1970), p. 219.
25. Jack Chen, *The Chinese of America* (San Francisco: Harper & Row, 1980), p. 4.
26. Ibid.
27. Anthony B. Chan, op cit., p. 33.
28. Ibid.
29. Betty Lee Sung, *The Story of the Chinese in America* (New York: Collier Books, 1967), p. 35.
30. Edgar Wickberg, op cit., p. 16.
31. Anthony B. Chan, op cit., p. 67.
32. Stanford M. Lyman, *Chinese Americans* (New York: Random House, 1974), p. 63.
33. Edgar Wickberg, op cit., p. 53.
34. Anthony B. Chan, op cit., p. 13.
35. Edgar Wickberg, op cit., p. 83.

Chapter 2

1. *Calgary Herald*, January 23, 1886.
2. Ibid., June 6, 1888.
3. Ibid., June 13, 1888.
4. Ibid., October 3, 1888.
5. Ibid., October 10, 1888.
6. Stuart C. Miller, *The Unwelcome Immigrant* (Berkeley: University of California Press, 1969), p. 36.
7. Ibid., p. 11.
8. Anthony B. Chan, op cit., p. 11.
9. Ibid., p. 16.
10. James Morton, *In the Sea of Sterile Mountains* (Vancouver: J.J. Douglas, 1974), p. 172.
11. *Calgary Herald*, July 15, 1892.

12. Ibid., July 19, 1892.
13. Ibid., July 20, 1892.
14. Ibid., August 3, 1892.
15. Ibid., July 19, 1892.
16. Ibid., July 21, 1892.
17. Ibid., July 23, 1892.
18. Ibid., August 3, 1892.
19. Canada. Sessional Papers, 1893, XXVI, Vol. 10, No. 15, "Annual Report Inspector R. Cuthbert," Appendix J, Calgary, December 1, 1892, p. 128.
20. Ibid.
21. Ibid.
22. *Calgary Tribune*, August 3, 1892.
23. Max Foran and Heather MacEwan Foran, *Calgary: Canada's Frontier Metropolis, An Illustrated History* (Burlington: Windsor Publications, 1982), p. 57.
24. Canada. Sessional Papers, 1893, XXVI, Vol. 10, No. 15, "Annual Report Inspector R. Cuthbert," Appendix J, Calgary, December 1, 1892, p. 128.
25. *Calgary Herald*, August 3, 1892.
26. Ibid., August 5, 1892.
27. *Calgary Tribune*, August 5, 1892.
28. Ibid.
29. *Calgary Tribune*, August 17, 1892.
30. *Calgary Herald*, August 17, 1892.
31. Ibid.
32. *Calgary Herald*, August 24, 1892.
33. Ibid., August 10, 1892.
34. *Calgary Tribune,* August 10, 1892.
35. *Calgary Herald*, August 19, 1892.
36. The term "garrison mentality" has been employed by Northrop Frye as an important concept in analyzing Canadian cultural history. See: Northrop Frye, "Conclusion," in Carl F. Klinck, *Literary History of Canada: Canadian Literature in English* (Toronto: University of Toronto Press, 1965), especially pp. 830-834.
37. Howard D. Palmer, "Anti-Oriental Sentiment in Alberta, 1880-1920," *Canadian Ethnic Studies*, Vol. II, No. 2, December, 1970, passim.
38. Cheng Tien-fang, *Oriental Immigration in Canada* (Shanghai: Commercial Press, 1931), p. 181.
39. *Medicine Hat Times*, March 26, 1887.
40. Ibid., April 16, 1887.
41. Ibid., April 14, 1892.
42. Ibid., September 17, 1891.
43. *Medicine Hat News*, February 3, 1910.
44. *Lethbridge News*, August 10, 1892.
45. *Lethbridge Herald,* December 6, 1905.
46. Ibid., November 22, 1905.
47. Ibid., October 17, 1907.
48. *Lethbridge News,* October 3, 1905.
49. Ibid., October 6, 1905.
50. *Lethbridge Herald*, January 1, 1908.
51. Ibid.
52. Ibid.
53. *Lethbridge Herald*, February 26, 1909.
54. Ibid., March 9, 1909.
55. Ibid., September 7, 1909.
56. *Lethbridge News*, September 8, 1909.
57. *Lethbridge Herald,* September 21, 1909.
58. J.H. Carpenter, T*he Badge and the Blotter* (Lethbridge: The Whoop-Up Country Chapter, Historical Society of Alberta, 1975), p. 34.
59. *Edmonton Bulletin*, December 1, 1883.
60. J.G. MacGregor, *Edmonton, A History* (Edmonton: Hurtig Publishers, 1975), p. 114.
61. *Edmonton Bulletin*, May 23, 1908.
62. *Edmonton Journal*, February 8, 1909.
63. *Edmonton Bulletin*, August 15, 1892.
64. Ibid., September 14, 1907.

65. *Edmonton Journal*, October 4, 1907.
66. Ibid., August 28, 1907.
67. Ibid., March 25, 1908.
68. Ibid., May 23, 1910.
69. *Calgary Herald*, September 24, 1884.
70. Ibid., November 5, 1884.
71. Ibid., February 10, 1885.
72. Ibid., June 13, 1888.
73. Ban-Seng Hoe, "Structural Changes of Two Chinese Communities in Alberta, Canada" (Vanderbilt University, 1974). Unpublished Ph.D. Dissertation, p. 91. Hereafter, referred to as Ban-Seng Hoe, Ph.D.
74. Ibid.
75. *Calgary Herald*, September 10, 1907.
76. *Calgary Albertan*, September 12, 1907.
77. Ibid., August 19, 1910.
78. *Lethbridge Herald*, October 3, 1907.
79. Ibid., October 24, 1907.
80. Ibid., March 20, 1909.
81. *Macleod Gazette*, December 23, 1898.
82. Ibid.
83. Ban-Seng Hoe, Ph.D., p. 91.
84. *Edmonton Journal*, July 28, 1910.
85. *Calgary Albertan*, October 4, 1910.
86. Ibid., October 11, 1910.
87. *Calgary Herald*, October 13, 1910.
88. *Calgary Albertan*, October 14, 1910.
89. Ibid.
90. Ibid.
91. Paul Dofoo, Interview.
92. June Jay Chang, Interview.
93. *Calgary Herald*, October 11, 1910.
94. *Calgary Albertan*, October 14, 1910.
95. *Calgary Herald*, October 7, 1910.
96. Ibid.
97. *Calgary Albertan*, October 15, 1910.
98. *Calgary Herald*, October 14, 1910.
99. Ibid., October 13, 1910.

Chapter 3

1. King Loo, Interview.
2. Seto Gan, Interview.
3. Charlie Chew, Interview.
4. Joe How, Interview.
5. Ibid.
6. Charles Lee, Interview.
7. Stanford M. Lyman, "Contrasts in the Community Organization of Chinese and Japanese in North America," *Canadian Review of Sociology and Anthropology*, Vol V, No. 2, May, 1968, p. 59.
8. Ibid.
9. Ibid.
10. Toe You Mah, Interview.
11. Ook Wah Yee, Interview.
12. Charlie Chew, Interview.
13. Joe How, Interview.
14. Ook Wah Yee, Interview.
15. June Jay Chang, Interview.
16. King Loo, Interview.
17. Henry C. Klassen, "Life in Frontier Calgary," in Anthony W. Rasporich and Henry C. Klassen, eds., *Western Canada: Past and Present* (Calgary: McClelland and Stewart West, 1975), p. 46.
18. Fred Yee, Interview.
19. *Chinatown News*, October 3, 1975.
20. Emely Johnston, Corbet Locke, John Mayer, Tom Moore, Dalwin Stanford and Lou Zeer, *Communities Six* (Calgary: Century Calgary, 1975), p. 38.
21. Nanton and District Historical Society, *Mosquito Creek Roundup* (Nanton: Nanton and District Historical Society, 1976), p. 103.
22. *Edmonton Journal*, February 14, 1930.
23. David Bercuson, *Settling the Canadian West* (Toronto: Grolier, 1984), p. 42.

24. Edna Appleby, *Canmore* (Canmore: Author, 1975), p. 66.
25. A.H. Clark, "The Conquering Cook," *Canada West*, Winter, 1979.
26. Crowsnest Pass Historical Society, *Crowsnest and Its People* (Coleman: Crowsnest Pass Historical Society, 1979), p. 86.
27. *Edmonton Journal*, March 23, 1911.
28. *Chinatown News*, December 3, 1976.
29. *Saint John's Calgary Report*, August 14, 1978.
30. Paul C.P. Siu, "The Sojourner," *American Journal of Sociology*, Vol. LVII, July, 1952, p. 34.
31. Jin Tan and Patricia E. Roy, op cit., p.4.
32. Ibid.
33. Stanford M. Lyman, "The Chinese Diaspora in America, 1850-1943," *The Asian in North America* (Santa Barbara: ABC-Clio, Inc., 1970), p. 15.
34. Jack Chen, op cit., p. 61.
35. Anthony B. Chan, "The Myth of the Chinese Sojourner in Canada," K. Victor Ujimoto and Gordon Hirabayashi, eds., *Visible Minorities and Multiculturalism: Asians in Canada* (Toronto: Butterworth, 1980), p. 35.
36. Ibid., p. 38.
37. Anthony B. Chan, "'Orientalism' and Image Making: The Sojourner in Canadian History," *Journal of Ethnic Studies*, Vol. 9, Fall, 1981, p. 43.
38. Betty Lee Sung, op cit., p. 133.
39. Ibid.
40. Ibid.
41. Lyman, "Contrasts in the Community Organization...," *pp. 53-54.*
42. Paul Dofoo, Interview.
43. Ibid.
44. Cheng Tien-fang, op cit., p. 18.
45. Stanford M. Lyman, "The Structure of Chinese Society in Nineteenth-Century America" (Berkeley: University of California, 1961). Unpublished Ph.D. Dissertation, pp. 329-330.
46. *Calgary Albertan*, May 26, 1913.
47. *Calgary Herald*, December 18, 1973.
48. James H. Carpenter, Interview.
49. Ibid.
50. Joe How, Interview.
51. James H. Carpenter, Interview.
52. Ibid.
53. Emily Murphy, *The Black Candle* (Toronto: T. Allen Co., 1922), p. 287.
54. Terry L. Chapman, "Drug Use in Western Canada," *Alberta History*, Vol. 24, No. 4, Autumn, 1976, p. 18.
55. J.H. Carpenter, op cit., p. 24.
56. Joe How, Interview.
57. Ibid.
58. George Fong, Interview.
59. Charlie Chew, Interview.
60. J.H. Carpenter, op cit., p. 25.
61. *Chinatown News*, May 18, 1981.
62. Ibid., June 3, 1976.
63. Ibid., August 3, 1984.
64. Ban-seng Hoe, "Adaptive Change and Overseas Chinese Settlements, With Special Reference to a Chinese Community in the Canadian Prairies" (Edmonton: University of Alberta, 1971). Unpublished M.A. Thesis, p. 186.
65. *Chinatown News*, September 18, 1976.
66. *Medicine Hat News*, February 3, 1910.
67. Ibid., February 1, 1911.
68. *Lethbridge News*, February 18, 1904.
69. *Lethbridge Herald*, January 22, 1909.
70. *Calgary Albertan*, Centennial Edition, May, 1975, p. 7B.
71. *Calgary Albertan*, February 8, 1967.

72. Ibid., January 31, 1911.
73. Ms. in the possession of the author by J. Fraser Perry, author of a history of Central Methodist Church.
74. *Calgary Albertan*, January 28, 1956.
75. Chinese United Church, *Dedication Service*, December 19, 1954, p. 2.
76. *Calgary Albertan*, January 25, 1922.
77. Rev. David Wen, Interview.
78. Chinese United Church, op cit., p. 2.
79. G. Baureiss, "The City and the Sub-community: The Chinese of Calgary" (Calgary: University of Calgary, 1971). Unpublished M.A. Thesis, pp. 36-37.
80. Ibid., p. 44.
81. *Calgary Albertan*, January 25, 1922.
82. Ibid.
83. Ban-Seng Hoe, Ph.D., p. 179.
84. *Calgary Albertan*, January 25, 1922.
85. Ibid., November 1, 1921.
86. W. Peter Ward, "The Oriental Immigrant and Canada's Protestant Clergy, 1858-1925," *B.C. Studies*, No. 22, Summer, 1974, p. 44.
87. Betty Lee Sung, op cit., p. 218.
88. *Calgary Albertan*, September 16, 1913.
89. Ibid.
90. Ibid.
91. Chinese United Church, op cit., p. 6.
92. Ibid.
93. *Edmonton Bulletin*, May 23, 1908.
94. Ban-Seng Hoe, *Structural Changes of Two Chinese Communities in Alberta, Canada* (Ottawa: National Museum of Man, 1976), National Museum of Man Mercury Series, Canadian Centre for Folk Culture Studies, Paper No. 19, p. 79. Hereafter Ban-Seng Hoe, Book.
95. *Calgary Albertan*, March 6, 1912.
96. Ibid., January 4, 1913.
97. Ibid., November 1, 1921.
98. Ibid., December 21, 1921.
99. Ibid.
100. *Calgary Albertan*, March 7, 1921.
101. Ban-Seng Hoe, Ph.D., pp. 214-215.
102. Ibid., p. 215.
103. G. Baureiss, op cit., p. 45.
104. Ibid
105. Ban-Seng Hoe, Ph.D., p. 184.

Chapter 4

1. Betty Lee Sung, op cit., p. 134.
2. W.E. Willmott, "Approaches to the Study of the Chinese in British Columbia," *B.C. Studies*, Vol. XIV, No. 1, Spring, 1970, p. 39.
3. Stanford M. Lyman, *Chinese Americans*, p. 9.
4. Ibid., p. 17.
5. T.C. Fan, "Chinese Residents in Chicago" (Chicago: University of Chicago, 1926). Unpublished Ph.D. Dissertation, pp. 76-77.
6. Ban-Seng Hoe, Book, p. 126.
7. William E. Willmott, "Chinese Clan Associations in Vancouver," *Man*, Vol. LXIV, No. 49, 1964, p. 34.
8. G. Baureiss, op cit., p. 50.
9. Jimmy Lee, Interview.
10. Joe How, Interview.
11. Jimmy Lee, Interview.
12. Charlie Chew, Interview.
13. Stanford M. Lyman, *Chinese Americans*, pp. 17-18.
14. Ibid., p. 18.
15. Edgar Wickberg, op cit., p. 106.
16. Jimmy Lee, Interview.
17. Stanford M. Lyman, *Chinese Americans*, p. 37.
18. Charles Drage, *Two-Gun Cohen* (London: Jonathan Cape, 1954), p. 37.

19. Rose Hum Lee, *The Chinese in the United States of America* (Hong Kong: Oxford University Press, 1960), p. 169.
20. Stanford M. Lyman, "Chinese Secret Societies in the Occident: Notes and Suggestions for Research in the Sociology of Secrecy," *Canadian Review of Sociology and Anthropology*, Vol I, No. 2, May, 1964, p. 84.
21. William E. Willmott, "Some Aspects of Chinese Communities in British Columbia," *B.C. Studies*, No. 8, Winter, 1968, p. 32.
22. J. Brooks Joyner, "Lethbridge Chinatown: An Analysis of the Kwong On Lung Co. Building, the Bow On Tong Co. Building, and the Chinese Free Masons Building," Historic Sites Service, Alberta Culture, endnote no. 72.
23. J. Brian Dawson, "The Chinese Community of Lethbridge," Historic Sites Service, Alberta Culture, pp. 8-9.
24. Ibid., p. 8.
25. Stanford M. Lyman, *Chinese Americans*, p. 39.
26. James Morton, op cit., p. 195.
27. *Calgary Herald*, April 27, 1939.
28. *Medicine Hat News*, February 5, 1903.
29. Ibid.
30. *Calgary Albertan*, November 18, 1919.
31. Ibid., March 5, 1921.
32. Ibid.
33. *Calgary Herald*, October 15, 1923.
34. Ibid.
35. Ibid.
36. *Lethbridge Herald*, June 7, 1915.
37. Ibid.
38. Ibid.
39. Ibid.
40. Ibid.
41. *Lethbridge Herald*, June 4, 1917.
42. Ibid.
43. Ibid.
44. *Lethbridge Herald*, June 1, 1917.
45. Ibid., June 16, 1919.
46. Ibid.
47. Ibid.
48. Jimmy Lee, Interview.
49. Ibid.
50. Ibid.
51. *Edmonton Journal*, April 25, 1919.
52. Paul L. Voisey, "Two Chinese Communities in Alberta: An Historical Perspective," *Canadian Ethnic Studies*, Vol. II, No. 2, Spring, 1972, p. 20.
53. William E. Willmott, "Some Aspects of Chinese Communities in British Columbia," p. 34.
54. From a letter of James Short, K.C., to the Hon J.R. Boyle, Attorney-General of Alberta, dated February 28, 1919. Department of the Attorney-General of Alberta, Criminal Files, 1915-1928 (Edmonton: Provincial Archives of Alberta), Acc. No. 72.26, f.f. 1962/c. Hereafter, this acquisition will be referred to as *Criminal Files, 1915-1928.*
55. Ibid.
56. From a letter of James Short, K.C., to the Attorney-General of Alberta, dated October 29, 1920, *Criminal Files, 1915-1928*, f.f. 3083/c.
57. *Calgary Albertan*, February 13, 1919.
58. From a letter of W.A. Begg to the Office of the Attorney-General of Alberta, dated February 17, 1917, *Criminal Files, 1915-1928*, f.f. 637/c.
59. Ibid.
60. From a letter of C.F.P. Conybeare to Deputy Attorney-General A.G. Browning, dated May 13, 1918, *Criminal Files, 1915-1928*, f.f. 1430/c.
61. From a telegram of D.H. Elton to the Office of the Attorney-General, dated June 21, 1918. Ibid.

62. From a letter of C.F.P. Conybeare to Deputy Attorney-General A.G. Browning, dated August 24, 1918. *Criminal Files, 1915-1928*, f.f. 1337/c.
63. *Calgary Albertan*, March 7, 1921.
64. Ibid., March 18, 1921.
65. Joe How, Interview.
66. Ibid.
67. Ibid.
68. Willmott, "Some Aspects of Chinese Communities...," p. 34.

Chapter 5

1. Howard D. Palmer, "Anti-Oriental Sentiment in Alberta, 1880-1920," p. 31.
2. Ibid., p. 47.
3. Ibid., p. 34.
4. Patricia E. Roy, "The Oriental 'Menace' in British Columbia," Susan Trofimenkoff, ed., *The Twenties in Western Canada* (Ottawa: National Museum of Man, 1972), p. 243.
5. *Calgary Herald,* February 3, 1908.
6. *Calgary Albertan*, May 3, 1922.
7. Ibid., January 25, 1913.
8. Peter S. Li, *The Chinese in Canada* (Toronto: Oxford University Press, 1988), p. 65. Supporting this conclusion, see: Ibid., p. 138, Note 3, Chapter 4. One newspaper remarked in this respect: "We do not want to see white girls becoming the wives of Chinamen—especially the class of Chinamen inhabiting this country." *Lethbridge Herald*, June 20, 1912.
9. *Calgary Albertan*, November 27, 1913.
10. Ibid., December 1, 1913.
11. Calgary Eye-Opener, May 18, 1912.
12. Paul Voisey, op cit., p. 19.
13. Howard D. Palmer, "Anti-Oriental Sentiment in Alberta, 1880-1920," p. 40.
14. *Calgary Albertan*, June 12, 1913.
15. Howard D. Palmer, "Anti-Oriental Sentiment in Alberta, 1880-1920," p. 36.
16. *Calgary Albertan*, July 3, 1920.
17. From a letter of the Hon. V.W. Smith, Minister of Railways and Telephones, to R.W. Jones, Managing Director, Mackenzie Basin Fisheries Company, dated November 30, 1921, *Premier's Office* (Edmonton: Provincial Archives of Alberta), Acc. 69.239.
18. From a letter of R.W. Jones to the Hon. V.W. Smith, dated December 15, 1921, ibid.
19. Ibid.
20. From a letter of J.E. Young to the Hon. H. Greenfield, dated February 2, 1922, ibid.
21. *Calgary Albertan*, June 27, 1916.
22. Ibid., July 30, 1919.
23. Ibid.
24. Ibid.
25. *Lethbridge Herald,* June 19, 1916.
26. Howard Palmer, "Patterns of Racism: Attitudes Towards Chinese and Japanese in Alberta 1920-1950," *Social History*, Vol. 8, No. 25 (1980), pp. 140-141.
27. *Edmonton Journal*, June 29, 1914.
28. *Calgary Herald*, September 22, 1909.
29. Ibid., October 13, 1910.
30. James H. Gray, *Red Lights on the Prairies* (Scarborough: The New American Library of Canada Ltd., 1973), pp. 167-168.
31. *Calgary Albertan*, February 4, 1911.
32. Ibid.
33. *Calgary Herald*, March 23, 1910.
34. James H. Gray, op cit., p. 175.
35. Ibid., pp. 175-181.
36. *Calgary Herald*, March 11, 1912.
37. *Calgary News-Telegram*, April 30, 1912.
38. Ibid.
39. *Calgary Albertan*, January 7, 1914.
40. Ibid., July 9, 1914.
41. *Calgary Herald,* January 4, 1915.

42. *Calgary Albertan*, May 15, 1914.
43. Ibid., May 16, 1914.
44. Ibid., May 18, 1914.
45. Patricia E. Roy, "Educating the 'East': British Columbia and the Oriental Question in the Interwar Years," *B.C. Studies,* Vol. XVIII, Spring, 1973, p. 52.
46. *Calgary Albertan*, May 4, 1920.
47. Ibid., June 10, 1920.
48. Ibid., February 23, 1921.
49. Ibid., March 3, 1921.
50. Ibid., April 18, 1921.
51. Ibid.
52. Ibid.
53. James H. Gray, *The Roar of the Twenties* (Toronto: Macmillan of Canada, 1975), p. 7.
54. James Morton, op cit., p. 234.
55. Ibid., p. 231.
56. Ibid., p. 236.
57. Ibid., p. 239.
58. Cheng Tien-fang, op cit., pp. 96-97.
59. Ibid., p. 97.
60. Ibid., pp. 97-98.
61. *Calgary Herald*, April 28, 1923.
62. Ibid.
63. *Calgary Herald,* July 11, 1923.

Interlude

1. Jin Tan and Patricia E. Roy, op cit., p. 16.
2. Freda Hawkins, *Canada and Immigration: Public Policy and Public Concern* (Montreal: McGill-Queen's University Press, 1972), p. 102.
3. Jin Tan and Patricia E. Roy, op cit., p. 16.
4. Phat Wu and Hong Tai Au, "Facts about Ethnic Chinese from Vietnam," *Refugees from Southeast Asia: Their Background* (Toronto: Ontario Ministry of Culture and Recreation, 1980), p. 17.
5. Peter S. Li, "The Economic Cost of Racism to Chinese-Canadians," *Canadian Ethnic Studies*, Vol. XIX, No. 3, 1987, p. 106.
6. Jin Tan and Patricia E. Roy, op cit., p. 16.
7. Edgar Wickberg, ed., op cit., p. 245.
8. Ibid.

Chapter 6

1. Joe How, Interview.
2. Jimmy Lee, Interview.
3. Fred Yee, Interview.
4. Ibid.
5. James H. Carpenter, Interview.
6. Howard Palmer, "Patterns of Racism: Attitudes Towards Chinese and Japanese in Alberta 1920-1950," p. 146.
7. Ibid., p. 148.
8. Ban-Seng Hoe, Ph.D., p. 99.
9. *Calgary Herald*, April 27, 1939.
10. Ibid.
11. Howard Palmer, "Patterns of Racism: Attitudes Towards Chinese and Japanese in Alberta 1920-1950," p. 159.
12. *Calgary Herald*, September 25, 1952.
13. Edgar Wickberg, ed., op cit., p. 260.
14. *Calgary Herald*, June 21, 1987.
15. Ibid., July 16, 1987.
16. Ibid.
17. G. Baureiss, op cit., p. 97.
18. *Chinatown News*, December 18, 1976.
19. Ibid.
20. Ban-Seng Hoe, Ph.D., p. 237.
21. Dr. Kok-Wah Chang, Interview.
22. *Calgary Herald*, June 21, 1987.
23. Ibid.

Chapter 7

1. Bing K. Mah, Interview, 1990.
2. Ibid

3. *Edmonton Journal*, February 26, 1980.
4. Ibid., October 31, 1987.
5. Ban-Seng Hoe, Book, p. 183.
6. Ibid., p. 203.
7. City of Edmonton, Planning and Building Department, *Edmonton's New Chinatown*, 1986, p. 2 (not numbered).
8. *Edmonton Journal*, February 18, 1985.
9. Ed Lam, Interview.
10. Alderman Lance White, Interview, 1988.

Chapter 8

1. Lyman, "Contrasts in the Community Organization...," p. 55.
2. Willmott, "Some Aspects of Chinese Communities...," p. 34.
3. Li, *The Chinese in Canada*, p. 25.
4. Charlie Chew, Interview.
5. Li, *The Chinese in Canada*, p. 30.
6. Fred Yee, Interview.
7. Ibid.
8. Mrs. Helen Mock, Interview.
9. Frank Lung, Interview.
10. Mrs. Alice Louie-Byne, Interview.
11. Ibid.
12. Buck Doo Yee, Interview.
13. Li, *The Chinese in Canada,* p. 33.
14. Charles Lee, Interview.
15. Charlie Chew, Interview.
16. Ibid.
17. Ibid.
18. Paul Dofoo, Interview.
19. Mrs. Tenie Quan, Interview.
20. Arthur Yee Mock, Interview.
21. June Jay Chang, Interview.
22. Ibid.
23. Buck Doo Yee, Interview.
24. Ook Wah Yee, Interview.
25. Ibid.
26. Jimmy (Hon Men) Lee, Interview.
27. Ibid.
28. Byng Lee, Interview.
29. Charles Lee, Interview.
30. Paul Dofoo, Interview.
31. Jimmy (Hon Men) Lee, Interview.
32. Ibid.
33. Fred Yee, Interview.
34. Johnny Long, Interview.
35. Fred Yee, Interview.
36. Peter S. Li, "Chinese Immigrants on the Canadian Prairie, 1910-47," *Canadian Review of Sociology and Anthropology* (No. 4, 1982): p. 534.
37. Ibid., p. 535.
38. Joe How, Interview.
39. Kim Dong, Interview.
40. Ibid.
41. Toe You Mah, Interview.

Chapter 9

1. Paul Dofoo, Interview.
2. Chan, *Gold Mountain*, p. 146.
3. Watts D. Lee, Interview.
4. Charlie Chew, Interview.
5. Paul Tse, Interview.
6. Peter Ng, Interview.
7. Johnnie Chui, Interview.
8. Ng Yuk Sum, Interview.
9. Ibid.
10. Mrs. Agatha Lim, Interview.
11. José Khu, Interview.
12. Khuu Biuh Phu, Interview.
13. Wickberg, ed., *From China to Canada*, p. 250.

14. Margaret Cannon, *China Tide: The Revealing Story of the Hong Kong Exodus to Canada* (Toronto: Harper & Collins, 1989), p. 46.
15. Ibid., p. 16.
16. Dr. Kok-Wah Chang, Interview.
17. José Khu, Interview.
18. Ibid.
19. Excluding Mr. Khu and Dr. Chang, of the contemporary immigrants interviewed for this study, the following have been active in Chinese organizations and have held the positions, or had the affiliations, listed:

    Dr. Nicholas Choi (president, Chinese Soccer Club); Michael Ho (member, United Calgary Chinese Association); Hornby Jear (principal and teacher, Chinese Public School; director, Sien Lok Society; member, Chinese United Church); Rev. Dr. John Kong (minister, Chinese Pentecostal Church; member, Sue Yuen Tong); Mrs. Virginia Lui (vice-principal, Chinese Public School); Sen Mah (chairman, Mah Association; chairman, Chinese Freemasons); Rev. Father John Mak (priest, serving Cantonese-speaking Catholics); Ng Yuk Sum (member, Ng Association; adviser to: Calgary Toi Shan [Toi-san] Association, Canada Chinese Television Ltd., and Taiwan Alumni Association; member, Chinese Freemasons; director, Chinese Public School).

20. In regard to Canadian-born Chinese interviewed for this study, the following have been active in Chinese organizations and have held the positions, or had the affiliations, listed:

    Paul Dofoo (treasurer, Chinese United Church); Mrs. Violet George (president, Sien Lok Society); George Ho Lem (member, Chinese United Church; chairman, Chinatown Development Task Force; chairman, Chinatown Development Foundation; chairman, Oi Kwan Foundation); Jimmy (Hon Men) Lee (president, Chinese National League); Raymond T. Lee (member, Lee Association); Mrs. Annie Louie (elder, Chinese United Church; director, Sien Lok Society; director, Wai Kwan Foundation; director, Chinatown Development Foundation; president, Chinese Curling Club); Mrs. Alice Louie-Byne (member, Chinese United Church; member, Sue Yuen Tong; member, United Calgary Chinese Association; member, Chinese Public School Association); Frank Lung (member, Wong Family Association); Mrs. Helen Mock (steward, Chinese United Church; member, Sue Yuen Tong; director, Sien Lok Society); Mrs. Tenie Quan (member, Lee Association; member, Chinese United Church; member, United Calgary Chinese Association).

    With one possible exception (someone who might be third-generation), all of the above-mentioned are second-generation Chinese Canadians and, except for Raymond T. Lee, all are over sixty years of age.

    Growing up as they did during the Exclusion Era, this second generation naturally forged powerful emotional, psychological, and intellectual bonds to their own community, its cultural heritage, and the various means by which its essence was expressed.

    Though acculturated to quite an extent, then, in many ways this group was also very much traditionally Chinese. So, it was to be expected that, as adults, they would conduct many of their social, religious, recreational, and cultural activities in the world they felt closest to and knew best—the Chinese community.

21. Watts D. Lee, Interview.

Selected Bibliography

A. Primary Sources

Government Documents

Canada. Dominion Bureau of Statistics. "Census," 1881, 1891, 1901, 1911 and 1921.

——. Dominion Bureau of Statistics. "Census of the Prairie Provinces," 1906, 1916 and 1926.

——. Sessional Papers. 1893, XXVI, Vol. 10, No. 15, "Annual Report Inspector R. Cuthbert," Appendix J, Calgary, Dec. 1, 1892.

Manuscripts, Document Collections and Pamphlets (Archival Collections)

Glenbow Archives. *City of Calgary Papers*, 1886-1957.

——. *Gronlunds' Calgary Directory*, 1902.

——. *Henderson's Alberta Directory*, 1914 and 1924.

——. *Henderson's Calgary Directory*, 1906, 1911, 1915, 1916, 1917, 1918, 1919, 1920 and 1925.

——. *Wrigley's Alberta Directory*, 1920.

Provincial Archives of Alberta. Department of the Attorney-General of Alberta, *Criminal Files*, 1915-1928.

——. Premier's Office, *Files*.

Contemporary Books

Cheng, Tien-fang. *Oriental Immigration in Canada*. Shanghai: Commercial Press, 1931.

Murphy, Emily. *The Black Candle*. Toronto: T. Allen Co., 1922.

Newspapers

Calgary Albertan, 1895; 1902-1925; 1956; 1967; 1975.

Calgary Eye-Opener, 1912.

Calgary Herald, 1885-1990.

Calgary News-Telegram, 1912.

Calgary Tribune, 1885-1895.

Chinatown News, 1975; 1976; 1981; 1984.

Edmonton Bulletin, 1883; 1892; 1908; 1921.

Edmonton Journal, 1885-1990.

Lethbridge Herald, 1905-1925.

Medicine Hat News, 1900-1925.

Medicine Hat Times, 1886-1899.

Interviews

1974: June Jay Chang; Luey Dofoo; Kim Dong; Charles Lee; King Loo; Toe You Mah; Seto Gan; Rev. David Wen; Buck Doo Yee; Ook Wah Yee; Poy Yee.

1975: Dr. Thomas Y. Huang; Fred Wong.

1984: James Leong.

1985: James H. Carpenter; Rev Paul Chan; Dr. Kok-Wah ("K.W.") Chang; Charlie Chew (Leung Chew Thang); Dr. Nicholas Y.K. Choi; L. Chong; Johnnie P.H. Chui; Paul Dofoo; George Fong; Mrs. Violet George; Michael L.L. Ho; George Ho Lem, Sr.; Joe (L.) How; Hornby Jear; Jack L. Kheong; Joe Kheong; José (Joe) Khu; Khuu Biuh Phu; Rev. Dr. John W.S. Kong; Dr. Patrick C.W. Lai; Vincent Lau; Byng Lee; Lee Hoy; Jimmy Lee (Lee Hon Men); Raymond T. Lee; Watts D. Lee; Albert Leong; Tony C.F. Leong; Mrs. Agatha Lim; Charles Liu; Johnny Long (Leung Kung Nan); Mrs. Annie Louie; Mrs. Alice Louie-Byne; Charles Lui; Mrs. Virginia Lui; Frank Lung; Sen Mah; Rev. Father John E.K. Mak; Arthur Yee Mock; Mrs. Helen Mock; Peter Ng; Ng Yuk Sum; Allan Poon; David Quan; Mrs. Tenie Quan; Raymond Sung; Paul Tse; Dr. Stephen Tse; Peter Wong; Fred Yee (Yee Sue Yen); Paul Yee; George Yip.

1988: Rev. Paul Chan; Ed Lam; Kulbir Singh (Senior Downtown Planner, City of Edmonton); Alderman Lance White; Frank Wong.

1990: Dr. Steven K.H. Aung; Ken Chen; Kan Ki Chiu; Games Choy; Frank Gee; Jimmy Gin; Kim Hung; Bing K. Mah; Henry Mah; Kim Mah; Can Thieu Pho; Ching-Wah Tse; Joe Wong.

B. Secondary Sources

Books

Adelman, Howard. *Canada and the Indochinese Refugees*. Regina: L.A. Weigl Educational Associates Ltd., 1982.

Appleby, Edna. *Canmore*. Canmore: Author, 1975.

Barth, G. *Bitter Strength*. Cambridge: Harvard University Press, 1964.

Bercuson, David. *Settling the Canadian West*. Toronto: Grolier, 1984.

Burnet, Jean R. with Howard Palmer. *"Coming Canadians:" An Introduction to a History of Canada's Peoples*. Toronto: McClelland and Stewart, 1988.

Berton, Pierre. *The Last Spike*. Toronto: McClelland and Stewart, 1971.

Cannon, Margaret. *China Tide*. Toronto: Harper & Collins, 1989.

Carpenter, J.H. *The Badge and the Blotter*. Lethbridge: The Whoop-Up Country Chapter, Historical Society of Alberta, 1975.

Chan, Anthony B. *Gold Mountain: The Chinese in the New World*. Vancouver: New Star Books, 1983.

Chen, Jack. *The Chinese of America*. San Francisco: Harper & Row, 1980.

Choo, N.K. *The Chinese in London*. London: Institute of Race Relations, 1958.

Coye, Molly Joel and Jon Livingston, eds., *China Yesterday and Today*. New York: Bantam Books, 1975.

Crowsnest Pass Historical Society. *Crowsnest and Its People*. Coleman: Crowsnest Pass Historical Society, 1979.

Dabbs, Frank, and Bev Wotton. *Oi Kwan Endowment Trust Fund Commemorative Book*. Calgary: Oi Kwan Foundation, 1987.

Dillon, R.H. *The Hatchet Men*. New York: Coward-McCann, 1962.

Drage, Charles. *Two-Gun Cohen*. London: Jonathan Cape, 1954.

Foran, Max and Heather MacEwan Foran. *Calgary: Canada's Frontier Metropolis, An Illustrated History*. Burlington: Windsor Publications, 1982.

Grant, Bruce. *The Boat People*. Markham, Ontario: Penguin, 1979.

Gray, James H. *Booze*. Toronto: Macmillan of Canada, 1972.

——. *Red Lights on the Prairies*. Scarborough: The New American Library of Canada, 1973.

——. *The Roar of the Twenties*. Toronto: Macmillan of Canada, 1975.

Guimond, Pierre S. and Brian R. Sinclair. *Calgary Architecture: The Boom Years 1972-1982*. Calgary: Detselig Enterprises, 1984.

Hawkins, Freda. *Canada and Immigration: Public Policy and Public Concern*. Montreal: McGill-Queen's University Press, 1972.

Hoe, Ban-Seng. *Structural Changes of Two Chinese Communities in Alberta, Canada*. Ottawa: National Museum of Canada, 1976.

Hsu, Immanuel C.Y. *The Rise of Modern China*. London: Oxford University Press, 1970.

Klinck, Carl F. *Literary History of Canada: Canadian Literature in English*. Toronto: University of Toronto Press, 1965.

Lai, David C.Y. *Chinatown: Towns Within Cities in Canada*. Vancouver, UBC Press, 1988.

Lee, R.H. *The Chinese in the United States of America*. Hong Kong: Oxford University Press, 1960.

Li, Peter S. *The Chinese in Canada*. Toronto: Oxford University Press, 1988.

Lyman, Stanford M. *Chinatown and Little Tokyo: Power, Conflict, and Community Among Chinese and Japanese Immigrants in America*. Millwood, N.Y.: Associated Faculty Press, 1986.

——. *Chinese Americans*. New York: Random House, 1974.

MacGregor, J.G. *Edmonton, A History*. Edmonton: Hurtig Publishers, 1975.

Miller, Stuart C. *The Unwelcome Immigrant*. Berkeley: University of California Press, 1969.

Morton, James. *In the Sea of Sterile Mountains*. J.J. Douglas Ltd., 1974.

Nanton and District Historical Society. *Mosquito Creek Roundup*. Nanton: Nanton and District Historical Society, 1976.

Nee, Victor G. and Brett de Bary. *Longtime Californ'*. New York: Pantheon Books, 1972.

Palmer, Howard. *Land of the Second Chance: A History of Ethnic Groups in Southern Alberta*. Lethbridge: The *Lethbridge Herald*, 1972.

——. *Patterns of Prejudice: A History of Nativism in Alberta*. Toronto: McClelland and Stewart, 1982.

Palmer, Howard, and Tamara Palmer, eds. *Peoples of Alberta: Portraits of Cultural Diversity*. Saskatoon: Western Producer Prairie Books, 1985.

Schurmann, Franz and Orville Schell, eds., *Imperial China*. New York: Vintage Books, 1967.

Stevens, S. *Chinese Americans*. Stockton: Relevant Instructional Materials, 1970.

Sung, Betty Lee. *The Story of the Chinese in America*. New York: Macmillan, 1967.

Tepper, Elliot L. *Southeast Asian Exodus: From Tradition to Resettlement. Understanding Refugees from Laos, Kampuchea and Vietnam in Canada*. Ottawa: Canadian Asian Studies Association, 1980.

Tsai, Shih-shan Henry. *China and the Overseas Chinese in the United States, 1868-1911*. Fayetteville, Arkansas: University of Arkansas Press, 1983.

Wickberg, Edgar, ed. *From China to Canada: A History of the Chinese Communities in Canada*. Toronto: McClelland and Stewart, 1982.

Pamphlets and Booklets

Chinese United Church. *Dedication Service*, December 19, 1954.

City of Edmonton, Planning and Building Department. *Edmonton's New Chinatown*, 1986.

Johnston, Emely and Corbet Locke, John Mayer, Tom Moore, Dalwin Stanford, and Lou Zeer. *Communities Six*. Calgary: Century Calgary, 1975.

Tan, Jin and Patricia E. Roy. *The Chinese in Canada*. Ottawa: Canadian Historical Association, 1985.

Articles

Ball, J.C., and M.P. Lau. "The Chinese Narcotic Addict in the United States," *Social Forces*, Vol. XLV, No. 1, 1966.

Barnett, Milton L. "Kinship as a Factor Affecting Cantonese Economic Adaptation in the United States," *Human Organization*, Vol. XIX, Spring, 1960.

Baureiss, G. "The Chinese Community in Calgary," *Alberta Historical Review*, Vol. XXII, No. 2, Spring, 1974.

——. "The Chinese Community of Calgary," *Canadian Ethnic Studies*, Vol, III, No. 1, June, 1971.

——. "Chinese Immigration, Chinese Stereotypes, and Chinese Labour," *Canadian Ethnic Studies*, Vol.XIX, No. 3, 1987.

——. "Chinese Organizational Development—A Comment," *Canadian Ethnic Studies*, Vol. XII, No. 3, 1980.

Caley, Peter. "Canada's Chinese Columbus," *The Beaver*, Spring, 1983.

Chan, Anthony B. "The Myth of the Chinese Sojourner in Canada," K. Victor Ujimoto and Gordon Hirabayashi, eds., *Visible Minorities and Multiculturalism: Asians in Canada*. Toronto: Butterworth, 1980.

——. "Neither French nor British: The Rise of the Asianadian Culture," *Canadian Ethnic Studies*, Vol. X, No. 2, 1978.

——. "'Orientalism' and Image Making: The Sojourner in Canadian History," *Journal of Ethnic Studies*, Vol. 9, Fall, 1981.

Chan Kwok B. and Denise Helly. "Coping with Racism: A Century of the Chinese Experience in Canada," *Canadian Ethnic Studies*, Vol. XIX, No. 3, 1987.

Chapman, Terry L. "Drug Use in Western Canada," *Alberta History*, Vol. 24, No. 4, Autumn, 1976.

Clark, A.H. "The Conquering Cook," *Canada West*, Winter, 1979.

Dawson, J. Brian. "The Chinese Experience in Frontier Calgary: 1885-1910," Anthony W. Rasporich and Henry C. Klassen, eds., *Frontier Calgary: Town, City, and Region 1875-1914*. Calgary: McClelland and Stewart West, 1975.

Fang, Zhongpu. "Did Chinese Buddhists Reach America 1,000 Years Before Columbus?", *China Reconstructs*, August, 1980.

Hoe, Ban-Seng. "The Chinatown in Alberta: Architectural Adaptation, Urban Renewal and Community's Needs," Christina Cameron and Martin Segger, eds., *Selected Papers from the Society for the Study of Architecture in Canada*. Ottawa: Society for the Study of Architecture in Canada, 1981.

——. "Chinese Cultural Traditions in Canada: Main Themes of an Ethnic Hall Exhibition at a Federal Museum," *Canadian Ethnic Studies*, Vol. XIX, No. 3, 1987.

Indra, Doreen. "Khmer, Lao, Vietnamese, and Vietnamese-Chinese in Alberta," Howard Palmer and Tamara Palmer, eds., *Peoples of Alberta: Portraits of Cultural Diversity*. Saskatoon: Western Producer Prairie Books, 1985.

Klassen, Henry C. "Life in Frontier Calgary," Anthony W. Rasporich, ed., *Western Canada: Past and Present*. Calgary: McClelland and Stewart West, 1975.

Lai, David C.Y. "Home County and Clan Origins of Overseas Chinese in Canada in the Early 1880s," *B.C. Studies*, No. 27, Autumn, 1975.

Li, Peter S. "Chinese Immigrants on the Canadian Prairie, 1910-47," *Canadian Review of Sociology and Anthropology*, Vol. 19, No. 4, 1982.

——. "The Economic Cost of Racism to Chinese-Canadians," *Canadian Ethnic Studies*, Vol. XIX, No. 3, 1987.

——. "A Historical Approach to Ethnic Stratification: the Case of the Chinese in Canada, 1858-1930," *The Canadian Review of Sociology and Anthropology*, Vol. 16, No. 3, 1979.

——. "Immigration Laws and Family Patterns: Some Demographic Changes Among Chinese Families in Canada, 1885-1971," *Canadian Ethnic Studies*, Vol. XII, No. 1, 1980.

——. "Income Achievement and Adaptive Capacity: An Empirical Comparison of Chinese and Japanese in Canada," K. Victor Ujimoto and Gordon Hirabayashi, eds., *Visible Minorities and Multiculturalism: Asians in Canada*. Toronto: Butterworth, 1980.

Lyman, Stanford M. "The Chinese Diaspora in America, 1850-1943," Stanford M. Lyman, *The Asian in North America*. Santa Barbara: ABC-Clio, Inc., 1970.

——. "Chinese Secret Societies in the Occident: Notes and Suggestions for Research in the Sociology of Secrecy," *Canadian Review of Sociology and Anthropology*, Vol. I, No. 2, May, 1964.

——. "Contrasts in the Community Organization of Chinese and Japanese in North America," *Canadian Review of Sociology and Anthropology*, Vol.V, No. 2, May, 1968.

——. "Overseas Chinese in America and Indonesia," *The Asian in North America*. Santa Barbara: ABC-Clio, Inc., 1970.

Palmer, Howard D. "Anti-Oriental Sentiment in Alberta, 1880-1920," *Canadian Ethnic Studies*, Vol II, No. 2, December, 1970.

——. "Patterns of Racism: Attitudes Towards Chinese and Japanese in Alberta 1920-1950," *Social History*, Vol. 8, No. 25, 1980.

Roy, Patricia E. "Educating the 'East': British Columbia and the Oriental Question in the Inter-War Years," *B.C. Studies*, No. 18, Spring, 1973.

——. "The Oriental 'Menace' in British Columbia," Susan Trofimenkoff, ed., *The Twenties in Western Canada*. Ottawa: National Museum of Man, 1972.

Siu, Paul C.P. "The Sojourner," *American Journal of Sociology*, Vol. LVII, July, 1952.

Verma, Ravi, Kwok B. Chan and Larry Lam. "The Chinese-Canadian Family: A Socio-Economic Profile," K. Ishwaran, ed., *Canadian Families: Ethnic Variations*. Toronto: McGraw-Hill Ryerson, 1980.

Voisey, Paul. "Two Chinese Communities in Alberta: An Historical Perspective," *Canadian Ethnic Studies*, Vol. IV, No. 2, Spring, 1972.

——. "Chinatown on the Prairies: The Emergence of an Ethnic Community," Christina Cameron and Martin Segger, eds., *Selected Papers from the Society for the Study of Architecture in Canada*. Ottawa: Society for the Study of Architecture in Canada, 1981.

Ward, Peter. "The Oriental Immigrant and Canada's Protestant Clergy, 1858-1925," *B.C. Studies*, No. 22, Summer, 1974.

Wickberg, Edgar. "Chinese and Canadian Influences on Chinese Politics in Vancouver, 1900-1947," *B.C. Studies*, No. 45, Spring, 1980.

——. "Chinese Associations in Canada, 1923-47," K. Victor Ujimoto and Gordon Hirabayashi, eds., *Visible Minorities and Multiculturalism: Asians in Canada*. Toronto: Butterworth, 1980.

——. "Some Problems in Chinese Organizational Development in Canada, 1923-1937," *Canadian Ethnic Studies*, Vol. XI, No. 1, 1979.

Willmott, William E. "Approaches to the Study of the Chinese in British Columbia," *B.C. Studies*, No. 14, Spring, 1970.

——. "Chinese Clan Associations in Vancouver," *Man*, Vol. LXIV, No. 49, 1964.

——. "Some Aspects of Chinese Communities in British Columbia," *B.C. Studies*, No. 8, Winter, 1968.

Wolf, Eric R. "China," *Peasant Wars of the Twentieth Century*. New York: Harper & Row, 1969.

Wolfgang, Aaron and Nina Josefowitz. "Chinese Immigrant Value Changes with Length of Time in Canada and Value Differences Compared to Canadian Students," *Canadian Ethnic Studies*, Vol. X, No. 2, 1978.

Wu, Phat and Hong Tai Au. "Facts about Ethnic Chinese from Vietnam," *Refugees from Southeast Asia: Their Background*. Toronto: Ontario Ministry of Culture and Recreation, 1980.

Yee, Paul. *Saltwater City: An Illustrated History of the Chinese in Vancouver*. Vancouver/Toronto: Douglas & McIntyre, 1988.

Yu, Miriam. "Human Rights, Discrimination, and Coping Behavior of the Chinese in Canada," *Canadian Ethnic Studies*, Vol. XIX, No. 3, 1987.

Unpublished Manuscripts

Chapman, Terry. "The Non-Medical Use of Drugs in Alberta, 1900-1920," (The University of Calgary History Department, 1975).

Dawson, J. Brian. "The Chinese Community of Lethbridge." (Historic Sites Service, Alberta Culture, Government of Alberta, 1985).

Joyner, J. Brooks. "Lethbridge Chinatown: An Analysis of the Kwong On Lung Co. Building, the Bow On Tong Co. Building, and the Chinese Free Masons Building." (Historic Sites Service, Alberta Culture, Government of Alberta, 1985).

Theses and Dissertations

Baureiss, G. "The City and the Sub-community: The Chinese of Calgary." (Unpublished M.A. Thesis. Calgary: University of Calgary, 1971).

Dawson, J. Brian. "Chinese Urban Communities in Southern Alberta, 1885-1925." (Unpublished M.A. Thesis, The University of Calgary, 1976).

Fan, T.C. "Chinese Residents in Chicago." (Unpublished Ph.D. Dissertation. University of Chicago, 1926).

Hoe, Ban-seng. "Adaptive Change and Overseas Chinese Settlements, With Special Reference to a Chinese Community in the Canadian Prairies." (Unpublished M.A. Thesis. Edmonton: University of Alberta, 1971).

——. "Structural Changes of Two Chinese Communities in Alberta, Canada." (Unpublished Ph.D. Dissertation. Vanderbilt University, 1974).

Lyman, Stanford M. "The Structure of Chinese Society in Nineteenth-Century America." (Unpublished Ph.D. Dissertation. Berkeley: University of California, 1961).

Palmer, Howard D. "Responses to Foreign Immigration: Nativism and Ethnic Tolerance in Alberta, 1880-1920." (Unpublished M.A. Thesis. Edmonton: University of Alberta, 1971).

Index

R

S

T

U

V

W

Y